CARIBBEAN LITERATURE AFTER INDEPENDENCE: THE CASE OF EARL LOVELACE

CARIBBEAN LITERATURE AFTER INDEPENDENCE
The Case of Earl Lovelace

Edited by
BILL SCHWARZ

INSTITUTE FOR THE STUDY OF THE
AMERICAS

UNIVERSITY OF LONDON · SCHOOL OF ADVANCED STUDY

© Institute for the Study of the Americas, 2008

British Library Cataloguing-in-Publication Data
A catalogue record for this book is available from the British Library

ISBN 978-1-900039-91-8

Institute for the Study of the Americas
31 Tavistock Square
London
WC1H 9HA
Telephone: 020 7862 8870
Fax: 020 7862 8886
Email: americas@sas.ac.uk
Web: americas.sas.ac.uk

Contents

		Page
	Acknowledgements	vii
	Contributors	viii
	Introduction: 'Where is Myself?'	xi
	Bill Schwarz	
1	Being in the World	1
	Bill Schwarz	
2	'I Will Let Down My Bucket Here': Writers and the Conditions of Cultural Production in Post-Independence Trinidad	21
	Kate Quinn	
3	Nostalgia for the Future: The Novels of Earl Lovelace	41
	J. Dillon Brown	
4	Illusions of Paradise and Progress: An Ecocritical Perspective on Earl Lovelace	61
	Chris Campbell	
5	The Crisis of Caribbean History: Society and Self in C.L.R. James and Earl Lovelace	76
	Aaron Love	
6	Writing Trinidad: Nation and Hybridity in *The Dragon Can't Dance* and *Witchbroom*	94
	Patricia Murray	
7	Performance and Tradition in Earl Lovelace's *A Brief Conversion*: The Drama of the Everyday	111
	Nicole King	
8	'A Limited Situation': Brevity and Lovelace's *A Brief Conversion*	130
	James Procter	

9	'All o' We is One': Carnival Forms and Creolisation in *The Dragon Can't Dance* and *Salt* John Thieme	146
10	Engaging the World: Lovelace's *Salt* as a Caribbean Epic Louis James	161
11	'Beauty and Promise': Sonic Narrative and the Politics of Freedom in the Literary Imagination of Lovelace Tina Ramnarine	175
12	On the Road to Kumaca: A Reflection Lawrence Scott	191

Acknowledgements

We are grateful indeed to London University's Institute for the Study of the Americas which, from the outset, accommodated this project. In particular, we thank the Institute's Director, James Dunkerley, and its sole Caribbean cadre, Kate Quinn. Without their commitment, the volume would never have appeared. Karen Perkins, at the ISA, and Emily Morrell, at the Institute for Historical Research, ensured that the production of the book progressed smoothly and with great speed. We are indebted to both. The School of English and Drama at Queen Mary, University of London, and Earl Lovelace's UK publisher, Faber and Faber, each offered vital support when it was needed.

Thanks are due as well to Earl Lovelace. He devoted time to talk when I was in Port of Spain — when I am sure there was plenty more uppermost in his mind. He was a gracious, generous host. It was a pleasure to hear him discuss his work in the company of friends: Funso Aiyejina, Rhoda Bharath, Jenny Scott and Lawrence Scott. What he will make of this volume, coming from afar — from a region where Kumaca, Bonasse and the Hill do not loom large in the literary imagination — remains to be seen.

What can be said, though, is that all the contributors to the volume — who, in the way of these things, had many other urgent demands — determined to create the time to engage with Lovelace's writings, believing them to be of the first importance. This collective enthusiasm drove the project, and made it a pleasure from beginning to end.

Bill Schwarz

Contributors

J. Dillon Brown is an Assistant Professor in the English Department at Washington University in St Louis. His current research investigates the metropolitan contexts in which Anglophone Caribbean fiction was produced and published after World War II. He recently spent a year at the University of the West Indies at the Cave Hill campus in Barbados on a Fulbright research grant.

Chris Campbell is a Lecturer in Colonial and Postcolonial Writing at Queen Mary, University of London. He has co-edited, with Erin Somerville, *'What is the Earthly Paradise?' Ecocritical Responses to the Caribbean* (Cambridge Scholars Publishing, 2007) and is a contributor to the *Oxford Companion to Black British History* (Oxford University Press, 2007). Previously he has taught at the University of Warwick and at the University of Central England.

Louis James taught at the University of the West Indies, Mona, from 1963–66. Returning to England to the newly formed University of Kent, he introduced Caribbean writing into the English syllabus and was active in the Caribbean Artists Movement and the Association of Teachers in African and Related Literatures. His publications in the field include *Islands in Between: Essays on West Indian Literature* (1968), *Jean Rhys* (1978) and *Caribbean Literature in English* (1999). He is Emeritus Professor at the University of Kent.

Nicole King works at the English Subject Centre, Royal Holloway, University of London, a national body dedicated to the pedagogy of English in higher education. Previously she was Associate Professor of Literature at the University of California, San Diego and Assistant Professor of English at the University of Maryland. She is the author of *C.L.R. James and Creolization: Circles of Influence* (University Press of Mississippi, 2001) and is currently researching American representations of black authenticity at the turn of the twenty-first century.

Aaron Love is a PhD candidate in Comparative Literature at New York University.

Patricia Murray is Senior Lecturer in English and a member of the Caribbean Studies Centre at London Metropolitan University. She has travelled widely in Latin America and the Caribbean and has published on a range of pan-Caribbean and black British writing. She is editor (with Ashok Bery) of *Comparing Postcolonial Literatures: Dislocations* (Macmillan, 2000) and is completing a book entitled *Shared Solitude: The Fiction of Wilson Harris and Gabriel García Márquez*. Her research focuses on cultural theory and on new ways of exploring the interconnections between myth and science, politics and spirituality, indigeneity and Creolisation.

James Procter teaches in the School of English at Newcastle University. He is editor of *Writing Black Britain 1948–1998* (Manchester University Press, 2000), and author of *Dwelling Places: Postwar Black British Writing* (Manchester University Press, 2003) and *Stuart Hall* (Routledge, 2004). His most recent article, 'The Postcolonial Everyday', was published in *New Formations*. He is currently Principal Investigator on a large AHRC-funded project examining the relationship between reading, location and diasporic literature: www.devolvingdiasporas.com.

Kate Quinn teaches at the Institute for the Study of the Americas, University of London. She completed her doctorate on cultural policy and nationalism in Cuba and Guyana at the Department of History, University College London in 2005. Her current research focuses on Black Power in the Anglophone and Hispanic Caribbean. She is on the committee of the Society for Caribbean Studies.

Tina K. Ramnarine teaches at Royal Holloway, University of London and is author of *Creating Their Own Space: The Development of an Indian Caribbean Musical Tradition* (University of West Indies Press, 2001), *Ilmatar's Inspirations: Nationalism, Globalization and the Changing Soundscapes of Finnish Folk Music* (University of Chicago Press, 2003) and *Beautiful Cosmos: Performance and Belonging in the Caribbean Diaspora* (Pluto Press, 2007).

Bill Schwarz teaches in the School of English and Drama, Queen Mary, University of London. Most recently he has edited *West Indian Intellectuals in Britain* (Manchester University Press, 2003) and *The Locations of George Lamming* (Warwick University/Macmillan, 2007). He is an editor of *History Workshop Journal*.

Lawrence Scott is from Trinidad and Tobago. He is the prize-winning author of the novel *Aelred's Sin*, which won a Commonwealth Writers' Prize, Best Book in Canada and the Caribbean, 1999. *Night Calypso*, his most recent novel, was short-listed for a Commonwealth Writers' Prize, Best Book in Canada and the Caribbean, 2005, and nominated for the International Impac Dublin Literary

Award 2006; it was a One Book One Community Choice in 2006, and published in France in 2005 as *Calypso de Nuit*. His first novel, *Witchbroom*, was also short-listed for a Commonwealth Writers' Prize for Best First Book in Canada and the Caribbean in 1993. It was read on the BBC's 'Book At Bed Time' in 1993. His collection of short stories, *Ballad for the New World*, was published in 1994; it includes 'The House of Funerals', the prize-winning short story for the 1986 Tom-Gallon Award. His short stories have been read on the BBC and have been anthologised internationally, notably in *The Penguin Book of Caribbean Short Stories* and *The Oxford Book of Caribbean Short Stories*. His poetry is published in several anthologies. He moves between London and Port of Spain, where he was Writer in Residence at the University of the West Indies in 2004. He is presently a Senior Research Fellow at the Academy for Arts, Letters, Culture and Public Affairs at the University of Trinidad and Tobago. He divides his time between writing, researching and teaching literature and creative writing.

John Thieme teaches at the University of East Anglia. His books include *The Web of Tradition: Uses of Allusion in V.S. Naipaul's Fiction* (Hansib/Dangaroo, 1987), *The Arnold Anthology of Post-Colonial Literatures in English* (Arnold, 1996), *Derek Walcott* (Manchester University Press, 1999), *Post-Colonial Con-Texts: Writing Back to the Canon* (Continuum, 2001), *Post-Colonial Studies: The Essential Glossary* (Arnold, 2003) and *R.K. Narayan* (Manchester University Press, 2007). He edits *The Journal of Commonwealth Literature* and is General Editor of the Manchester University Press Contemporary World Writers Series.

INTRODUCTION: 'WHERE IS MYSELF?'

Bill Schwarz

> I am doomed to write about Nigeria. That is where my work is. What I want to say about the world, I can say in writing about Nigeria.
> — Chinua Achebe (2007)

Much of the energy of Earl Lovelace's writing derives from his determination to recuperate 'another' Trinidad.[1] His is not the Trinidad of official society, conforming to the historic protocols of the People's National Movement, but a more visionary and democratic — if more unruly — conception of what the independent nation might yet become. The Trinidad encountered in Lovelace is dispossessed, dark and vital. At every turn it confronts degradation. But in this fictive world the contraries of degradation and salvation are closely — historically — linked, the former serving as the precondition for the latter. Above all, Lovelace is preoccupied with the political and psychic struggles for selfhood. In his novels and stories we witness, in the midst of the degraded nation, occasions when a precarious possession of selfhood is maintained against the odds, or when — as if from nowhere — it is discovered anew. These moments — the 'brief conversions' of his short stories — also serve as the prerequisite for the social sovereignty of the future, for Lovelace seeks to take hold of the idea of salvation, to wrest it from any received notion of the ideal and the ethereal, and (literally in some instances) to bring it down to earth. His conception of salvation is persuasively profane.

The profanity of this other Trinidad, located in the lives of the dark-skinned dispossessed, is composed of social forces that cannot easily be translated into the generic conventions of prose writing with which, as readers, we are familiar or which we might expect. It is not that Lovelace's Trinidad is without its symbolic forms, or without the means to represent itself. The steelband, Carnival and calypso all attest to the complexity of its cultural expression. Yet, for all its complexity, this is a culture which works at some distance from the writerly world of the novelist; it is a culture with its own internal rules, codes and rhythms, existing close to the surface of popular life. As Kate Quinn suggests in Chapter 2, there are many points of crossover between the reading publics of Trinidad and Tobago and the predominantly oral, performative cultures of steelband,

Carnival, calypso and popular drama. Many of the nation's established writers have straddled the two worlds, and endeavoured to represent on the page the vitality of vernacular performance, organised around voice and music. Readers will be familiar with this from the novels of Sam Selvon, conceived as 'ballads' and chronicled in a version of the nation-language, written over 50 years ago. There is, moreover, a long tradition in Trinidad of barrack-yard literature, from which Lovelace's writing evolves. In Lovelace, however, the attempt to reconstruct in the novels and in the stories the rhythms of popular speech and the forms of calypso goes significantly deeper, producing in the later fiction especially a hybrid genre of performative epic.[2] This formal inventiveness is, I think, peculiarly Trinidadian, with its roots in a long tradition of the island's writing; as we read Lovelace, we can sense these literary antecedents crystallising, and generating new constellations of narrative forms.

Much has been made of the capacities of modern Caribbean writing — the literary formations which first cohered in the 1930s and 1940s, in the French- and Spanish-speaking Caribbean as much as in the Anglophone islands of the region — to recast the languages of the respective metropoles, and to reimagine them anew. Such a view, for example, drives advocates of *Créolité* in the Francophone Caribbean such as Edouard Glissant and Patrick Chamoiseau. The very 'lateness' of this national or regional literature served the emergent generation of Caribbean writers to good effect. In a welcome affirmation of the cultural virtues of combined and uneven development, Wilson Harris famously recognised that the budding regional Fieldings and Smolletts of the mid-twentieth century had entered the world of literature in the wake of Joyce, Proust and Faulkner (Harris 1963: 12). Many wonderful things happened as a result: the political energies invested in the struggle for Independence generated their aesthetic counterparts, and an incomparable body of Caribbean writing emerged, which has had far-reaching influence well beyond the region itself. For all the local, or putatively local, Trinidadian themes which structure his novels, Lovelace needs to be read through this broader optic, not only in aesthetic terms but as an author conscious of his location at the crossroads of the New World and whose writings are alive with a largeness of historical vision.

In summary terms, this is the argument of our collection. The volume offers a (mainly) non-Caribbean, North Atlantic reading of his fiction. All the contributors believe that his work is of general significance, and merits attention, outside the Caribbean as much as within. However, this raises a number of issues.

Like many or most writers perceived within the literary institutions of the metropolitan centres to arise from faraway locations, Lovelace's reputation is underwritten by a marked ambiguity. On the one hand, he is a globally recognised author. He wins international prizes; he is published by prestige houses; he has access to smart venues for his readings in cities across the Anglophone world. On the other, outside the Caribbean many an intellectual well versed in contemporary literature won't have read him, or maybe won't have come across him. His works are seldom available in bookstores — though this is hardly particular to him. The holdings in even the most generously endowed libraries are uneven. (It appears at the time of writing that his collection of non-fiction writings, published in the Caribbean four years ago, is not held in any of the major university libraries in the United States or in the United Kingdom.) And, while there are a handful of essays scattered across a small number of academic journals, there exist no volumes of published criticism.[3] To claim that he is best known by those with a knowledge of the Caribbean, and that those who don't have this knowledge generally feel no great obligation to read him, is to say no more than that his reputation is subsumed by his being received as a regional — a Caribbean — author.

'Regional', of course, is no innocent term. Nowhere is this more acutely illustrated than in the case of Lovelace's Trinidadian contemporary, V.S. Naipaul. In one sense, Lovelace is Naipaul's contrary, or his literary double. Naipaul has travelled to the ends of the earth in order to testify that his craft is properly worldly. He has devoted his life to the task of stripping away all remnants of his Caribbean patrimony, such that he can be appreciated as *a writer* with no need for prefix. His disquiet at being identified as a Caribbean writer is notorious. This act of repudiation has required sustained labour on Naipaul's part, and we might speculate that — notwithstanding the virtuosity of his prose — over the years the aesthetic costs have been mounting. Many might think that the Nobel citation, in which he was lauded as an Olympian, 'incorruptible' creator of 'suppressed histories', was a scandal in which error preened itself as truth (cited in the *Guardian* 2001). No doubt Naipaul himself thought differently. But while Naipaul determined to strip away his past — his regional, colonial past — in order to become properly worldly and cosmopolitan, Lovelace seeks the world in his own local habitus, and in so doing does much to incite his readers into questioning where 'the world' is to be located and what it constitutes.

There can be little doubt that Naipaul's belief in his entitlement to the accolade of writer, without the prefix, has also been due to the seemingly prosaic fact that he, unlike Lovelace, chooses to live in the metropolitan centre: in this instance, in England. England, it turns out, is — providentially — not 'a region' at all but a historic site of cultivation where literature and civilisation happen. Or, as Derek Walcott has it, with Naipaul in his sights: 'Press one foot on the soil of England and the phantoms spring' (1996: 121). It is well known that Naipaul's generation of writers felt compelled, as young men in the 1940s and 1950s, to leave the West Indies and head for London. This was not so much a choice than — as George Lamming has argued, the bitterness painfully present — a matter of survival, a journey undertaken 'for the specific purpose of staying alive' (2005: 213). Lovelace, born in 1935, did not make this journey, although it looked for a time as if he might. As a young boy he was a ferocious reader, and smart at school. As a consequence, his life came to be subject to the system of competitive examinations which dominated the colonial education of the time. But, unlike the fêted few who passed — the likes of C.L.R. James and Naipaul himself, for example, whose entry to the magnificence of Queen's Royal College provided them the means to believe themselves rightful participants in the intellectual life of the metropole — on two occasions Lovelace failed the national examinations. The notion that he might embark upon a professional career slipped away, and his life necessarily took on a new direction. 'Failure,' he writes in *Salt*, 'was not to escape. To fail to escape was defeat; defeat even before you began' (1996: 76). A few years later, in 1950 after the death of his mother, he was due to join his sister in London. The call never came, however, and he remained in Trinidad.[4] 'Of course, out there in the metropolitan centres,' he reflects, 'things might have been different. More might have been made of me, but which me? Without the experiences here, I would have been a different me' (Hewson, 2004: 5). Naipaul took his decision, and so too, in some sense, did Lovelace.[5] By refusing the life of an *émigré*, Lovelace — and others like him — did much to demonstrate that it was indeed possible to remain in the Caribbean and to follow the vocation of writing. What for a time many took to be an impossibility was, in the end, shown not to be so. Either way, by going or staying, the Lovelace 'me' was contingent upon these alternative decisions which lay before him. But that chilling formulation remains hanging in the air: 'More might have been made of me ...'. We can assume the likelihood that if he had left Trinidad, and if he had also discovered himself in his new environment to have been a writer, this other — virtual or hypothetical — Lovelace might well have fostered a more secure, elevated literary reputation, for as Naipaul had learnt even before he'd arrived in the metropole, in such matters the centre still holds.

Perceptions such as these — being worldly or local, being at the centre or at the periphery — carry in them, in our postcolonial times, the heavy imprint of the colonial past. Many of Lovelace's most astute intellectual forbears from Trinidad, not least among them C.L.R. James, believed deep in their souls that the only means by which they could become modern cosmopolitan citizens was to migrate to the metropole, and one can understand all that conspired to produce such a conclusion.[6] Lovelace himself was formed by colonialism and by its aftermath. In the strict sense of the term, though, he is a postcolonial writer. Unlike Selvon and Lamming, for example, his writings did not appear in the years which marked the prelude to Independence.[7] His first novel, *While Gods are Falling*, was published three years after Trinidad and Tobago gained Independence, in 1965, having the year before won, in manuscript, the British Petroleum Independence Literary Award.

But the fact that Lovelace first became a published writer after Independence is not merely a literal, or chronological, matter. It is a properly historical issue, which goes to the heart of his fiction. The great bulk of his protagonists have little to their names. They remain dispossessed and unrepresented. They struggle to maintain their dignity, to win for themselves an elemental, human recognition and, where possible, to outwit a social order which holds all the cards. The great irony is that the society in which, against all odds, they conduct these struggles for selfhood prides itself on the act of emancipation which freed it from colonial rule.

In Trinidad and Tobago, the People's National Movement (PNM), under the leadership of Eric Williams, created at breakneck speed a political movement whose overriding purpose was to win political power from London. To this end, the PNM was able to mobilise much of the population. It fought too on many fronts, most famously in the arena of political pedagogy, the public debates and lectures which came to be known as the University of Woodford Square, marking an extraordinary experiment in the attempt to recast intellectual culture on a popular axis.

In some beautiful pages in *Salt*, Lovelace conveys the transforming power of this educative project, in which the violence of the historical past from which the Caribbean had been formed was publicly acknowledged, translated into a vernacular idiom — a tragic history retold as *gossip* — and brought home so that it could acquire meaning within the imperatives of contemporary everyday life.[8] The passages are too long to be quoted here in full, but even a heavily edited version offers some sense of the intensity of the prose:

> That evening under Lorenzo Rumshop & Grocery in the bright
> dark sparkle of speeches from the National Party, Miss Myrtle began
> to see the world afresh and nearly five hundred years of time ...
>
> Miss Myrtle just stand up there. She felt her body tremble at the
> stories of the tortures, of the whips, of the chains and this great
> sorrow for the island, for the people, for the world and a shame.
> She hear dogs howling. She hear grieving parrots rise up as one fleet,
> cawing and squealing.

Miss Norma, also part of the crowd but fearful of what she hears, wonders whether the threat of violent retribution lies just around the corner, distressed that 'all these things' — the systematic indignities of the Caribbean past — are being brought into the present. 'They want us to commit murder?' she asks. 'They want us to fight?' In the manner of a classical chorus, those around her — positioned in, or close by, the Lorenzo Rumshop — respond:

> 'They want us to know.'
> 'They giving us power.'
> 'They making us wise.'
> 'They making us remember in order to forget.'
> 'They purging us out.'

To which Miss Myrtle, momentarily disorientated by too much history, can only ask herself:

> 'Where am I? ... Where is myself?'

But as Lovelace depicts the scene, there is no time for subjective disorientation:

> 'And what now after all this?' cried the leader. 'More brutality, more inequality, more injustice, more degradation?'
> 'No. Oh God, no!' cried Miss Myrtle. 'No!'
> 'No,' said the leader with finality. 'No.' These things were done in the dark ages of our past. These acts were done from a different vision of what is the world, of what is human, in a time when men and women did not have the right to vote, when there was no ideal of democracy by which to live. But today we have Democracy, Brotherhood, Unity. This land that belonged to a few now belongs to everybody ...
> 'Come and join us!' he cried. 'Come and help us make this one nation. Show us your support by raising your hands.'
> And before the words could leave his mouth Miss Myrtle had up her hand. And when the speaking finish she go and line up with the other people and get a form and fill out her name and address and give them a dollar for subscription. (Lovelace 1996: 154–7)

As elsewhere in his writing, here Lovelace insists on the transfigurative potential of the fictional 'National Party' and its fictional 'leader', which represent closely the historical PNM and the historical Eric Williams.[9] Williams himself, for Lovelace, has always been a figure composed of many contrary elements — part conventional politician, part Jouvay character:

> He was masked with dark shades. Nobody in public saw his real face. He was equipped with a hearing-aid. In the early days he had a cigarette dangling from his lips. His speaking voice was unique, his vocabulary and rhythms a kind of baroque Trinidadian, his cadences echoing the Midnight Robber, his repartee as swift and sharp as an extempore calypsonian's, his attitude that of the badjohn. In addition he was griot, historian, Obeah man, the third brightest man in the world. (Lovelace 2003: 41–2)

These contrary elements are not those of Williams alone, however. While Lovelace appreciates the radical power of the PNM's founding vision of the new nation, driven by the belief that the historical past could finally be overcome, he also knows well enough the degree to which the PNM itself worked to curb the self-activity of the people. It effected, largely, a passive break from the colonial past, in which the new national leadership planned to step into the shoes of the traditional governing elite. It inaugurated not only the independent nation but also a marked strain of clientelism and authoritarianism: 'badjohn', translated into the more sober categories of political science, evokes an apprehension of Bonarpartism.

Something of this larger history is caught in the juxtaposition between the leader, on the one hand, and the rumshop *philosophes* on the other. The rhetorical spell carries too a certain menace: 'They want us to know' ... 'They giving us power' ... 'They making us wise', the third person plural constituting the active subject, the first person the unwitting recipient, present only to be acted upon. (Indeed, these words echo the moment of Lovelace imagining in the passive voice his other, *émigré* self: 'More might have been made of me ...') These declarations are followed by another, altogether more ambiguous, one: 'They purging us out.' In this respect, despite the drama of the revelation she experiences, Miss Myrtle's disorientation may not be at all inappropriate. The words of the leader intervene to still her anxiety. 'The dark ages of our past' are over. The nation now is one. But in the turbulence of the moment, Miss Myrtle's questions — 'Where am I? ... Where is myself?' — remain unheard and forgotten.

For Lovelace, the mythic moment of Independence has bequeathed a troubled, continuing legacy. The social order that followed Independence organises the lives of his fictional protagonists, in which frustration and despair accumulate. He doesn't refrain from identifying those he holds responsible for the plight of his nation. His principal antagonists are close to home. They are Trinidadians. They are the same colour as him. At every opportunity, they are the ones who in public commit themselves to maintaining the integrity of the nation. Much of the tension of his writing derives from his determination to get inside these official rhetorics of the nation, and to turn them inside out.[10] At the same time, in exposing the myopia and bad faith of the post-Independence ruling caste, he is at pains to draw into the field of vision those other arenas of national life which have either been rendered invisible or unspeakable, or which only appear in public consciousness branded as the source of all manner of social ills. This act of symbolic recuperation, or reconstruction, brings into the imagination the 'other' Trinidad, in all its darkness and vitality. Indeed, what is this but — precisely — a narrative strategy which retrieves an entire underworld of 'suppressed histories', fashioning epics that move back and forth in time between the colonial and postcolonial epochs? One can search far and wide in the later corpus of Naipaul's writings in a bid to uncover the compassion and political will necessary for such an undertaking, to no avail. In Lovelace, they are there for all to see.

In giving voice to these histories, Lovelace not only creates in the imagination another Trinidad, a more contingent nation, with a greater array of possible futures before it. His complex, shifting narrative voices — the influence of Faulkner is never far away — also work to question the practices of representation themselves. In this regard, he is a purposively modernist writer. In presenting to his readers another Trinidad, he also offers them the means to know 'the world' differently.

Indeed, as the following chapters demonstrate, one of the most enticing aspects of Lovelace's novels and stories is his insistence that 'the world' is always local and always grounded, and that the Caribbean is as worldly as anywhere. His conception of the local and the worldly is a dialectical one, in which identity and difference operate in the same moment, each inextricably part of the other. While this has much going for it in the abstract, it can at the same time be demanding for those of his readers, from afar, who know neither the Caribbean nor Trinidad.

The distance between writer and critic is hazardous at the best of times, particularly in an age when criticism is lodged deeply in the academy. These hazards redouble when the respective locations of writer and critic vary as markedly as they do in this instance. Personally, I have never heard a parang band, danced the Bamboula, nor seen a stickfight, and I guess this is true for many of the contributors to this collection. As readers familiar with Lovelace will know, these and kindred practices feature prominently in the lives of his fictional characters. Our social distance from the Lovelace environment was readily apparent when we, the authors, met to discuss our chapters. We convened in Bloomsbury in the heart of London, a locale once famed for the pursuit of metropolitan refinement and for the high-minded cultivation of its habitués. It was a strange experience to look out on to the well-tended town squares while discussing the fate of

Fisheye or Bolo.[11] Although classic Bloomsbury is not our world, it nonetheless focused the mind, requiring of us the effort to create for ourselves a double vision, encompassing both us, in our contemporary locations, and Lovelace in his. What were we to make, in our world, of the moral and epistemological value that he invests in the popular customs of an Afro-Caribbean underclass?

Certainly, the stories Lovelace tells do much to unsettle a metropolitan provincialism which so readily masquerades as universal. However, they also work to disrupt conventional dichotomies: 'the world' and the local; past and present; salvation and degradation; the sacred and the profane; lightness and darkness; self and other. To think in this manner is always instructive — not least because the polarities which underwrite Lovelace's writings themselves are easy to overdraw. When C.L.R. James, in his bid — quite properly — to highlight Lovelace's locality as a specifically Trinidadian writer, goes on to suggest that his prose is free from the influence of European literary precursors, there is room for legitimate doubt. When I suggest that he can be positioned as Naipaul's double, this too needs to be qualified: not only are there important affinities between Naipaul's early stories and the fiction of Lovelace (a point discussed later by John Thieme) but, as we know, doubles have the habit of becoming the other. What are we to make, after all, of the fictive dimensions of Naipaul's own life, in which he struts his pose as literary badjohn? Or again, the elemental Caribbean decision — whether to 'stay' or to 'leave' — in reality often proves a more complicated business, in which movements back and forth repeatedly punctuate a life.

These points, perhaps, don't need rehearsing. They simply remind us of the complexities of the various worlds we all inhabit. But one final point does need to be emphasised. While the contrasts between Lovelace's Trinidad, on the one hand, and the predominantly North Atlantic locales of the majority of the authors represented here, on the other, are real enough, they cannot be taken as absolute. The protean, diasporic qualities of the Caribbean preclude any definitive distinction between 'here' and 'there'. For all its modern history, the Caribbean has functioned, symbolically as well as in a more strictly material sense, as a constituent of the metropolitan societies. Shared histories have been intertwined from the outset. At the start of the twenty-first century, the Creolisation of many a northern city continues apace. This is not to say that stickfighting has now been adopted by the inhabitants of Bloomsbury. But it does attest to the locations of blackness in the contemporary metropole. Traces — more than traces — of Lovelace's world are now visible, and audible, in the urban landscapes of the North: transformed, recast, but nonetheless recognisable. And how Lovelace imagines blackness as a resource for the future is not a matter confined to the traces of Bonasse.

The following chapters make no attempt to offer a comprehensive reading of Lovelace's work. The focus is weighted on his later novels and short stories. We don't address his musical and radio dramas, his screenplays, or the short film in which he was involved based on his story 'Joebell and America'. Nor do we discuss his writing for children and the great quantity of his essays and journalism. Of particular interest is Lovelace's practice (like Selvon before him) of rewriting the novels for dramatisation; a more complete account would need to review these performative aspects of his work and would, we imagine, generate significant new readings of the published fiction. There is, we know, a great deal more to be said.

Notes

1. I would like to thank the British Academy for financing my travel to Trinidad so that I could both conduct an interview with Earl Lovelace and also consult the Lovelace papers at the St Augustine campus of the University of the West Indies.
2. For a good account of the language of Lovelace's fiction, see Hodge (2006).
3. Recently Funso Aiyejina, a close friend of Lovelace's and an indefatigable promoter of his writings, edited a special issue of the online journal devoted to his work and life, *Anthurium. A Caribbean Studies Journal*, vol. 4, no. 2 (2006). This comprises a selection of the papers from the celebration of Lovelace's 75th birthday, which took place in Port of Spain (and elsewhere in Trinidad) in 2005. There are plans to publish a more comprehensive version of the papers in book form, as well as to produce an accompanying critical volume. The birthday celebrations, and the publications which have so far followed, offer a magnificent insight into the Trinidadian and Caribbean reception of Lovelace. Nadia Johnson's 'Select Bibliography', included in the *Anthurium* special issue, gives the most reliable indication of the current critical literature, citing in all nearly 50 articles. In addition, in the Lovelace archive at St Augustine, there are six graduate dissertations and four unpublished, mimeographed papers, including one by Kenneth Ramchand and one by Carolyn Cooper.
4. Had he left in 1950, he would have arrived in England in the same year as Selvon and Lamming, though he was some years younger than both of them.
5. We should note, though, Lovelace's own declaration: 'I have not chosen to remain in Trinidad', which occurs in Marie-Alice (1989: 144).
6. In an ambiguous formulation, James once referred to Lovelace as a 'native' writer. This was envisaged as a compliment, and even perhaps as something

of a self-criticism on James's part, for he went on to explain that he meant it 'in the sense that the prose and the things that they [James refers here to Earl Lovelace and to the novelist Michael Anthony] are dealing with, spring from below, and are not seen through a European-educated literary sieve, as some of the finest writing in the West Indies up to today has been' (James, 1980: 243). Even so, the description of Lovelace as a 'native' writer, it seems to me, cuts both ways: native in this context may well connote a specifically Trinidadian writer, but it is too a heavily weighted term, resonating with older, colonial perceptions. In an interview with Melle Troudart Marie-Alice, Lovelace indicated that, in the context of his remaining in Trinidad, 'C.L.R. James once asked me: "Who do you talk to?"' (1989: 144).

[7] And, unlike Lamming and Selvon, Lovelace is of a different generation of authors who (as Nicole King puts this in Chapter 7) 'are not concerned with explaining and introducing the Caribbean to a foreign readership. Their particular critical perspective looks inward rather than outwards and places the lives of the Caribbean people, wherever they may be in the world, centre stage.'

[8] This rich idea of a vernacular political rhetoric functioning as 'gossip', directly drawing from the Williams years in Trinidad, comes from George Lamming (1993: 322–3).

[9] See too the momentary conversion of Fisheye to the PNM in *The Dragon Can't Dance*:

'But the PNM was its own happening. Something like a religion, it was capturing people. Old women were bouncing. Muscles swelled on the arms of young men and a glint of battle was coming into their eyes. Fellars was talking. He couldn't understand the words. He doubted that they could explain them; but you didn't really need words to understand the roaring of an ocean. Words were just a kind of background dressing, a kinda screen, a sound, the sounds. Manifesto, Nationhood, Culture, Colonialism.' (1979: 57).

[10] From this perspective, *Salt*, for example, can be read as a rewriting of Eric Williams' memoirs, *Inward Hunger. The Education of a Prime Minister* (1969).

[11] We might recall, though, that in the early 1930s the inner core of the Bloomsbury group did make contact, albeit fleetingly, with C.L.R. James, recently arrived from Trinidad. We can be sure, however, that in his dealings with Leonard Woolf, James didn't expatiate on the aesthetic wonders of stick-fighting, nor insist that Virginia learn the Bamboula.

References

Achebe, Chinua (2007) 'Interview', BBC Radio 4, *Front Row*, 27 June.

Guardian (UK) (2001) 'Nobel Citation from the Swedish Academy', 11 October.

Harris, Wilson (1963) *Tradition and the West Indian Novel* (London: West Indian Students' Union).

Hewson, Kelly (2004) 'An Interview with Earl Lovelace. June 2003', *Postcolonial Text*, vol. 1, no. 1.

Hodge, Merle (2006) 'The Language of Earl Lovelace', *Anthurium: A Caribbean Studies Journal*, vol. 4, no. 2.

James, C.L.R. (1980 [1969]) 'Discovering Literature in Trinidad: The 1930s', in C.L.R. James, *Spheres of Existence. Selected Writings* (London: Allison and Busby).

Johnson, Nadia I. (2006) 'Earl Lovelace: Select Bibliography', *Anthurium: A Caribbean Studies Journal*, vol. 4, no. 2.

Lamming, George (1993 [1956]) 'Trinidad and the Revolution in Political Intelligence', *PNM Weekly*, 30 August, republished in Selwyn R. Cudjoe (ed.), *Eric E. Williams Speaks: Essays on Colonialism and Independence* (Wellesley, MA: Calaloux).

—— (2005 [1960]) *The Pleasures of Exile* (London: Pluto Press).

Lovelace, Earl (1979) *The Dragon Can't Dance* (London: Faber and Faber).

—— (1996) *Salt* (London: Faber and Faber).

—— (2003) *Growing in the Dark: Selected Essays*, ed. Funso Aiyejina (San Juan, Trinidad: Lexicon).

Marie-Alice, Melle Troudart (1989) 'Interview with Earl Lovelace' in M.T. Marie-Alice, *From Non-Entity to Selfhood: Earl Lovelace's Approach in While Gods are Falling, The Dragon Can't Dance and The Wine of Astonishment* (Maitrise Anglais: Université de Antilles-Guyane).

Walcott, Derek (1998 [1987]) 'The Garden Path: V.S. Naipaul' in D. Walcott, *What The Twilight Says: Essays* (London: Faber and Faber).

Williams, Eric (1969) *Inward Hunger: The Education of a Prime Minister* (London: André Deutsch).

1
BEING IN THE WORLD

Bill Schwarz

> If Mr [Alfred] Mendes ever feels an urge to be glamorous,
> I suppose he works it off by writing a romantic tale about life in
> South Kensington, or a glowing work-picture of Dorking or Skegness.
> — Aldous Huxley (1934: 7)

In 1943 Earl Lovelace turned eight years old.[1] In itself, so far as we know, there was nothing of great significance in this event. There is no reason to suppose that there exists from this time, say, a great juvenile verse drama, which precociously anticipates *The Dragon Can't Dance* or *Salt*. There is no record of some cataclysmic occurrence which shaped the future life of the writer. Its importance can only have been as a private, family affair — or maybe, if we recall the arrival of the fictional G.'s ninth birthday at the beginning of George Lamming's *In The Castle of My Skin*, it wasn't even important as a family matter. In conventional biographical or literary terms, 1943 is a conspicuously uneventful moment in Lovelace's life.

Yet I want to make a historical argument, or at least an oblique historical argument, for making this my starting-point, which has to do with the configurations of an emergent cultural politics.

Lovelace had been born in Toco, in Trinidad, but — following a common pattern of Caribbean family life — as a very young boy he moved to the neighbouring island of Tobago in order to live with his grandparents. They were Methodists; he attended Scarborough Methodist Primary School; on Saturdays he went to the market with his grandmother, who sold homemade delicacies. His was a life of black Victorian respectability, devoted, in his own words, to 'Work and Church': 'in the house we couldn't sing calypso, nobody played mas, Carnival; these were the activities of the Devil'. 'I didn't know it then,' he comments, but 'everything bad was black'. This was not, he emphasises, a 'subservient' culture: rectitude and respectability signalled independence, a sense of collective selfhood marking a triumph in the face of the adversity with which his grandparents, whose memories of slavery were proximate, had to contend. Like many children brought up in such a household, in the Caribbean and elsewhere, Lovelace turned to books. 'I read every book in the small library (bookshelf at home) then I went to the public library. By ten I had read the Bible, had read all about American Negroes as they were called then, Frederick Douglass, etc. I had a book on pirates, which I read last of all because it didn't have pictures.' At this point: 'I was heading for a pleasant middle-class existence that I was going to achieve by becoming a doctor (every child was going to be a doctor) and this I would embark upon when I passed the college exhibition examination that I would sit at the age of eleven.' When the moment came, though, to his initial 'horror' he failed this first time in Tobago, and then failed again the following year in Trinidad (Lovelace 2003: 2–3).

Yet, while Lovelace was immersed in the Bible and reading up on American Negroes and pirates, across the water in Port of Spain a public debate was taking off concerning the origins and forms of Trinidad's traditions of calypso and popular music. Discussion turned on the questions of whether calypso could be regarded as an authentic indigenous or folk form and, if so, whether it was specifically Trinidadian or whether it could claim a wider, pan-Caribbean significance. The purpose of these inquiries into the contending conceptualisations of folk culture was explicitly nationalist in orientation. As one prominent (Saint Lucian) folklorist, Harold Simmons, had put it in a letter to the *Trinidad Guardian* early in 1943:

> A nation in the making should have its own music, art, literature and culture — a frank admission and self-criticism will dictate to the West Indian a true concept of himself, free from external influences. (Cited in Rohlehr and Brereton 2007: xxviii)[2]

The surest voice to intervene in this debate was that of Edric Connor. Connor was to have an illustrious future ahead of him as singer, stage and screen actor, radio broadcaster and filmmaker. Just before this moment, though, he had been an impoverished young man who had been studying railway engineering at the Royal Victoria Institute in Port of Spain, living a hand-to-mouth existence and prepared to do anything for an income, from journalism to joining the police force. During this time, he became familiar with many of the popular street celebrities of the city — tricksters, preachers, singers — including the heterodox, pantomime evangelist 'Teacher' Nosegay, who later appears as Taffy in Lovelace's *The Dragon Can't Dance* (and also in the work of Selvon and Naipaul, as John Thieme discusses in Chapter 9). At the same time, Connor was connected to the cluster of intellectuals, more respectable and publicly influential, who were organic to the emergent nationalist movement, including Albert Gomes, Ralph de Boissière and Carlton Comma. A resourceful man with an entrepreneurial flair, by the time the public discussion of Trinidad's folk past got going in the press in the latter part of 1943, Connor had set up his own contracting firm and was serving as a foreman on the construction site of the new US military base at Chaguaramas.

He was, in addition, also one of the island's foremost ethnomusicologists. As Rohlehr and Brereton (2007) suggest, his location as 'an intermediary between classes, castes and cultures' in Trinidad provided him with a privileged vantage point from which to comprehend the mix of elements which went into the makeup of vernacular musics (2007: xxix). Connor endeavoured to speak for a new generation who wished to reconcile their love for classical European traditions with their appreciation that, deep in the interstices of black Trinidad, there existed an emergent form — a peculiar articulation of the old and the new — which could become an organic, necessary part of the new nation. One way of achieving this, conceptually, was for him to argue that what might appear to be debased — the product of the urban barrack-yard — had an older, more noble ancestor in the Negro spiritual of an earlier time. Connor's reply to Simmons, in this vein, generated a number of responses, suggesting the degree to which arcane questions of ethnomusicology had an urgent topicality. Among these were commentators (including the Guyanese novelist then living in Trinidad, Edgar Mittelholzer) who refused to countenance the idea that calypso could be regarded as art, and who believed that, in consequence, such a visceral aesthetic should never become the means by which the new nation would be represented.

In July and December 1943, Connor delivered two public lectures on Trinidadian folk songs. These had an immediate impact, while Connor led himself to believe that the hand of history was upon him, declaring later that the occasion of the first of these lectures was the day when 'West Indian nationalism was born' (2007: 53). The hyperbole itself can be disregarded, but it could be said that it does demonstrate the degree of political investment in the recovery of folk forms. During the first lecture, Connor had some 50 'ordinary people' from villages and city sing traditional songs and demonstrate Limbo, Belé, Bongo and Shango dancing — even though the Bongo and Shango were prohibited by law. They also played steelband, a new phenomenon for the respectable classes of Port of Spain, which had only previously entered their field of vision as the object of concerted social derision (see Stuempfle, 1996). And throughout, Connor strove to emphasise the centrality of Africa to these contemporary Caribbean forms. Later in the year, he was asked to repeat the performance for an audience composed, in part, of the colonial elite, including the governor, Sir Bede Clifford. There they were confronted by steelbands, and by pleas from Connor to lift the bans on the Spiritual Baptists — an important cultural force amongst Trinidad's poor, particularly during the labour rebellion six years earlier — and also on the dancing of the Bongo and Shango.[3] When the mayor called for the national anthem, a number of the audience chose instead a rendition of the 'Internationale'. Included in the repertoire was one ancient Haitian song that can only have been included in order to have given maximum offence:

> Pain nous ka mange [The bread we eat]
> C'est viande beké [Is white man's flesh]
> Di vin nous ka boué [The wine we drink]
> C'est sang beké [Is white man's blood]
> Hé St Domingo [Hey St Domingo]
> Songé St Domingo [Remember St Domingo]

Remembering the events of the slave rebellion of St Domingo was the last thing the colonial audience would have wished for. Canon Farquhar reported in the *Sunday Guardian* that the song had produced 'instant and spontaneous applause' from a section of the audience. He continued:

> Many natives like myself were not a little embarrassed, and conscious
> of a sense of deep humiliation. It was unpardonably bad manners,
> and ill became the generous spirit which is the more natural heritage
> and instinct of the African race. Yet here again the incident furnishes
> more than an ordinary straw in the wind of public opinion.
> (Cited in Rohlehr and Brereton 2007: xxxiv)

A collapse in social etiquette is one way of looking at it. Rohlehr and Brereton offer an alternative view: 'If his first lecture was the beginning of West Indian nationalism, his second, disclosing as it had the stark divisions in the society and the age-old antagonism between contesting ethnicities and classes, was like a declaration of war' (2007: xxxv). The governor saw to it that Connor was moved on at the first opportunity — arranging a scholarship for him to complete his City and Guilds diploma in England, clearly not worrying where he went so long as it was a long way away.

On many matters, Connor was no great radical. We don't have to take at face value the idea that he was the forgotten progenitor of West Indian nationalism, nor see the occasion of these lectures as the decisive breakthrough for a new politics. What the recovery of this event does convey, however, is a vivid dramatisation of two contrary ideas of the nation directly confronting one another. On the one hand, we can see the idea of the colonised nation which, even in the moment when formal colonial authority was about to be dispatched, held true to the deepest imperatives of the colonial order. To recognise Africa and the tribulations of the Caribbean past as a means to assert blackness could only, within this scheme of things, be a cause of embarrassment, humiliation or shame. The alternative conception, on the other hand, envisaged a Trinidad which would heed the syncretic symbolic forms which were a conspicuous, active element in Afro-Caribbean social life — in religion, music and dance particularly — and draw upon these as a vehicle by which the new nation, after colonialism, could be imagined. The Connor lectures represent a moment when this idea assumed a public form. Of course, the terms of this dialogue between the official languages of the nation and the syncretic cultures of the black dispossessed were various, complex and open-ended; this was never a conversation between equals, it was always multivocal, and it remains unfinished. But as it has unfolded, Lovelace has been a critical voice within it.

The Folk Dynamic

In Lovelace's published essays, there occur a number of autobiographical reflections. Some of these turn on what he *didn't* do. He didn't pass his exams. He didn't cross the seas and make the journey to London. The first of these, certainly, was the cause of much pain at the time. But subsequently he came to rejoice both in his educational 'failure' and in the fact that he never migrated, for the alternative life which opened up to him presented him with a new world at home. Two episodes in particular reverberate through his writings.

After he failed his college exhibition for the first time, he left the Methodist household of his grandparents in Tobago and went to live with his mother in Trinidad. One night his mother took him to a Spiritual Baptist church. The Spiritual Baptists (commonly known, for obvious reasons, as the Shouters) were plebeian and for long had been outlawed by the colonial state, a prohibition which was only lifted in 1951. In the eyes of officialdom, the Shouters were at best a nuisance and at worst a source of indecency, politically suspect and the cause of unmitigated social evil. At the church, a girl a little older than Lovelace was either being prepared for baptism or had just been baptised — the accounts differ. Before the congregation, she acted out the spiritual journey of her life. 'She was,' Lovelace recalled, 'very energetic and the energy filled the whole place' (2003: 10). The experience was powerful; the memory stayed with him and the telling of the story keeps recurring:

> Even now I experience again that night and the thick energy exuded by that girl as she cried and laughed and danced and screamed as she relived her journey into the regions of the dream/spirit world, telling where she had been, the rivers she had crossed, the people she had met, speaking in tongues, in languages, that night, flooding the church with the electricity of a transfigurating power that drew other devotees in, moving them to their own dancing and screams and their own languages, making me feel more of a stranger, that more distant, remote from what I had no fear of. I was not afraid. It was something I had no way to embrace as much as I wanted to. I did not know it then but I had visited the darkness that the light had kept from me. (Lovelace 2003: 222–3)

The contrast to the Methodism to which he had been habituated could not have been more pronounced, not least because the historical resource of blackness was embraced by the Shouters as a welcome, necessary affirmation of their faith.

The second episode occurred some years later. When Lovelace left school, he took a job as a proofreader on the *Trinidad Guardian*: after a short while he abandoned both the job and Port of Spain to start a new life as a forest ranger in Valencia, deep in rural Trinidad, and for the next 12 years, as his career as a writer took off, he worked in various capacities for the Department of Forestry and the Ministry of Agriculture, throughout both Trinidad and Tobago. In the countryside he found a new life: drinking, gambling, playing makeshift cricket and football, storytelling, stick-fighting, and dancing hitherto obscure, unknown dances:

> Then one night I attended a wake and suddenly there, before me, at its most brilliant, was the darkness that I had glimpsed in the Baptist church years before. Everything that had been banned was here: fine play, stories, beating bamboo, dancing bongo, stickfights, the ribald songs of the wake. No wonder everything of this native culture had been associated with the dark, with death, and because they were associated with death, you didn't sing them everyday, and gradually they came associated with the grave, with death, but that very association recalled them; every time somebody died they were recalled, they were strengthened. It was something I had never seen before. Here was something the light had not penetrated to. It had its own rough strength, its violence, its ignorance.

In this environment he discovered a new freedom in which he could divest himself of his prior self — his Methodist and scholarly boyhood, with all the attendant expectations they carried — and fashion for himself a new sense of selfhood. 'I was free to go anywhere,' he says (2003: 224 and 4; see also 10–11).

There are a number of examples of similar occurrences in a generation of writers in the Caribbean, when young men trained to enter the middle class confronted what they experienced as an elemental blackness. In turn, this was internalised and became a means by which they could articulate their discontent with the values of the colonial system in which they had been educated. The opening pages of George Lamming's *The Pleasures of Exile*, for example, recount the author's experience of the ceremony of the Souls that he witnessed in Port au Prince in the latter part of the 1950s, the ceremony triggering for Lamming a sense of another world comparable to that which Lovelace experienced at the wake.[4] These pages detail the conflict between what Lamming identifies (upper case) as 'the Law' and a peasantry which determined to maintain what he calls 'a racial, and historic, desire to worship their original gods' (2005: 9–13). As much as in Lovelace's novel *The Wine of Astonishment*, which can be read as a sustained reflection on the intensity of his childhood experience in the Shouter church, 'the Law' in *The Pleasures of Exile* is no abstract concept but refers explicitly to the arrival of the police and to the violence which ensues. For Lamming as much as for Lovelace, making the cognitive leap from an attachment to the values of the educated middle class to an identification with the lives of the darker-skinned dispossessed was, in many respects, a demanding threshold to cross. Notwithstanding the powerful sense of personal liberation that a transformation of this kind promised, the subjective consequences were not always comfortably accommodated.[5]

Even so, these individual recastings of the self were impressive, and the history of anti-colonialism in the Caribbean cannot be grasped without appreciating the profundity of their consequences. For Lovelace, this encounter with the culture of the 'underworld class' came to him as a revelation (it was, he explicitly states, 'revealed to me'), the idea of a spiritual conversion not far distant. This was a culture in which he discovered 'meaning and possibility'. In turn, it prompted an engagement and a politics, for he came to realise that 'my task lay in validating the lives of these people, because they were indeed the salt of the earth' (Lovelace 2003: 4, 11).

In his essays — especially the early ones — he refers to this 'underworld' explicitly as a 'folk' culture (Lovelace 2003: 2, 5, 25).[6] The editor of the collection, Funso Aiyejina (2003) emphasises this line of argument in identifying what he believes to be particular about Lovelace's aesthetic. 'In essence', he writes, 'no matter how profound his thoughts, their founts and legitimising agencies are to be found in the world-view of the folk; and his vision, no matter how unique, echoes, clarifies, problematises, and extends folk preoccupations, wisdom, and philosophy' (Aiyejina 2003: v). He quotes from Lovelace:

> the philosophical support I called upon was to be found in the activities of the very people, and in the very culture that gave meaning to their actions. It is this culture I call the folk culture. I see the folk culture not as a rural culture conceived in the context of an agrarian society, or has having to so with the nature of the seasons but as resistance. (Lovelace 2003: 5)

'Folk' is a notoriously awkward term which can too easily slide into validating the kind of nationalist project to which Lovelace himself is hostile. In both its literary and political manifestations, as Gordon Rohlehr (1988) has detailed, it can lead to damaging sociological simplifications. It is a term which can essentialise that which needs to be rendered complex, effacing difference in favour of imaginary unities. Rohlehr, in his critique, focused principally on issues of social class and of ethnicity. But it isn't only a matter of class and ethnic difference. As we can see from Lovelace's initial encounters with rural Trinidad, it is clear that many of the practices he tells us that he most prized were predominately male, resulting in an overly partial, exclusive interpretation of what the folk might, or could, comprise. These difficulties need to be acknowledged. Yet it isn't as if Lovelace is unaware that these problems are present. In an interesting observation, Rohlehr (1988) suggests that, in the case of George Lamming, what can appear to be too one-dimensional or polemical in the essays is invariably more complex and multi-dimensional in the fiction. The same is true in the case of Lovelace. In the journalism and in the transcribed talks, complex arguments are often necessarily compressed, dependent on formats where economy and immediacy of communication are at a premium. But even here, I think, there are many interesting tensions. Aiyejina is right to say that in Lovelace we witness the idea of folk 'problematised' and 'extended'. The question, though, is how.

When Lovelace reconstructs his past life, and rehearses his early encounter with the rural forest workers, the location of the folk assumes an empirical, palpable reality: it is there embodied in the lives of those with whom he lived. When he indicates that he also understands folk culture to be 'resistance', this is a more complicated, abstract rendition for (as we know from the novels) the social practices of popular life are various, and even taking the most expansive conception of resistance, there is no necessary conformity between the two. But we should note the particular, characteristic rendition that he gives to the idea of 'resistance', unifying in a single formulation significant aspects of his thought:

> The principal philosophical concerns of the folk culture have centred around the affirmation of self in the face of the oppressive and powerful other; it has stressed the individual's place within the group, as well as the sense of a moral order, a hope for redemption and salvation. (Lovelace 2003: 28)

Self and other; moral order; redemption and salvation: these issues are decisive for Lovelace, the essentially Christian structure of his thinking transformed into a tough, this-worldly intransigence.

A third possibility arises, however: that the folk is essentially a contingent, symbolic arena that has been shaped by the histories of social struggles. This sense of folk, as I see it, is elaborated most persuasively in Lovelace's fiction. He is careful, for example, to insist that what he terms the folk is not the contrary to modernisation: folk and modernity operate less as antinomies than in a relation of reciprocity. 'It is ... with a consciousness of loss, but with a greater emphasis on gain, that I find it most profitable to look at the question of Caribbean folk culture within the process of modernisation' (2003: 25). This theme is explored with great subtlety in his early novel, *The Schoolmaster*.

As the opening of the novel demonstrates, the village of Kumaca, isolated from the rest of the nation, is composed of people 'whose needs are simple, desires few'. Only three of its inhabitants have ever ventured to the capital city. In these circumstances, the community itself is definitive; uppermost 'in the minds of all Kumaca is that big fête at the end of the harvest when Easter is beginning'. But in a finely etched counterpoint, Lovelace makes it clear that other desires impinge, which makes it difficult to conceive the village as a conventional folk idyll.[7] Kumaca, self-contained as it is, is still dependent on the abstractions of a money economy, the harvest bringing 'money into the humblest household'. Indeed, 'money is a great something', allowing not just subsistence but the possibility of possessing a radio or, for young men with more erotic passions to attend to, perhaps providing the means to purchase coveted new clothes. The allure of the nearest town is a constant presence — with 'many radios playing in the shops of the clean streets and the green painted cinema house where for a price you can go in and watch men on horses shoot guns off and make fine talk and kiss pretty girls, and where in the crowded rumshops it is easy to get drunk again with friends of the year before' (Lovelace 1979: 3–5). Although Lovelace hints that the pleasures associated with the fête may in some sense be more immediate, more real, he doesn't at all discount the power of those desires which look beyond the confines of the known community. They too have their own reality. This interplay between the lived relations of the village and the fantasised wishes associated with an urban modernity is delicately poised in the novel. That the coming of modern life to the village — the school and its master, literacy, the prospect of the road — brings catastrophe cannot be in doubt, but this is not to say that Lovelace embraces a folkish anti-modernity. In *The Schoolmaster* and in much of his fiction, the social arena which he describes as folk signals a dynamic, historical set of relations in which an alternative counter-modernity can be apprehended — a site, precisely, of 'meaning and possibility'. Or, to borrow from the great historian, E.P. Thompson, Lovelace's concept of folk represents the domain where distinct 'customs in common' pertain (Thompson 1993).

Yet if Lovelace presents the folk as an arena where, potentially, simple human virtues — dignity, self-respect, recognition of others — can be realised, in making such an affirmation there occurs a twofold paradox. First, as his fiction demonstrates, the psychic journey undertaken by his characters in their bid to realise their humanity is anything but simple: much conspires, from both inside and outside the individual persona, to undermine its attainment. Achieving 'simple human virtues' is anything but 'simple'.

Second, Lovelace's own relation to the forms of popular life on which he places such a premium is both mediated and complex.[8] He entered the world of the forest as a stranger to it; the fact that it turned out to be a 'revelation' to him attests precisely to its strangeness for him. It *became* a home for him, which he learnt to appreciate. The intensity of his initial encounters with black vernacular life as he recounts them, in the church and in the forest, comprises a pedagogy based on direct lived experience.

But through the 1960s he also became attuned to a pedagogy of a different order, in different locales, in which the experiences of racial oppression gave birth to a systematic 'philosophy' in the Gramscian sense: Black Power.[9] From their earliest incarnations, Lovelace was engaged in the nascent Black Power groupings in Trinidad which later, in the emergency of 1969–70, moved to the very centre of national life.[10] These years were alive with political contention: like many black militants of the time, he read the full corpus of black and Third World writings which circulated with speed, and with spectacular effect, from group to group. Nor was his experience confined to Trinidad. In the late 1960s he lived for a period in Washington DC and then later, from 1971 to 1974, he was based in Baltimore.[11] This complicates, too, an immediate identification with the folk. And it also complicates an interpretation based on the binary distinction between those West Indians choosing 'to stay' or 'to leave'. Lovelace may be counted as one who 'stayed', but even so the diasporic communities of the Caribbean — some distance from the villages of rural Trinidad — were open to him, and known by him. Living in the United States during this period offered a momentous experience, allowing him to participate close at hand in an authentic social and political crisis (as he had before during the Black Power moment in Trinidad) in which blackness operated as a critical agent of disorder. This political involvement, broadly understood, offered him a further set of resources by which he could invent himself anew, and divest himself of a prior colonial formation in which black was anything but beautiful. In this regard, despite the distinct pedagogies involved, there was a certain symmetry in experiential terms between the lessons he learnt in the Trinidadian countryside as a young man and the lessons he learnt as an active participant in the diasporic centres of urban black insurgency. But how they are put together conceptually is a matter of great interest.

Fanon and Dance

This can be illustrated by exploring the connections Lovelace establishes between Fanon on the one hand, and dance on the other. Fanon appears explicitly in minor key, as a thread running through his non-fiction essays. Ideas loosely associated with Fanon have a greater presence throughout the writings: relations between the black self and the other; the politics of recognition; the conviction that (in Lovelace's words) 'The colonised cannot lead us out of colonialism'; and, in the larger sense, the aspiration to create a new black subject who has sovereignty over the world and who rightfully belongs to the world (Lovelace 2003: 160).[12] Dance for Lovelace, on the other hand, is an integral moment of the folk, and it works too as an active element in his imaginary world, particularly in the later novels and stories.

In the famous opening chapter of *The Wretched of the Earth*, 'Concerning Violence', in an often-overlooked passage, Fanon addresses the question of dance. In what he identifies as 'underdeveloped communities', the native — as a means of surviving the power of the settler — will, according to Fanon, call upon a 'magical superstructure' which, he says, 'fulfils certain well-defined functions of the libido'. It is here that a collective belonging is established, existing out of reach of the colonial power. It is a sphere of social life which operates 'entirely under magical jurisdiction'. And it is within this region that Fanon locates dance and similar 'ecstatic' practices. Dance becomes equated for him with 'possession', and both need to be understood as decisive in the lives of the colonised.

The native's relaxation takes precisely the form of a muscular orgy in which the most acute aggressivity and the most impelling violence are canalised, transformed and conjured away. In dance 'may be deciphered as in an open book the huge effort of a community to exorcise itself, to liberate itself, to explain itself'.

As Fanon (1971) puts it, 'inside the circle' of such magical practices there can be no limits: all 'the hampered aggressivity' of the native dissolves 'as in a volcanic eruption'.

But during the struggle for freedom, other — more properly political — outlets emerge through which these accumulated, repressed reservoirs of nervous energy can be realised. The native 'will have no more call for his fancies'. 'After centuries of unreality,' Fanon writes, 'after having wallowed in the midst of the most outlandish phantoms, at long last the native, gun in hand, stands face to face with the only forces which contend for his life — the forces of colonialism' (1971: 43–5).

Fanon's argument at this point echoes a conventional Marxist orthodoxy. In 'underdeveloped' societies, dance functions as a lower — magical — form of collective self-knowledge, which in effect can offer only imaginary solutions to real social contradictions. Only when the transition from the 'phantoms' of 'unreality' to a truer consciousness of the politics of decolonisation has been accomplished, 'gun in hand', can these inherited social habits be seen for what they really are: a form of cathartic primitive rebellion.

Lovelace's position, arising from a different historical location, refuses this Fanonian distrust, or denigration, of putatively underdeveloped forms. For Lovelace, there exists a quality in the lived forms of the vernacular, in the very nature of their underdevelopdness, to use Fanon's terms, which needs to be nurtured. Indeed, for him it is dance — rather than violence — that enables the self to be realised, effecting the passage by which the colonised cease to *experience* themselves as colonised. Dance, in this sense, is invoked primarily as a metaphor, working as a means for imagining how the native can cease to imagine him or herself *as* a native. Yet in part also the argument is historical. In the enslaved Caribbean, Lovelace suggests, it was in dance that the racially oppressed established sovereignty over their own black bodies which otherwise, in all other departments of social life, belonged to the slaveholder:

> The body became an instrument over which they had control. And if you look at African dances you will see that they show the body in control of itself. The dancer is not seeking to traverse space, like in the waltz and other European dances, but concentrates on mastering his/her body within a limited space. The body becomes the universe. (2003: 32)

But principally Lovelace employs the idea of dance to express a distinctly postcolonial situation. He takes for his premise the (Fanonian) axiom that 'we cannot be liberated from colonialism by those who have been colonised', explaining this by use of the 'analogy' — or secular parable, perhaps — of arriving at a dance and dancing. Those he directly addressed, on this occasion, were a class of matriculating students:

> I don't know how many of you have ever lined up to get into a dance, where you are not certain of your welcome. Where, at the door, there is some kind of restriction, maybe it is the dress code, or your colour, or your class, or you don't know the people and they don't know you and all your energies are focused on getting past that door. And you fix your dress and you fix your smile and you try to calm yourself and eventually you get in ... And when you get in, it is as if you have carried the uncertainties with you, you can't really leggo, you feel inhibited, you feel you must behave in a certain way, you feel you must restrict your behaviour to what you believe they would expect of you. You go to move, the way you want to move, and you believe somebody is watching you ... You in the dance, but you acting as if you owe the people you meet there something, you acting as if they somehow have more rights than you. And so you will behave in accordance with how they behave. And you end up dancing how you think they dancing, nothing excessive, if you truly dance at all. That, I want to suggest to you, is the colonial perspective, restricted to what he has had to overcome in order to get into the dance ... He left home feeling that he will dance, but the experience at door has taken its toll ...
>
> You on the other hand have had no trouble at the door, you are inside the dance and your job is to dance ... The dance is yours. You have to take over the fete.
>
> This is the perspective that being a child of Independence, however flawed it is, has given you. (Lovelace 2003: 187–8)

Or, as he puts this elsewhere: 'Fanon says that each generation must, out of relative obscurity, discover its mission, fulfil it or betray it. Yours is to dance.' (Lovelace, 2003: 161)

The metaphorical properties of this mode of thought are clear, and it would be wrong to take them too literally: nowhere does Lovelace suggest that the material realities of exploitation can be resolved 'in the dance'. Yet nor, on the other hand, is the choice of metaphor only of secondary significance. The historical connections between the freedoms that dance offered the enslaved and the place that popular dance and song hold in contemporary Trinidad are always uppermost in his imagination. When, in addition, he argues that the limits of the

PNM's conception of the nation was the steelband, this is no metaphor. But in the larger sense, Lovelace's Fanonianism — his commitment to the struggle by which the dark-skinned colonised can cease to experience themselves as natives, and can recognise themselves and be recognised for what they are by others — takes a markedly un-Fanonian turn: his is a humanism underwritten not by violence characteristic of *The Wretched of the Earth* but, in all its complex subjective registers, by the idea of dance.

The Shouter church, the wake in the forest, the urban steelband, dance — all these, for Lovelace, represent the forces of darkness as revelation. 'I had found the darkness in which to grow' (2003: 11). Or, as he recalled his encounter at the Shouter church: 'I had visited the darkness that the light had kept from me.' In making these claims, Lovelace has come to conclude that the political time has arrived when it is necessary to reverse the journeys of a previous generation of Caribbean anti-colonial radicals: to spurn, in other words, the pull of colonial enlightenment and to reach instead for the subterranean 'darkness' of local popular life. This too can be understood as a further articulation of his preoccupation with the theme of 'folk', as it is within the 'folk' that 'darkness' is incubated. In particular, the banning by the state of a range of popular activities served to create new energies which, Lovelace suggests, were in themselves peculiarly syncretic and Caribbean. These proscriptions forced popular

> institutions underground and on the defensive. This called forth again the invention and creativity of the folk to maintain their cultural practices. For example, with the outlawing of the beating of African drums, used in stickfights, bongo dances and other dances, the folk utilised bamboos, cut to different lengths and of different sizes, to make drum sounds. Less than twenty years after the law against African drums, the same folk would produce in Port of Spain, a tuned steel drum, now known worldwide as steelband. From African drum to Caribbean steelband. This process is analogous to the transformation of the African into a Caribbean people and of what began as African culture to a culture that has to be seen as Caribbean. (Lovelace 2003: 27)

But, as ever, the situation is more complex than it first appears for, as Lovelace concedes, what he defines as 'darkness' is also — in part and inevitably — a construction of colonial authority. He reads Conrad's *Heart of Darkness* as a kind of blueprint in which the idea of 'darkness' was codified in the imaginative literature of empire. In this moment of Britain's empire, much ideological work was expended in organising colonial life by differentiating those domains of social life which could be considered to have been touched by light from those which remained in the thrall of darkness. Lovelace explains this larger history specifically in terms of Trinidad and the West Indies:

> One sure condition for bringing the light of their civilisation was the creation of the darkness in which their light could shine. So the colonisers had to establish as darkness the culture of the African and to do so they had to legislate darkness. The darkness became official. This continued through the entire period of the African's sojourn in the islands. As late as 1919 Shango and the Shouters were banned, the beating of the drums and certain dances were banned. Every single African institution was banned or made illegal or illegitimate. (Lovelace 2003: 3)

'Darkness', then, has a double role. It is not only a form of subterranean, Creolised knowledge, given life by the practitioners of steelband, calypso and so on. Historically, it has also been 'created' by the colonial authorities, 'legislated' by them, and it has become 'official'. In a fittingly Fanonian paradox we see that there is no aspect of 'native' life, even that which proves to be the most highly charged in generating new possibilities for emancipation, which escapes the imprint of the colonial order.

The World and the Self

In the Lovelace cosmos, there is an important counterpoint to the idea of the folk, and that is what he calls 'the world'. Although these — the folk and the world — carry distinct meanings, there are significant overlaps and interconnections between the two. Lovelace employs both to describe the possibilities for the realisation of the black self, as arenas where salvation can occur. But as in his use of the folk, the world in his writings is a concept given weight and complexity by the range of signification he requires of it.

Lovelace's usage of the term is at times close to the notion of modernity itself, or to the idea of 'the modern world' (Lovelace, 2003: 150). As we have seen, he is not hostile in the abstract to the coming of modern forms, recognising the gains as much as the losses they entail. In particular, in this context, the world for him suggests the social conditions which allow the possibilities for human fulfilment. To refer back to the beginning of *The Schoolmaster*, we can see that modern life — the world — signifies, in part, an erotic realm of movies, fashion and the upbeat tempo of contemporary urban culture. Notwithstanding the moral power of the customs in common held by the villagers of Kumaca, destroyed by the colonial instincts of the incoming schoolmaster, Lovelace makes it clear that the isolation of the village imposes its costs: as he emphasises, modernisation can only be grasped by understanding its contrary, contradictory movements, where gain and loss are delicately imbricated.

But at the same time his political wager turns on the conviction that the possibilities of collective fulfilment do not at all depend on the dispositions given by the divides between the overdeveloped and the underdeveloped societies of current times. Eric Williams, he notes, at the time of Independence held out the promise of creating the world 'at home', in Trinidad and Tobago. Williams's project may not have been that of Lovelace, though both shared the belief that what constituted the world need not be restricted to the power-centres of the metropole. In *Salt*, the reader follows Alford George's shift in consciousness. As he gains education, 'he began to feel himself bound for *the world* and to look at his stay in Cunaripo as temporary, as a state from which he would graduate in the same effortless way in which one grew old, as a stop, a halt, a station to refine and purify himself and straighten out his defects, ever conscious that it was never to be his final home'. But when he hears the Leader promising the coming of the world, here in Trinidad, he begins to wonder whether, after all, 'the world was right here'. Later on, 'it came to him afresh that he had to work to make this island a place where people didn't have to leave to find the world' (1996: 34–5, 90). The world, in this sense, is contingent, as the set of questions which Lovelace poses makes clear:

> What then is the world? Who qualifies for the world? Who decides what is the world? Is there a world? Is there one world? Why are we not an automatic part of the world?

It this contingency which leads him to conclude that: 'Nobody is born into the world. Every one of is born into a place in the world, in a culture, and it is from that standpoint of the culture that we contribute to the world' (Lovelace 2003: 150, 152).

We also know that, to a degree at least, Lovelace establishes a connection between the world and the word. There are many instances in the fiction where education is presented as a vehicle which functions to destroy the inherited customs and ethics of the common people. This is one of the dominating themes of *The Schoolmaster*. Ivan Morton, in *The Wine of Astonishment*, is a renegade to his people, the ostentation of the pen in his top pocket a sign of the social distance he has travelled and the malevolent instrumentalism he now embraces. 'Under colonialism,' Lovelace argues, 'two sets of persons had a sense of self: the schoolmaster and the Bad-John' and both, he suggests, became agents of destruction (Marie-Alice 1989: 146). But literacy, and the consequent command of self, are also means by which Lovelace's characters can be in the world. An element of the early tragedy of Alford in *Salt* is that he 'couldn't take his words out into the world' (Lovelace 1996: 33). What he had learnt by rote offered him no possession of his own self. Or again in *The Schoolmaster*, the villagers' desire for the school was itself authentic. Paulaine Drandrade, condemning the priest for his fear of change, insists that 'a man must live in his times'; to be active in the world — in Port of Spain, but before too long, he surmises, in Kumaca too — must depend on attaining literacy; 'a man must keep up with the world'. Drandrade gives books to his children, bringing the word into the village. 'You have to care to improve yourself,' he tells one of his sons, 'not only for you but for the place you live in. A man does have to carry the world with him' (Lovelace 1979: 37–8).

'A man does have to carry the world with him.' The gendering of the world in this way, such that entering and making the world is essentially the predicament encountered by men, is characteristic of Lovelace. But he also hints that the world, far from being only an exterior manifestation, is also a matter of interior life. It is both inside and outside. If the exterior idea of the world in Lovelace, attached to an idea of the modern world with its promise of fulfilment, is one aspect, another is the interior sense of the realisation of the self. Both these external and the internal conceptions of the world are predicated on the notion of *becoming*.

The tension here lies between the world in its historicist, or world-historical, conceptions, on the one hand, and on the other the more phenomenological or existential renderings, in the Heideggarian sense of 'being-in-the-world'. One can imagine that Lovelace himself would baulk at this latter identification, sceptical of the value of systematised, abstract thought.[13] But whatever the reservations, in Lovelace's imagination to be in the world is to be part of human reciprocity, in which the world enters us as much as we enter the world.[14] This is underwritten by a temporality, not of the political masses mobilising across the globe, but by the time of the everyday — everydayness — in which subjective lives are necessarily incomplete and in process, as a function of their perpetual becoming. It is in part in this realm of social life that meanings and values are fought out and established. If Lovelace dispenses with the hyphens which populate the English translations of Heidegger, he nonetheless introduces new words ('aliveness', 'equalness') or new constructions ('people is people', 'more person') which not only seek to capture the elemental values in a human life, but also aim to do so in a peculiarly folk idiom — as if entirely estranged from the abstractions of high philosophy.

It is in this 'local' world that the Lovelaceian struggle takes place between survival and defeat. But here there is a politics which *isn't* Heidegger's, for Lovelace demonstrates the degree to which the local, everyday world is a place where great social forces conspire to suborn, to imprison and to break individual lives, particularly the lives of those who carry the burden of having once been designated 'natives'. It is a struggle which is both inside and outside the self. In the protracted process of resurrection, or potential resurrection, of Aldrick and Sylvia in *The Dragon Can't Dance*, the tempo of the story turns on the drama fought out between the forces of defeat and the forces of survival and, as a function of that struggle, between bad faith and good faith. In the wonderful, surprising concluding paragraph of *The Wine of Astonishment*, a miracle occurs, but it is marked as much by its unexpected displacement — realised not in the congregation but in the steelband tent — and by its vital, unyielding profanity. At such moments the reader can apprehend what is at stake in making the leap of faith which opens to us the world.

Notes

[1] With thanks to Louis James for his comments on this chapter.
[2] In these opening pages, I stick closely to this impressive, illuminating account by Rohlehr and Brereton (2007), though in the space here I can't convey the full complexity of their argument.
[3] For the interplay between the Spiritual Baptists and calypso, see Rohlehr (2004).
[4] Indeed, Webb (1992) makes the connection, principally through her reading of Alejo Carpentier's encounter with Haiti, between this discovery of the folk and a form of narrative (broadly, that of 'marvelous realism') which can apprehend the mythic dimensions of New World history. See, too, Carpentier (1995). It would be fruitful to address Lovelace's conception of the folk within this larger discussion.
[5] With Lamming, as with some others of his generation, this also encompassed a re-recognition of the prior life which the education system had alienated them from: see particularly Lamming's 'Author's Note' in *Season of Adventure* (1960: 330–2).
[6] At the time he was preparing *The Dragon Can't Dance*, Lovelace drafted many versions of a paper he entitled 'Notes on Creole Culture', though nowhere does he elaborate on the conceptual distinctions between the key terms 'Creole' and 'folk'. See the St Augustine archive, Box 9 Ms #162.
[7] On this point more generally, see in particular J. Dillon Brown's chapter in this volume.

[8] Indeed, Lovelace himself has suggested that his adolescent experience in the Shouter church only acquired the meaning he gives it today retrospectively, in memory: 'When it was happening I didn't take a lot of notice of it.' Interview with the author, St Ann's, Port of Spain, 4 January 2007.

[9] See especially the St Augustine archive Box 11 Ms #5005 under the title 'English Curriculum', which shows both the insurrectionary texts Lovelace was using as an English instructor in Washington, and at the same time his concern with quite traditional aspects of classroom pedagogy. Box 9 Ms #231A, '*Dragon* Notes', also contains important reflections on Black Power in Trinidad.

[10] Paquet (2006) offers a compelling account of the essays, reading them historically rather than — as they are currently arranged — thematically: in this, she depends on the Black Power moment in Trinidad as a pivotal interpretative device.

[11] Fragments of his first impressions of Washington can be found in the St Augustine archive, Box 9 Ms #69/2. On arriving at Howard University in the late 1960s, what most immediately struck him was less any formal manifestation of Black Power rather than the women who styled their hair as 'a natural': interview with the author, St Ann's, Port of Spain, 4 January 2007.

[12] 'On the evidence of these essays here,' writes their editor, Funso Aiyejina, 'Frantz Fanon appears to have been one of his [Lovelace's] favourite political thinkers' (2003: xiv), while Paquet notes the elements of 'anguished Fanonian self-awareness' which punctuates Lovelace's addresses and essays (2006: 4).

[13] 'He didn't need CLR [James] comparing his ideas to Heidegger's or to any other European philosopher's' (Rigsby, 2006). A slightly different picture emerges from a reading of the various papers collected together in the St Augustine archive in Box 11 Ms#42a, 'Earliest Beginnings of *Salt*', with its emphasis on the philosophical conceptions of the relations between self and other, and the many versions of the essay 'Liberation and the Reclamation of the Self', which can be found in Boxes 9 and 11.

[14] In turn, this leads Lovelace to his important considerations on the concept of reparation, based on his starting-point that the violated cannot be unviolated. This theme is explored, with great insight, in *Salt*.

References

Aiyejina, Funso (2003) 'Introduction: Finding the Darkness in Which to Grow — The Journey Towards Bacchanal Aesthetics', in Earl Lovelace, *Growing in the Dark: Selected Essays*, ed. Funso Aiyejina (San Juan, Trinidad: Lexicon).

Carpentier, Alejo (1995 [1949]) 'On the Marvelous Real in America', in Lois Parkinson Zamora and Wendy B. Faris (eds), *Magical Realism: Theory, History, Community* (Durham NC: Duke University Press).

Connor, Edric (2007) *Edric Connor: Horizons — The Life and Times of Edric Connor, 1913–1968: An Autobiography* (Kingston: Ian Randle).

Fanon, Frantz (1971 [1961]) *The Wretched of the Earth*, trans. Constance Farrington (Harmondsworth: Penguin).

Huxley, Aldous (1934) 'Introduction', in Alfred Mendes, *Pitch Lake: A Story from Trinidad* (London: Duckworth).

Lamming, George (2005 [1960]) *The Pleasures of Exile* (London: Pluto Press).

—— (1960) *Season of Adventure* (London: Michael Joseph).

Lovelace, Earl (1979 [1968]) *The Schoolmaster* (London: Heinemann).

—— (1996) *Salt* (London: Faber and Faber).

—— (2003) *Growing in the Dark: Selected Essays*, ed. Funso Aiyejina (San Juan, Trinidad: Lexicon).

Marie-Alice, Melle Troudart (1989) 'Interview with Earl Lovelace' in M.T. Marie-Alice, *From Non-Entity to Selfhood: Earl Lovelace's Approach in While Gods are Falling, The Dragon Can't Dance and The Wine of Astonishment* (Maitrise Anglais: Université de Antilles-Guyane).

Paquet, Sandra Pouchet (2006) 'The Vulnerable Observer: Self-Fashioning in Earl Lovelace's *Growing in the Dark — Selected Essays*', *Anthurium: A Caribbean Studies Journal*, vol. 4, no. 2.

Rigsby, Greg (2006) 'Earl Lovelace's Years in Washington, DC: A Personal Memoir' *Anthurium: A Caribbean Studies Journal*, vol. 4, no. 2.

Rohlehr, Gordon (1988) 'The Folk in Caribbean Literature', in Susheila Nasta (ed.), *Critical Perspectives on Sam Selvon* (Washington DC: Three Continents Press).

—— 2004. 'Calypso Reinvents Itself', in Milla Cozart Riggio (ed.), *Carnival: Culture in Action — The Trinidad Experience* (New York: Routledge).

Rohlehr, Gordon and Brereton, Bridget (2007) 'Introduction', in E. Connor, *Edric Connor: Horizons — The Life and Times of Edric Connor, 1913–1968: An Autobiography* (Kingston: Ian Randle).

Stuempfle, Stephen (1996) *The Steelband Movement: The Forging of a National Arts in Trinidad and Tobago* (Philadelphia: University of Pennsylvania Press).

Thompson, E.P. (1993) *Customs in Common* (London: Penguin).

Webb, Barbara J. (1992) *Myth and History in Caribbean Fiction: Alejo Carpentier, Wilson Harris and Edouard Glissant* (Amherst: University of Massachusetts Press).

2
'I WILL LET DOWN MY BUCKET HERE': WRITERS AND THE CONDITIONS OF CULTURAL PRODUCTION IN POST-INDEPENDENCE TRINIDAD

Kate Quinn

'Emigrate or Vegetate'

Casting his eye over the cultural scene in 1970, the Jamaican writer Andrew Salkey (1972) painted a cheerless picture of the opportunities available to the 'culturally committed few' in the Caribbean (1972: 344). Such was the cultural impoverishment of the region, he lamented, that writers were forced to confront an unspoken choice: to go into voluntary exile, with a chance of making a living from their craft in the unwelcoming metropolis; or to remain at home and face the precarious existence offered to the writer in the 'peripheral' societies of the Caribbean — a bleak choice, in Salkey's words, of 'emigrate or vegetate' (1972: 29). Salkey speaks, however, as a member of that generation of Caribbean writers who chose — or who believed that they had no option but to take — the former course: writers such as Edgar Mittelholzer (Guyana), George Lamming (Barbados), Roger Mais (Jamaica), Samuel Selvon and V.S. Naipaul (Trinidad). This was the generation of the *émigré* artists on whom so much scholarly attention has been focused, and who arguably still retain a privileged position within the Caribbean literary canon. But by 1970, when Salkey recorded his pessimistic observations in his famous *Georgetown Journal*, a new generation of writers — including Earl Lovelace in Trinidad — were living and working in the Caribbean nations (still in the early years of Independence), actively rejecting the ambivalent condition of the artist-in-exile in order to stake their chances on the uncertain future offered at home. Consciously writing as national (though not necessarily nationalist) intellectuals of the post-Independence Caribbean, they sought to distinguish themselves from the postwar writers of the Caribbean boom, whose works were for the most part produced and consumed outside the region they describe.[1]

Lovelace's pride in the decision he took to stay in Trinidad and 'write about the Caribbean from the inside' is reflected both in his interviews and in his literary works. Contrasting himself explicitly to his *déraciné* compatriot, V.S. Naipaul, he states:

> Naipaul's ... is the view from someone who lived outside, from a point of superiority ... [he] didn't live in the society and understand the difficulties ... I've had the advantage over other writers [in] that I lived among the people as one of them ... [I] have respect for them, and insight. (Cited in Sankar 1988: 42)

Lovelace's self-identification as a man of the 'ordinary people' is typical of the self-consciously anti-elitist strand that pervaded debates on the role of the intellectual in the Anglophone Caribbean in the years after Independence. Across the region, a new generation of radical intellectuals attempted to distance themselves from their classic role as 'scholarship boys' — products of the colonial system which, through education and the scholarship system, geared the Caribbean to export its talents while condemning the majority left behind as 'failures'.[2] For Lovelace, his own conventional failure in this regard (as a schoolboy, he twice failed the exams that would have allowed him to attend one of Trinidad's 'prestige schools') offered him instead an escape from colonial mimicry and the 'civilising mission' of 'formal colonising education'. It was precisely outside this system, he believed, that the 'native elements' of Trinidad's cultural patrimony were born (Lovelace 2003: 10; 1998: 56). For the *intellectuel engagé* of the postcolonial Caribbean, then, the decision to stay was constructed as both a moral obligation and a political act: a refusal to play out the role of the intellectual minority who joined the ranks of *émigrés* or bolstered the bureaucracies of government administration without making any 'tangible contribution to national intellectual life'. In the underdeveloped societies of the Caribbean, it was argued, intellectuals could no longer accept that 'the only options [were] the eternal dispossession of the novelist abroad, or the Robinson Crusoe solitude of the poet at home' (Best 1968: 5–6).

Such distinctions between *émigré* and non-*émigré* writers, however, can be misleading. Many non-*émigré* writers have, like Lovelace, spent extensive periods abroad, while many *émigré* writers have maintained strong connections with, and in some cases residences in, the region. Those who made the Caribbean their base, as this chapter will show, were still heavily tied in to metropolitan cultural circuits, not least in the matter of publishing their works. Independence did not eliminate the powerful lure of the metropolis, or the uneven distribution of cultural resources characteristic of the Caribbean's 'branch plant' relationship with the West (Wynter 1996: 307). Writers may consciously have chosen to 'define themselves within their homeland' (Allis 1981: xxx–xxxi), but the desire to be a self-sustaining Caribbean writer, freed from the demands of the metropolis and oriented towards a local audience, was not always facilitated by the conditions in which they worked. Here I will sketch the conditions for writers in post-Independence Trinidad, focusing briefly on the cultural policy of the Eric Williams administration, and then primarily on the vexed question of publishing.

Cultural Policy and the Role of the State

The initial optimism that accompanied the granting of Independence in the Anglophone Caribbean brought with it a small reversal in the usual flow of outward cultural migration. Writers and artists like Donald Locke (Guyana), Karl Parboosingh (Jamaica), and Clifford Sealy and Michael Anthony (Trinidad) returned to the region, ending their periods of voluntary exile in the hope of contributing to the cultural development of the newly emerging states. However, while many of the new governments acknowledged that political independence should be accompanied by efforts towards cultural independence, they were most immediately concerned with the more pressing problems of economic development and the basic consolidation of the instruments and institutions of the state. Provision for cultural development was low in terms of government priorities; cultural policies were generally made piecemeal, and were financed by a low share of total public spending. However, the state had a potentially key role to play in facilitating cultural development in the Caribbean, and it was under the aegis of the state that many Caribbean artists and writers found employment as the administrators and directors of the new cultural agencies and ministries that sprang up across the region after Independence. In Trinidad, figures such as Derek Walcott, Michael Anthony, Isaiah Boodhoo and George Bailey all held posts at various times within state agencies such as the National Cultural Council and the Ministry of Education and Culture — indeed, the directorship of the Ministry was held for many years by the artist, poet and broadcaster M.P. Alladin. Appointments such as these, as well as some positive government pronouncements on provision for the arts, encouraged an initially 'favourable' impression of Eric Williams among West Indian writers — a perception given a certain credence by Williams' own standing as a distinguished man of letters, a reputation he himself was not shy in proclaiming (King 1995: 42).

However, with regard to encouraging literary production, it soon became clear that the policies of the Williams administration fell dramatically short of writers' expectations or demands. First, in terms of providing the infrastructure for the promotion and dissemination of culture on a national scale, Williams's 'miserable' performance in this area has been described as nothing short of gross neglect (Ryan 1988: 156). Despite early promises to construct a national cultural centre, 'after thirty years [in] power ... the PNM demitted office without leaving a national theatre for the performing arts, a national museum for carnival, a national gallery for the visual arts, a national library or a proper national archive system'. 'Quite simply,' states Selwyn Ryan:

> [Williams] ... left no monuments to the cultural genius of the people of Trinidad and Tobago. The man of culture revealed himself to be a philistine. (Ryan 1988: 156–7)

In the absence of state provision, the creation of spaces that could form the foundations of a cultural community fell instead to the efforts of individuals: Derek Walcott's Trinidad Theatre Workshop, Beryl McBurnie's Little Carib Theatre and Clifford Sealy's Book Shop on Frederick Street, for example, all provided physical meeting places where writers and artists could gather to share their work with each other and with a wider audience, creating in the process the makings of a local market for their work.[3] The problem of cultural infrastructure, meanwhile, has still not been solved in Trinidad. For some four decades, artists, writers and performers have lobbied the government to construct the so-called 'Missing Cultural Institutions' of Trinidad and Tobago, most recently in a petition submitted to the government in March 2006. Summarising 44 years of 'outstanding artist demands ... not one [of which] has ever been met', the petition expresses the 'profound marginalisation' felt by cultural workers who have long felt excluded from the decisions of the state in the areas that most affect their work.[4]

The roots of contemporary shortcomings in cultural provision may at least partially be traced to the style of cultural policy-making that evolved under the Williams administration. As is well known, cultural policy in the Williams era focused primarily on the 'folk arts', namely calypso, Carnival and Best Village (an annual competition promoting performances of theatre, dance, music and skits at village level). This latter initiative, founded in 1963 as a consequence of Williams's 'meet-the people' tours of the early 1960s (Yawching 1991: 141), achieved some measure of success, evolving into a national festival that both showcased local talents and provided a stimulus to new and established writers to produce new works of theatre. Earl Lovelace, whose *My Name is Village* won the 1976 award for Best Play, contributed for many years to Best Village, writing and producing plays, and campaigning for the Friends of Best Village Committee when the 'treasured institution' was threatened with extinction (Lovelace 2003: 18–21; 1988: 335–42). But while Lovelace saw the potential of Best Village for validating and preserving the indigenous cultural forms and traditions he believed formed the true basis of Trinidad's national patrimony, others saw the festival as a PNM showcase promoting a limited conception of national culture at the expense of 'elite arts' such as creative writing and theatre. Taking an explicitly 'hierarchical' conception of culture, 'based on an inequality of talent', Derek Walcott warned against destroying the 'freshness and vitality' of folk arts while creating 'the illusion that people can be artists without the discipline of art'. Walcott, who had struggled to create a national theatre for Trinidad since the founding of the Trinidad Theatre Workshop in 1959, suggested that 'a scholarship for the training of a real artist [had] more value than any Best Village programme' (cited in King 1995: 154–5), a position clearly at odds with Lovelace's anti-elitist belief in the cultural and political force of the 'indigenous arts'.

Walcott's critique points to wider concerns that Williams's seemingly democratised approach to cultural policy amounted to a limited promotion of 'grassroots' culture for reasons of political expediency and cheap cultural nationalism. Writing at a time of heightened anxieties about the repressive powers of the state, Walcott suggests that the 'assimilation of folk culture to the state, and the manifestation of the state's image through folk-costumes, folk-parades and folk-circuses' was no less than a sign of cultural 'fascism', valorising 'mass arts' above individual creativity and promoting a narrow cultural 'decolonisation' as a means of appeasing radicals in the wake of Trinidad's Black Power rebellion (cited in King 1995: 154). Lovelace, too, has been highly critical of state policy in this area, though — unlike Walcott — he emphasised the bureaucratisation and 'officialisation' of culture that resulted from government intervention. For Lovelace, the establishment's embrace of cultural forms like calypso and Carnival emptied them of their emancipatory potential: Carnival was now run by 'government bureaucrats' wielding the 'sanitised rules and regulations of the colonial middle class'; the cultural expressions of the 'ordinary people' were packaged as 'national exotica' to be consumed by tourists; while the calypsonian, once the 'mouthpiece of the people', was now the 'prisoner of the Carnival Development Committee', composing pro-government songs and marching 'openly in support of the ruling party' (Lovelace 1998: 58; 2003: 66). In contrast to the belief that Williams ignored 'high' culture, for Lovelace it was precisely Williams's elitism that caused a true apprehension of Trinidad's popular cultural forms to elude him. Williams, the classic scholarship boy, could not, suggests Lovelace, 'elevate the indigenous above the educated, the creative over the imitative'; the 'genius of the people', as such, 'remained largely unexplored' (Lovelace 2003: 66).[5]

As for the genius of the writers, the shortcomings of government policy only served to confirm their pessimistic conclusions that the creative professions were not valued either by the state or by wider society. This was certainly true in the material sense of basic remuneration for their work: economic survival dictated that full-time creative employment was impossible for even the most successfully established writers. Those who remained in Trinidad '[had] to be content with the status of part-time writers and hobbyists' with the business of writing fitted in around a variety of day jobs (Eric Williams, cited in Gonzalez, 1974: 7). Earl Lovelace, for example, was working as an agricultural officer when he won the British Petroleum Independence Prize for literature. He subsequently worked as a sub-editor on the *Trinidad and Tobago Express*, and then as a lecturer at the University of the West Indies, even as his novels brought him acclaim at home and abroad. Even Derek Walcott, who was by this time well established both in Trinidad and internationally, lived under the constant pressures of financial insecurity, dependent on his job as a writer for the *Trinidad Guardian*, and frequently reliant on grants awarded by the Rockefeller Foundation to allow him to continue his work as a writer and as the driving force behind the Trinidad Theatre Workshop (King 1995: 37, 59–60, 70, 76).[6] The financial backing of the Rockefeller Foundation (and in other cases British Petroleum, Texaco, and Tate and Lyle) draws attention to the role of external agencies and private corporations in the cultural sector in the Caribbean.[7] Despite the rhetoric of cultural decolonisation, it was the Rockefeller, and not the Trinidadian government, that helped to keep the Trinidad Theatre workshop afloat throughout its frequent periods of financial crisis.

Publishing in the Anglophone Caribbean: The Colonial Experience

> the literary world is pragmatic like any other, and the canon of literary achievement, the very commerce of ideas, depends so largely on the development of outlets ... (Swanzy 1956: 249)

Of all the criticisms made of Williams's failure to establish the necessary cultural infrastructures, few mention the question of local publishing. This can perhaps partly be attributed to assumptions that overseas publishing houses (in London, New York or Toronto) would continue to provide the main outlet for Caribbean work, and partly to assumptions that writers are solitary creatures with simple needs, requiring only a desk and a typewriter (or these days a computer), rather than expensive physical structures — concert halls, cultural centres or studios — in order to produce their work. However, for the majority of

Trinidadian writers who did not have contracts with metropolitan publishers, viable local outlets for publishing were crucial if their manuscripts were not to be left to the 'devastating critique of moths and mice' (Castro 1967).[8]

In the decades before Independence, the Anglophone territories possessed little that could accurately be described as a publishing industry catering for creative writing, despite the flowering of West Indian literature in the period since the 1930s. Early ventures into book publishing tended to be small-scale and short-lived, dependent on the commitment and solvency of the individuals (often writers themselves) who had had the initiative to set them up: a key theme in Naipaul's *The Mystic Masseur* (1957) concerns the protagonist's attempts in the 1940s to get his various tracts and writings published, his first deal being struck with the Elite Electric Printery.[9] Not until the 1950s did the book publishing landscape in the region begin to experience subterranean shifts. The founding of Pioneer Press (Jamaica), the Jamaican Institute and the Extra Mural Studies Unit of the University of the West Indies provided local outlets for local works — the latter, for example, producing the invaluable *Caribbean Plays* series under the directorship of dramatist Errol Hill: a series 'which for many years provided the only available texts of West Indian drama' and whose existence underpinned the theatrical renaissance in Trinidad in the 1960s (King 1995: 13).[10] Nevertheless, as Kenneth Ramchand's figures for the West Indian novel show, the proportion of novels published locally between 1950 and 1964 actually decreased in the run-up to Independence and, notably, all of these were published in Jamaica (see Table 2.1). While the novel is not representative of all literary production (I discuss this later), these figures reflect a more generally applicable truth: book publishing, in the years before Independence, was an overwhelmingly metropolitan affair.

Within the region, the primary outlets for writers to place their work were the local newspapers and the famous 'little magazines', amongst which Trinidad's *The Beacon* (1931–33) and *Trinidad* (1929–30) were early pioneers (Sander 1988: 27–45). *Bim*, established in Barbados in 1942, was followed by A.J. Seymour's

Table 2.1: West Indian Novels published 1950–1964

Period	No. first published	UK	Jamaica	USA	Australia
1950–54	20	14	5	0	1
1955–59	32	28	2	1	1
1960–64	45	43	1	1	0

Source: Ramchand (1983: 63).

Kyk-over-Al (1945–62) in British Guiana, *Caribbean Quarterly* (Jamaica) in 1949, and the *Jamaica Journal* in 1961. Their contributions to the development of a consciously West Indian literature, aesthetic and political consciousness were all the more remarkable given the precarious conditions in which they were produced. Financing — whether secured through political patronage, advertising, or from the pockets of their founders — was a perennial problem, exacerbated by production costs outweighing sales. Hiring a dedicated production or editorial team was beyond the means of most of these local periodicals. Indeed, the demise of *Trinidad* in 1930 and the suspension of *Kyk-over-Al* in 1962 highlights the extent to which publishing ventures of this kind were wholly dependent upon the initiatives and dedication of committed individuals: neither *Trinidad* nor the original *Kyk* survived beyond the migration of their founders.[11] Nevertheless, along with the local newspapers, these magazines provided not only a means for writers to be remunerated for their work, but also a stimulus to creation and a sense of a wider literary community.

Given the obvious restrictions of space in these media, it is no surprise that it was poetry and the short story that flourished in this period. For those who wanted 'something other than the newspapers as a vehicle for [their creative] expression', however, the main option was to publish their work themselves, taking their manuscripts of poems, short stories and in a few cases novels to local printing firms or to the presses of the local newspapers, who took on paid printing jobs in limited runs (H.M. Telemaque, the Trinidadian poet, cited in Gonzalez 1974: 35).[12] Acting as both 'publisher and bookseller', writers would commonly visit friends or call door to door to sell print runs averaging less than 500 copies, paid for in irregular installments eked out from the salaries of their day jobs (Cameron 1965: 9). As Telemaque recalled, speaking of his 1947 publication *Burnt Bush* (a joint anthology with fellow poet A.M. Clarke):

> we had to seek out a man who would do it — a printer who would prepare the work [for] a fair price, because in those days we worked for very little as teachers. After selling so many, we paid up, and sold so many more, and paid up again, and so on. In the end we paraded the streets, in stores, in people's homes. We knocked at doors and we were able to meet the cost. This was the only way we could do it. (Cited in Gonzalez 1974: 35)

In most cases, however, the cost of publishing outstripped sales. Despite selling out his print run of 1,000 copies in three weeks ('a best seller in those days'), De Wilton Rogers's 1942 book *Lalaja*, one of the handful of novels published in Trinidad in the pre-Independence period, cost him, he recalls, 'a goodly sum from which I never recovered' (De Wilton Rogers, cited in Gonzalez 1974: 13). This gap between sales and costs hints at the limited local market into which writers launched their books, and also explains publishers' reluctance to take on creative works. Publication patterns in Trinidad in the period 1930–59 reveal that 21 out of 22 creative works were self-published in local printing firms, most popularly Frasers Printerie and the Guardian Commercial Printery (six publications each), despite the existence of a local publisher — College Press — established in 1929.[13] Given that the vast majority of these were works of less than a hundred pages, it is again evident that the costs and available medium favoured the slimmer and less expensive volumes of short stories and poems — indeed, not a single Trinidadian novel was published in Trinidad in the decade before Independence.[14] Jeannette Allis's observation that 'it is primarily the poets who have chosen to remain in their homeland, while the novelists tend to work abroad' (Allis 1981: xxx) may at least partially be explained by this basic inequality in the resources at their disposal.

Publishing in Post-Independence Trinidad

The first two decades after Independence brought some significant alterations to the publishing landscape in Trinidad. While the local newspapers continued to play an important role, a new breed of 'little magazines' expanded the avenues for publishing individual works, and intensified debates on the language, forms and, increasingly, politics of the literature of Independence. Region-wide, many of these new journals emerged as the organs of activist groups engaged in the political struggles of the 'postcolonial' Caribbean: Jamaica's *Abeng* (founded February 1969) and Trinidad's *Moko* (October 1968) and *Tapia* (September 1969), for example, all emerged in the aftermath of the Rodney riots which occurred in Jamaica in October 1968. The 1970s also saw the establishment of equally significant, if more strictly literary, journals — including Jamaica's *Savacou* (1974) — developed out of the Caribbean Artists Movement, and the focus of 'a particularly fierce debate about aesthetics, tradition, literary criticism and sensibility' (Donnell and Welsh 1996: 287); and Trinidad's *New Voices* (1973), a bi-annual literary review founded by the writer and publisher Anson Gonzalez, which — unusually — enjoyed an unbroken run of some 20 years. Like their pre-Independence counterparts, these journals provided a space for publishing the most significant Caribbean writers and intellectuals of the period.

Post-Independence Trinidad also witnessed a considerable expansion in the local publishing industry. Data from the 1985 survey of publishers, printers and booksellers in Trinidad and Tobago suggests that, whereas between 1900 and

1962 there were less than half a dozen publishing houses on the islands, in the period since Independence, some 39 publishing houses were founded, the majority in the 1970s.[15] Given the sensitivities about foreign ownership of Caribbean cultural resources, it is interesting to note that the vast majority of these publishers were in fact locally and privately owned: six were government owned or funded (including the publishers associated with the Ministry of Culture and Education, the National Cultural Council and the University of the West Indies); and just two were subsidiaries of foreign agencies or enterprises: Longman Caribbean, founded in 1970; and the United Nations Economic Commission for Latin America. While school textbooks and other educational materials were the mainstay of local publishing, niche markets were catered for by a variety of publishers specialising, for example, in Rastafarian history (Black Star Line Inc.), cricket and regional sport (Brunell Jones), and West Indian flora and fauna (S.M. Publications). For creative writing, the most important local publishers were the Extra Mural Studies Unit of the University of the West Indies (St Augustine), which continued its crucial work in publishing Caribbean drama, and the privately owned publishers Columbus (founded in 1969), Inprint Caribbean (1975) and New Voices, founded by Anson Gonzalez in 1974. The founding of these publishers did see some improvements in the fate of Trinidadian poetry and drama, while for the first time the presence of Inprint, Columbus and Longman meant that Trinidadian novels could be published on Trinidadian soil, albeit in very small numbers (see Table 2.2). Nevertheless, judged on quantity of output alone, these were small-scale enterprises, the vast

Table 2.2: **Trinidadian Literature Published in Trinidad and Tobago 1960–99, by Publisher and Genre**

Publisher	Novels	Poetry collections	Plays	Short story collections	Total
Self-published	14	135	51	14	214
Inprint Caribbean	4	3		1	8
Columbus Publishers	2	1		1	4
UWI Extra Mural Unit			31	1	32
UWI	1				1
National Cultural Council				1	1
New Voices		20		1	21
Longman Caribbean			1		1
Other	6	23	6	3	37

majority publishing on average less than five titles per year (including even the metropolitan-owned Longman Caribbean, with just two titles per year).

Moreover, as these figures demonstrate, publishing houses accounted for less than one-third of the total creative works published in Trinidad in the period 1960–99: the rest — just over two-thirds — were published by commercial printers. In other words, despite the expansions in domestic publishing described above, self-publishing continued to be the primary method of local publication.[16]

This reliance on commercial printers had a number of implications for writers and for the production of their work. Viewed in positive terms, using commercial printers meant that aspiring writers in small towns and villages were not as dependent on the capital city (at least for printing their work) as would traditionally be the case where cultural infrastructures are highly centralised. Anyone with access to a printing shop could put out their work and, as bibliographical data reveal, writers did indeed publish beyond Port of Spain, in Arima, Curepe, Diego Martin, Gasparillo, Port Cumana, Sangre Grande and St Ann's, to name a few of the recurrent locations. Publishing in this sense could be a truly local affair. However, commercial printers — especially those at the small end of the scale — simply did not have the same distribution networks as publishers, meaning that writers in the post-Independence period were still not freed from the constraints of having 'to hawk' their work themselves (De Wilton Rogers, cited in Gonzalez 1974: 13). Indeed, in some respects, modernisation of the industry left writers at a disadvantage compared with their pre-Independence counterparts: instead of paying in instalments, writers now had to pay the full cost in advance at a time when, as Anson Gonzalez recalled, recovering two-thirds of the cost was considered to be 'quite a success' (Gonzalez 1974: 13). Further, if the ability to pay the printing costs was the only prerequisite for seeing your work in print, then the quality of output would inevitably be highly uneven. Without the critical eye of a professional editor, in other words, publishing of this type might well produce 'a large number of poems, but very little poetry' (Gonzalez 1974: 21).

Nor did the expansion of local publishing facilities eliminate the high degree of dependency on external publishing firms. While the ratio of local to non-locally published works improved in the post-Independence period, more Trinidadian literature was published outside Trinidad than within it in the period from 1960 to 1999 (see Table 2.3). As would be expected, 'abroad' meant primarily the UK, followed by the United States, Canada and, at a considerable distance behind, by other destinations in the Caribbean, continental Europe and Australia. The most notable discrepancy between home and abroad becomes evident when these figures are broken down by genre: while poetry and drama were fairly well served by local publishing, novels were still overwhelmingly published

Table 2.3: Trinidadian Literature Published 1960–99, by Place of Publication and Genre

	Novels	Poetry collections	Plays	Short Story collections	Total
Trinidad	27	182	89	22	220
UK	76	38	9	19	142
USA	36	29	7	3	75
Canada	11	22	5	4	42
Other Caribbean	-	3	-	1	4
Western Europe	-	1	-	-	1
Australia	-	2	-	-	2

abroad. Continued external dependency in this area was a matter of some sensitivity and indeed debate in the region in the decades after Independence, but while both writers and nationalist governments could agree on the ironies of having to re-import their national literature — at expense — from the metropolitan publishing firms, no local publisher had the resources to lure established writers away from the 'fairly substantial' advances and royalties they could obtain elsewhere, 'unless', as A. J. Seymour observed, 'their patriotism is to be [seriously] strained' (Seymour, undated manuscript). Hence while the national novelists of post-Independence Trinidad may have claimed they wrote for and to an imagined Trinidadian audience, their novels — and other works — in fact continued to be published in the metropolis. This is the case, for example, for Michael Anthony, whose novels were published by André Deutsch and Heinemann, and for Earl Lovelace, all of whose novels — and his collection of plays — were first published either in London or the United States.[17]

Given the constricted size of the local market, it is not surprising that the metropolitan publishers, with all of the comparative advantages they enjoyed, remained the primary outlet for Caribbean writing, even in the decades when the large firms were retracting their commitments to so-called 'Third World' or 'minority' literature.[18] Yet, if local publishing was to be commercially viable, and if writers were not to be wholly dependent upon the fluctuating tastes and demands of metropolitan cultural industries and markets, it was crucial to foster a book-buying public in the region itself. In Trinidad, however, the high degree of literacy since Independence (94.9 per cent in 1980) (UNESCO 1991) had not, as even Eric Williams conceded, been translated into a society with a strong 'culture of reading'. Indeed, while the massive expansion of education under the Williams administration helped to create a far larger reading public than the 'illiterate mass' confronting writers in the colonial period, other educational reforms had more ambivalent effects (Lamming 1992: 40).[19] Educational priorities were reoriented in the mid-1960s with the specific aim of overturning the 'literary bias' of the colonial curriculum in favour of the vocational and technical subjects required to meet the development objectives of Trinidad's economy (Williams 1981: 245). English language and literature, once the most popular subjects for the Cambridge Certificate O-Levels, were gradually displaced by subjects such as science, economics, commerce and agriculture (Harvey 1988: 361). Even a decade into Independence, the chairman of the National Cultural Council could complain that 'literature', on the school and college curriculum, still connoted 'English Literature', meaning not merely 'written in English, but produced by British writers' (Elder, cited in Gonzalez 1974: 2). Reviewing educational attainment after two decades of expansion and reform, policy-makers admitted that the 'level of achievement' at primary and secondary levels was 'unacceptably low' — most gravely manifested, they noted, 'as a serious deficiency in the teaching of reading skills' (Harvey 1988: 346).

It is difficult to assess the direct effects of these educational shifts on the local market for West Indian literature. While, relative to the pre-Independence period, the potential readership 'was wider now for local fiction than [ever] before' (De Wilton Rogers, cited in Gonzalez 1974: 13), what writers now had to confront, suggests Kevin Baldeosingh, was 'a mostly literate culture where most of the people who can read, do not read. Not books, at any rate, and often not anything they don't have to' (Baldeosingh 1998).

For Baldeosingh, writers themselves were partly to blame if only 'a tiny intellectual elite' read their novels: 'thriving sales' of popular fiction (Mills and Boon and John Grisham thrillers, for example) indicated a market for popular literature that had not been met by Caribbean writers seeking intellectual and critical esteem (Baldeosingh 1998). For Eric Williams, however, such popular preferences (in his day, manifested in the appetite for 'the latest James Bond novel') supplied further evidence of the 'steady bastardization of [Trinidad's] limited literary tastes', blamed — in characteristic Williams style — on 'foreign capital' and the 'constant emphasis on imported rubbish' (Williams 1981: 257-8). Many writers shared something of Williams's pessimism in their assessment of their local audience, berated for its putative 'colonial' tastes and the 'excessively bulky non-Caribbean diet' of its reading (Salkey 1972: 287). Across the region, writers bemoaned the miserable domestic sales figures for Caribbean writing in a market where even a writer as established and acclaimed as George Lamming managed to shift a mere 'fifty-eight copies of a particular edition of a book sold up and down the length of the Caribbean countries' (Seymour 1977) and where booksellers justified '[going] easy on importing Caribbean novels' on the grounds they would end up 'shop-soiled and unsold' (Salkey 1972: 285–8). 'Hardly anything,' stated the Guyanese writer Denis Williams, 'could seem more depressing to a Caribbean writer than the "overseas" [that is, Caribbean] column of his royalty statements' (Williams 1973: 107).

Other developments, however, suggested a greater appetite for local writing than the pessimists acknowledged or than book sales alone would reflect. The founding of bookshops selling local work, the introduction of West Indian texts to the school curriculum and the borrowing habits of members of Trinidad's new National Library all indicated the existence of a local market — albeit modest in both size and income. De Wilton Rogers, for example, felt sufficiently confident of a readership to re-launch both his *Chalk Dust* (in 1973) and *Lalaja* (in 1976), both self-published, despite the financial difficulties he admitted this method had caused him in the past.[20] Further, as Baldeosingh indicates, Trinidad may not have been a 'book-reading' society, but it was a 'newspaper-reading society' and newspapers continued to play a highly significant role in the publication of local work (Baldeosingh 2005). Several of Lovelace's short stories, for example, were published in the *Trinidad Guardian* in the mid-1960s, and most recently his 1979 novel, *The Dragon Can't Dance*, was serialised in the *Trinidad Express*, an initiative specifically aimed at engaging 'those for whom reading is not a habit' (*Trinidad Express*, 20 February 2005). Other media have also been important in securing an audience for local literature, including the radio (notably the radio plays series sponsored by Texaco, and the National Cultural Council's series of literary readings, broadcast in the 1970s); village theatre and Carnival (where Lovelace premièred several of his dramatic works); and other spaces, public and private, where literary readings brought Trinidadian works to life, in some cases long before they rolled off the presses of the metropolitan publishers. Dramatised readings of Lovelace's *Dragon*, for example, were performed in Trinidad before the novel was published by André Deutsch in London in 1979. Trinidadians were not then, to borrow Ramchand's phrase, 'imprisoned in a life without fiction' and, despite the evident restrictions, writers continued to write and to publish their work in ever-increasing numbers (Ramchand 1983: 74).

Conclusion

As De Wilton Rogers' case reminds us, life as a writer in Trinidad involved a certain quality of resilience — a will to produce the work within the available resources, and a hope that if the work was there, the audience would come. Writers' contributions, on the whole, were made without substantive support from the state. Educational reforms, gaps in the cultural infrastructure, and the government's focus on popular culture all appeared to downgrade the literary, confirming writers' belief that 'the decision-makers of ... society [had] no real understanding of the value of [their] contribution' (Lovelace 2003: 76). In this sense, little had changed since the pre-Independence period when writers universally complained of their sense of isolation; the disinterest of the elite; and the low status of the creative professions. '[Society] has not felt itself responsible to have people living here and writing,' stated Lovelace in 1998, '[we have] grown up seeing our writers being taken care of elsewhere' (Cited in Sankar 1988: 43). In contemporary Trinidad, writers continue to lament the lack of 'institutional support for aspiring writers', calling on the government to support the promotion of literature through concrete measures (subsiding local publishers to produce novels; reinstating literary competitions) that would require only modest amounts of state funding. Without such initiatives, it is feared, the lure of the metropolis remains strong. 'Forty years after independence,' writes Kevin Baldeosingh, '[almost] every single one of the younger generation (i.e. 45 and under) of Trinidadian-born novelists live in the metropolitan countries, just as our writers had to do before independence' (Baldeosingh 2002). Cultural development in post-Independence Trinidad, then, has rested primarily on the Herculean efforts of committed individuals — individuals like Walcott, who created not just a theatre but a whole cultural scene in Trinidad; Clifford Sealy, owner-manager of the Book Shop and founder of *Voices* magazine; Beryl McBurnie, director of the Little Carib Theatre; Anson Gonzalez, publisher and founder of *The New Voices*; Owen and Rhona Baptiste, founders of Trinidad's Inprint Publishing Company; De Wilton Rogers and many like him, paying money out of their own pockets to see the publication of their work. These and the legion of anonymous and unsung poets, writers, publishers, performers and general enthusiasts all chose — despite the difficulties — to let down their bucket on Caribbean soil. It is against this backdrop of individual resilience and scant resources that we might best measure the extent of Lovelace's achievements.

Notes

[1] On Lovelace as a 'native and national' writer, see Harney (1996: 33, 38–9).

[2] For Lovelace's fictional representation of this dilemma, see *Salt* (Lovelace 1996: 76).

[3] Private spaces were also important. Lovelace's home in Matura, for example, was frequently host to informal gatherings of writers from Trinidad and the Caribbean, as memorialised by Trinidadian writer Lawrence Scott in 'Matura

Days — A Memoir'. Likewise, the Pelican bar in Port of Spain witnessed many animated discussions of 'politics, art, theater, music, writing and language' (Scott 2007). On the development of theatre in Trinidadian society, see King (1995), and on the role played by Clifford Sealy's Book Shop, see Salkey (1972: 33).

[4] Amongst the signatories to the petition were Earl Lovelace, poet LeRoy Clarke and 'mas-man' Peter Minshall, alongside a roll-call of Trinidad and Tobago's many cultural contributors, including artists, writers, performers, archivists, musicians and former cultural directors. Lovelace has drawn attention to the deficiencies of cultural provision over a number of years (see Lovelace 2003: 63–4, 74–7, 158–62).

[5] Williams was indeed critical of the 'vulgarity' of Carnival and what would now be called the 'dumbing down' of culture in Trinidad. His critique of surface 'egalitarianism' — 'society cannot afford the illusion that one person is as good as another to do a particular job' — perhaps places him closer to Walcott's notion of cultural hierarchies and the inequality of talents (Williams 1981: 257–9).

[6] Walcott and Lovelace's stints on the *Express* and the *Guardian* also highlight the significant role played by the newspapers in providing employment for writers. The *Guardian*, in particular, 'has always been a haven and a helping hand for many creative writers in the Caribbean ... most of the writers who have become famous have passed through its portals — Mittelholzer, Lamming, Selvon, Naipaul, Ismith Khan, Michael Anthony, Eric Roach and Derek Walcott have all, at one time or another, worked at the *Guardian* or written for it' (Gonzalez 1974: 105).

[7] British Petroleum sponsored a literature prize in Trinidad; Texaco sponsored a series of radio plays in the 1970s; and Tate and Lyle financed Samuel Selvon's return trip to Trinidad in 1969, the result of which was his 1970 novel *The Plains of Caroni* (King 1995: 155; Fabre 1988: 69).

[8] My translation.

[9] One early pioneer was the All-Jamaica Library, founded by the writer Thomas MacDermot. Intended to publish cheap editions of local works, MacDermot's venture lasted from 1904 to 1909, publishing four titles, two of which were his own works (Donnell and Welsh 1996: 27).

[10] In the decade before Independence, the Extra Mural Department of the Mona campus of the University of the West Indies provided a valuable outlet for Trinidadian plays, publishing, for example, seven out of 11 plays by Trinidadian authors between 1950 and 1962. Figures compiled from the works listed in Wharton-Lake (1988).

[11] C.L.R. James and Alfred Mendes left Trinidad for England and New York in 1932 and 1933 respectively; A.J. Seymour left for Puerto Rico in 1962, seconded to a post in the Caribbean Organization by Cheddi Jagan's PPP government. On the suspension of *Kyk*, see Seymour (1987: 159–60).

[12] H.M. Telemaque, DeWilton Rogers and other writers were interviewed for the National Cultural Council's radio series *National Identity in Our Literature*, broadcast in Trinidad in 1973. Programmes included *A Leading Poet: H.M. Telemaque*, *DeWilton Rogers and the 1940s*, *Poetry in Trinidad* and *An Adopted Son: Derek Walcott*. Pre-production scripts are reproduced in Gonzalez (1974).

[13] Figures compiled from Wharton–Lake (1988). Works counted for this article comprise the following genres: collections of poems, short stories, novels and plays — all published as freestanding works (that is, outside the newspapers and journals) in Trinidad and Tobago, of more than 10 pages in length.

[14] Anson Gonzalez's *Bibliography of Creative Writing in Trinidad and Tobago* (http://users.rcn.com/alana.interport/bibindex/bibindex.html, accessed 23 January 2007) lists eight Trinidadian novels published between 1952 and 1962, four in the United Kingdom and four in the United States. Beverly Wharton-Lake's *Bibliography* (1988) lists 26 published novels (including reprints of the same title) between 1950 and 1961: of these, 14 were published in the United Kingdom, nine in the United States, two in Australia and one in Germany.

[15] These figures are based on publishers still in existence in 1985 and therefore do not account for any businesses which had folded before the survey period. All figures in this section are based on the *Directory of Publishers, Printers and Booksellers in Trinidad and Tobago* (1985) and the *Bibliography of Creative Writing in Trinidad and Tobago*, compiled by Anson Gonzalez.

[16] These statistics, moreover, do not take into account the 'small … quickly forgotten or poorly recorded editions' produced on 'miniscule presses or mimeograph machines of a school system, employer, or local group' that have been lost to bibliographical records. Taking these into account, the proportion of all self-published materials would undoubtedly be considerably higher (Wharton-Lake 1988: ix).

[17] Anthony has also published other works with Trinidad's Columbus publishers: *Folk-Tales and Fantasies* (1974 and 1976) and *Glimpses of Trinidad and Tobago* (1974). Individual short stories by Lovelace as well as extracts from his novels have also been published in Trinidad in such outlets as the *Trinidad Guardian*, *Voices* and the *Trinidad and Tobago Review*.

[18] Since the focus of this chapter is primarily on local rather than metropolitan publishing, no space has been given here to the pioneering specialist

publishers founded in the United Kingdom, such as New Beacon Books (founded by the Trinidadian John La Rose in 1966) or Bogle L'Ouverture (founded by Guyanese *émigrés* Eric and Jessica Huntley in 1969). John La Rose's struggle to establish outlets for Caribbean writing — both in the region and in the United Kingdom — underlines the fact that a purely national focus is insufficient to tell the story of Caribbean cultural production, whose networks have long been international.

[19] The number of students in secondary education increased from 7,040 in 1964 to 61,680 in 1985. The St Augustine campus of the University of the West Indies likewise saw dramatic expansion in enrolment figures. The number of students registered increased tenfold in the first five years of its existence, from just 67 students in 1960–1 to 780 in 1964–5. Student numbers continued to rise in the period, reaching 3,428 by 1984–5 (Harvey 1988: 347; Goulbourne 1992: 25).

[20] De Wilton Rogers based his belief in a local readership on previous sell-outs of his fiction and from his observation of Trinidad's reading habits derived from his eight years as Chair of the Trinidad National Library (Gonzalez 1974: 13).

References

Allis, Jeannette (1981) *West Indian Literature: An Index to Criticism, 1930–1975* (Boston, MA: G.K. Hall).

Baldeosingh, Kevin (1998) 'Do Books Matter?', First published August 1998 in the *Trinidad and Tobago Review*, www.caribscape.com/baldeosingh/literature/sober/1999/criticism4.html, accessed 10 April 2007.

Baldeosingh, Kevin (2002) 'State of the Art', 25 September, www.caribscape.com/baldeosingh/literature/sober/2002/independent.html, accessed 10 April 2007.

—— (2005) 'Write and Wrong', 2 February, www.caribscape.com/baldeosingh/literature/sober/2005/writers.html, accessed 10 April 2007.

Best, Lloyd (1968) 'Guest Editor's Statement: The Next Round', *New World Quarterly*, vol. IV, no. 2, Crop Time.

Cameron, Norman (1965) 'Looking Backwards in the Cultural Field' *Kaie* 1.

Castro, Fidel (1967) 'Discurso de Fidel Castro, Pinar del Rio 29 de abril de 1967' *Resumen Semanal Granma*, 7 May.

Donnell, Alison and Welsh, Sarah Lawson (eds) (1996) *The Routledge Reader in Caribbean Literature* (London: Routledge).

Elder, J.D. (1974) 'Foreword' to Anson Gonzalez, *Trinidad and Tobago Literature On Air* (Gasparillo: National Cultural Council of Trinidad and Tobago, Rilliprint).

Fabre, Michael (1988) 'Samuel Selvon: Interviews and Conversations', in Susheila Nasta (ed.), *Critical Perspectives on Sam Selvon* (Washington DC: Three Continents Press).

Gonzalez, Anson (n.d.) *Bibliography of Creative Writing in Trinidad and Tobago*, http://users.rcn.com/alana.interport/bibindex/bibindex.html, accessed 23 January 2007.

—— 1974. *Trinidad and Tobago Literature on Air* (Gasparillo: National Cultural Council of Trinidad and Tobago, Rilliprint).

Goulbourne, Harry (1992) 'The Institutional Contribution of the University of the West Indies to the Intellectual Life of the Anglophone Caribbean', in Alistair Hennessy (ed.), *Intellectuals in the Twentieth Century Caribbean, Volume 1: Spectre of the New Class: The Commonwealth Caribbean* (London: Macmillan Caribbean).

Harney, Stefano (1996) *Nationalism and Identity: Culture and the Imagination in a Caribbean Diaspora* (London: Zed Books/Kingston: University of the West Indies Press).

Harvey, Claudia (1988) 'Educational Change and its Impact on National Development in Trinidad and Tobago, 1962–1987', in Selwyn Ryan (ed.), *The Independence Experience, 1962–1987* (St Augustine: Institute of Social and Economic Research, University of the West Indies).

'Join the Battle to Build the Missing Cultural Institutions!', March 2006, www.geocities.com/natalie_tt/trinidad_and_tobago_arts.htm, accessed 4 April 2007; full petition forwarded by electronic mail from rubadiri@yahoo.com, 29 March 2006.

King, Bruce (1995) *Derek Walcott and West Indian Drama: 'Not Only a Playwright but a Company' — the Trinidad Theatre Workshop, 1959–1993* (Oxford: Clarendon Press).

Lamming, George (1992 [1960]) *The Pleasures of Exile* (Michigan: University of Michigan Press).

Lovelace, Earl (1988) 'The On-Going Value of Our Indigenous Traditions', in Selwyn Ryan (ed.), *The Independence Experience, 1962–1987* (St Augustine: Institute of Social and Economic Research, University of the West Indies).

—— (1996) *Salt* (London: Faber and Faber).

—— (1998) 'The Emancipation-Jouvay Tradition and the Almost Loss of Pan', *Trinidad Drama Review (TDR)*, vol. 42, no. 3, Autumn.

—— (2003) *Growing in the Dark: Selected Essays*, ed. Funso Aiyejina (San Juan, Trinidad: Lexicon).

Ramchand, Kenneth (1983 [1970]) *The West Indian Novel and Its Background* (London: Heinemann).
'A Regional Bow to Our Writers' (2005) *Trinidad Express*, 20 February, www.trinidadexpress.com/indix.pl/article_archive?id=62702104, accessed 10 April 2007.
Ryan, Selwyn (1988) 'Dr Eric Williams, the People's National Movement and the Independence Experience: A Retrospective', in Selwyn Ryan (ed.), *The Independence Experience, 1962–1987* (St Augustine: Institute of Social and Economic Research, University of the West Indies).
Salkey, Andrew (1972) *Georgetown Journal* (London and Port of Spain: New Beacon Books).
Sander, Reinhard (1988) *The Trinidad Awakening: West Indian Literature of the Nineteen-Thirties* (New York: Greenwood Press).
Sankar, Celia (1988) 'Earl Lovelace: Unsettled Accounts' *Americas*, vol. 50, no. 1, January–February.
Scott, Lawrence (2005) 'Matura Days — A Memoir', *Anthurium: A Caribbean Studies Journal*, vol. 4, no. 2, http://scholar.library.miami.edu/anthurium/volume_4/issue_2/scott-matura.html, accessed 10 April 2007.
Seymour, A.J. (n.d.) 'Proposals to Set Up a Publishing House in Guyana', manuscript, A.J. Seymour Collection, University of Guyana.
—— (1977) 'The Author and Society', 28 March, manuscript, A.J. Seymour Collection, University of Guyana.
Seymour, Elma (1987) *A Goodly Heritage: The Autobiography of Elma Seymour* (Georgetown: Guyana National Printers).
Swanzy, Henry (1996 [1956]) 'The Literary Situation in the Contemporary Caribbean', in Alison Donnell and Sarah Lawson Welsh (eds), *The Routledge Reader in Caribbean Literature* (London: Routledge).
UNESCO (1991) *World Education Report 1991* (Paris: UNESCO).
University of the West Indies (1985) *Directory of Publishers, Printers and Booksellers in Trinidad and Tobago* (St Augustine: University of the West Indies).
Wharton-Lake, Beverly (1988) *Creative Literature of Trinidad and Tobago: A Bibliography* (Washington DC: Columbus Memorial Library).
Williams, Denis (1973) 'Art and Society' *Kaie*, no. 11, August, pp. 100–115.
Williams, Eric (1981) *Forged from the Love of Liberty: Selected Speeches of Dr Eric Williams* (Harlow: Longman Caribbean).
Wynter, Sylvia (1996 [1969]) 'We Must Learn to Sit Down Together and Discuss a Little Culture — Reflections on West Indian Writing and Criticism', in Alison Donnell and Sarah Lawson Welsh (eds), *The Routledge Reader in Caribbean Literature* (London: Routledge).
Yawching, Donna (ed.) (1991) *Who's Who Handbook of Trinidad and Tobago* (Port of Spain: Inprint Caribbean).

3
NOSTALGIA FOR THE FUTURE: THE NOVELS OF EARL LOVELACE

J. Dillon Brown

> In every era the attempt must be made anew to wrest tradition away from a conformism that is about to overpower it.
> — Walter Benjamin

Within the discourse of most left-leaning politics, nostalgia is generally given less than fulsome praise. Indeed, at first glance, the resolute longing for an always better, never retrievable past seems inherently reactionary in the most foundational sense: anti-progressive in its desperate attempts at preserving (what is perceived as) a rapidly retreating status quo from any further corruption. Susan Stewart (1984), in her literary study *On Longing*, goes so far as to discuss nostalgia as a 'social disease', a radical denial of the lived present with implications of stagnation and a misplaced desire for authoritarian control (1984: ix).[1] There seems little doubt, of course, that the structure of nostalgia is in fact based in large part on a repudiation of the present, holding up an idealised, even exoticised, past as a rebuke to the disappointments of the contemporary, perhaps even arising from an unproductively neurotic fear of the future. Far more overtly polemical in its nature than other approaches to the past, such as history, memory, reminiscence, and memorialisation, nostalgia, in the view of one commentator, appears most immediately as an insidious obstacle to reform or revolution, something that 'looks backward rather than forward, for the familiar rather than the novel, for certainty rather than for discovery' (Davis 1979: 108). In such a view, nostalgia at best takes on the appearance of a relatively harmless, self-indulgent escape to a benignly comforting sentimentality; at worst it is a resolute refusal to face up to the challenges of the present, making the progressive political prospects for nostalgia seem all but nonexistent.

In contrast, Fredric Jameson (1974), in his examination of that most nostalgic of Marxists, Walter Benjamin, questions this conventional view of nostalgia, suggesting that the politics of nostalgia have been given short shrift in leftist thought. Jameson muses, 'but if nostalgia as a political motivation is most frequently associated with Fascism, there is no reason why a nostalgia conscious of itself, a lucid and remorseless dissatisfaction with the present on the grounds of some remembered plenitude, cannot furnish as adequate a revolutionary stimulus as any other' (1974: 82). Jameson here suggests nostalgia as a chronological inversion of the utopian thinking about which he has written in much more detail: the inexorable duty of paradoxically holding on to ideals that are impossibly far off and essentially unrealisable (either in the never to be realised future for utopian thinking or the never to be regained past in the case of nostalgia). For Jameson, an important value of utopian thinking lies in its ability to 'play a diagnostic and critical-substantive role' with regard to the present and to provide a notion of 'systemic otherness, of an alternate society', upon which any progressive political programme necessarily relies (2004: 38, 36). Jameson thus troubles any purely disaffirmative evaluations of nostalgia and, following Benjamin, opens up the (perhaps inevitable) range of emotional attachments humans form with the past as an agonistic field whose definitional stakes involve important political ramifications.[2] These competing views of nostalgia — a forthright rejection of it on ethical grounds, as well as a more cautious affirmation of its potential usefulness — contend with each other in the novels of Earl Lovelace.

One does not have to look very far into the novels of Earl Lovelace to detect a deeply held suspicion of the nostalgic. Indeed, in his first novel, *While Gods are Falling* (1965), such a suspicion seems to form the very basis of the moral worldview of the book, whose narrative arc traces Walter's heroic transition from a disaffected state of nostalgic withdrawal from the world around him to a hopeful, forcefully future-oriented engagement with it. In Lovelace's later novels, a similar characterisation of nostalgia as unhelpfully backward looking and retrograde emerges, such as in *The Wine of Astonishment* (1986), whose primary moral seems to be the necessity of discarding the old, tested and comfortably familiar means of capturing the Spirit via Spiritual Baptist worship in favour of a new form of folk-based communion — the steelband — or the similarly critical assessments of any obdurate and unchanging presumptions about Carnival's political efficacy articulated in *The Dragon Can't Dance* (1979). In *The Schoolmaster* (1997), nostalgia is mainly associated with Father Vincent's condescending (and implicitly imperialising) suggestion to Paulaine Dandrade that the people of Kumaca should resist any actions that endanger their quaint rustic traditions. Conversely, *Salt* (1996), critiques a nostalgic world-view by valorising both Bango and JoJo for making difficult but indubitably necessary adjustments in response to changing times: as JoJo notes with emancipation in the air, 'he had to re-examine all the old questions, to look again at the old songs, the old sayings, the stories — the meanings' (Lovelace 1996: 172). At this point in the novel, dense with its representation and analysis of history, both personal and national, there seems to be little room — or indeed time — for a rose-coloured lingering on the beauties and the peaceful continuities of the past.[3] Nostalgia in Lovelace's novels, then, is seen on one level to be unproductive and undesirable. And in the larger context of the Caribbean and its colonial heritage that the novels depict, Lovelace frequently allies nostalgia with an oversimplified and unrealistic overlooking of the complexities of history and identity. To side with nostalgia in this way is to accept either the hidden oppression of rural tradition, a whitewashed account of a painful colonial history, or an unrealistic and exclusionary embrace of an ethnically absolute pre-colonial past, all with negative implications for social solidarity in the here and now.

On the other hand, for an author like Lovelace, the insistence on an icy, ratiocinative relation to the world suggested by such a resolutely anti-nostalgic stance does not seem to match up with the deep human sympathy and lyricism that animate much of his writing; as Lovelace's novelistic career advances, the relative value of nostalgia becomes much more ambiguous in nature.[4] The image of Aldrick's dignified holiness as he makes his dragon costume in which 'every thread he sewed, every scale he put on the body of the dragon, was a thought, a gesture, an adventure, a name that celebrated' his past and his forebears (1979: 36); or the description of Bolo evoking a time-honoured African spirit of warriorhood 'with love and respect, more as if he was making a gift of himself, offering himself up with his quick speed and rhythm' (1986: 22); or May's Thanksgiving feast in *Salt*, which allows her 'to place herself within the shelter of a new and ancient force' (1996: 22); or the redemption inherent in Bango's having 'crossed the chasm into that past to link up with Jo-Jo, to carry still his sense of violation after the granting of the "Emancipation"' (1996: 257) — all these suggest a much more emotional and affective relation to the past, a veneration that could well come across as a type of nostalgia. These scenes intimate that something redemptive might be found in an emotional, almost sentimental, relationship to the past, hinting at the possibility of a progressive politics of nostalgia envisioned in Lovelace's fiction.[5] Although it seems the case that Lovelace's first novel takes an almost completely negative approach to the trap of nostalgia, his later works — especially *Salt* and *The Dragon Can't Dance* — seem to serve as a careful recalibration of this approach, keeping the initial suspicion of nostalgia clearly in mind while fleshing out some more redemptive aspects to their characters' very human yearning for the glories of a vanished, creatively imagined past.

The critique of nostalgia in *While Gods are Falling* (1965) is resolute and clear. The novel's first chapter begins with a desolate description of Port of Spain, in which there is 'something dark, poisonous and stinking, something like a sore in this city' (1965: 9). Walter is introduced discussing the sad state of the city with Mr Cross, who diagnoses the problem as one specific to modernity, saying 'it's the way of the world. It's progress' (1965: 11), setting up the primary tension in the novel: Walter's escapist desire to leave the modern city and retreat to the countryside versus his wife Stephanie's attempts to help Walter find meaning in his present situation, at his present location. So dire is modern-day life to Walter's mind that he even argues against the future, answering his wife's forward-looking hopes with the dismissive retort: 'There's no tomorrow. Every day's today. And as to hope! What the hell I keep wasting my breath for?' (1965: 17). Walter's refusal even to finish his thoughts marks the depth of his nihilism in the face of the apparent abjection of life in contemporary Trinidad.[6] A considerable portion of the rest of the novel is structured around Walter's deferral of present problems by his dreamy, solitary immersion in his past. Lovelace directly suggests the stagnation of Walter's reminiscing by emphasising his absolute lack of forward motion: in the first instance, Walter is *about* to get up to comfort his infant son, but as soon as he 'moves to get up the child stops crying; so he sinks back into the chair, draws up the cushions like a pillow at his head, stretches out his legs and closes his eyes' (1965: 21). When Walter remerges from this reverie, it is only to have a tense exchange with his wife, who leaves the room expecting him to follow. Walter, however, 'does not follow. He sinks backwards into the chair. And again his mind goes back to days past' (1965: 74). In both instances, the emphasis is on regression and lack of engagement with the people who should be important to him: Walter, it is clearly suggested, is running — or perhaps exhaustedly sinking — back to the past as a means of avoiding the present.

Indeed, the very content of Walter's memories seems to suggest that he is using them as a nostalgic template for his current predicament. Once in the past, Walter had escaped the trouble and contention of the city by going away to Nuggle, a place characterised as simple and timeless, where 'they don't think of tomorrow or yesterday' (1965: 103). Far from most pressures of twentieth-century life, Walter recalls, the people of Nuggle live a life of rustic virtue removed from historical change. Nuggle — or, more precisely, his nostalgia-tinged memories of it — is exactly what Walter conceives to be the solution to his current ennui. When asked by Stephanie precisely where he wants to run away to, Walter's mind evokes the pastoral peace he associates with Nuggle:

> In his mind he sees the countryside so quiet. The earth is wet, and the grass is green and glistens with dew and sunlight. The corn is tall and the ears are long, and blonde hair hangs out from the tassles.
> Birds are singing in a mango-tree, the mist is disappearing ...
> The children bathe in the river and lie down on the bank and laugh ... the doves coo and walk on the ground, in pairs. (1965: 127)

In using such an impossibly lyrical tone to describe Walter's vision of the countryside, Lovelace makes clear how much of a fairytale Walter's plan really is.[7] Walter himself at one point seems to realise that his relationship to Nuggle had been largely imaginary, a fictional relationship, confessing 'he had looked on, looked on like it was a book he was reading, moved by the language, and then he had closed the book' (1965: 129). Even when he lived there, Walter realises, Nuggle's function in his life only took effect at the level of a storybook. Moreover, when Walter's memories take on a somewhat less nostalgic bent — concentrating more on the historical roots of his relationship with Stephanie, for example — his relation to them is conveyed as distant and fictionalised, as if they do not make up a part of his present actuality: 'so many things a man remembers, so many things, like a professor. He could write a book on memories alone. He could write about the things he had seen and heard and not take one thing from his imagination' (1965: 180). Yoking Walter's memories with this sense of an uncreative lack of imagination, Lovelace establishes a clear critique of 'living in the past', of an inability to deal with the present or future palliated only by a return to fond, foolish memories — or, in a word, nostalgia.[8]

It is perhaps the narrative structure that brings Lovelace's critique of nostalgia in *While Gods are Falling* into the greatest relief. The first two-thirds of the book are dominated by long sections of nostalgic reminiscence, punctuated by much briefer, anguished discussions about the meaning of life between Walter and various of his friends and family. Lovelace underscores Walter's stasis and stagnation via this device: the only action in the novel's present during these sections, aside from Walter's moping, dreaming, resting and arguing, is his disconsolate journey to the rum bar, where he indulges in another familiar form of escapism: drunkenness. It is as if Walter is paralysed by his nostalgic visions of the past, and the book's narrative mirrors this paralysis: Walter shambolically attempts to make sense of his life, as the title suggests, 'while gods are falling' all around him. It is only at the end of the novel that Walter regains his sense of well-being and purpose, focusing on his present (signalled in the text by a stream of consciousness narrative style) and working to unite the neighbourhood in the interests of social change.[9] The book ends on this optimistic note of progressive advance. In the novel's final line, Walter 'smiles at the wild thought and automatically quickens his step' (1965: 254), in sharp contrast to the despondent lassitude that characterised his earlier behaviour: Lovelace clearly suggests that Walter, in both physical and psychic ways, has given up his nostalgic escape from the reality of the everyday and is instead engaging fully with the present, while cocking an optimistic eye toward the future.[10]

The decisive rejection of nostalgia in *While Gods are Falling*, however, is moderated considerably in Lovelace's second novel, *The Schoolmaster* (1997 [1968]) which describes the ambiguous tension between the advancing forces of modernity and the more traditional rural values of Kumaca.[11] On one hand, the novel clearly criticises the nostalgia of Father Vincent's arguments against creating a school. In discussion with Paulaine Dandrade, Father Vincent observes: 'your people are different, Mr Dandrade. They are ... well ... simple ... yes, unsophisticated. They have grown up in a tradition which is not easy to break, nor perhaps wise to break ... I have seen your beautiful festival at the time of Easter' (1997: 35). Here, the priest's nostalgic praise is linked conspicuously to a dubious shouldering of 'the white man's burden' for the alleged benefit of childlike natives, enacting Frantz Fanon's observations that, at a certain point in the process of decolonisation, it is the agents of the colonisers themselves who 'rush to the rescue of indigenous traditions' (Fanon, 2004: 175). Paulaine Dandrade's succinct arguments for change — such as when he wryly notes that the villagers 'live just as our fathers live. But they are dead and their time gone' (Lovelace, 1997: 27) — provide a sharply valorised contrast to the retrogressive nature of Father Vincent's nostalgia at the beginning of the novel, suggesting the book's strongly anti-nostalgic viewpoint. However, the representative of progressive change in the novel, the schoolmaster, could hardly be said to have a beneficial effect on the lives of the villagers, and by the end of the novel Paulaine Dandrade's repeated assertions that 'changes must come' (1997: 107) ultimately take on the outlines of a mindlessly repeated cliché, especially in light of the morally bankrupt agents of change he so blindly trusts and supports. Indeed, it is Constantine Patron, the character identified with Kumaca's traditions and a suspicion of change, who commits the violent act that returns the village to their communal awareness, bringing a sense of stability back to the traumatised residents.[12]

The novel itself ends with a more equivocal image of *both* continuity with the past and an orientation toward change, detailing the priest's return from Kumaca with his acolytes: 'the donkey that had made the most runs between Kumaca and Valencia began to bray and broke into a trot and surprised the acolyte on its back who was completing his first trip' (1997: 187). This uneasy mixture of old and new complements and reinforces the donkey driver Benn's bittersweet knowledge that he 'will have again to learn how to live. They are building this road and will not need [his] donkeys any more' (1997: 187). Instead of dispensing with nostalgia for past ways and announcing triumphant progress forward, the book takes pains to suggest the doubtful nature of such progress: though the new road will probably make things better for the village and should even allow for another, more public-spirited schoolmaster, the priest ruefully notes that 'the opening of the road will bring its own difficulties' (1997: 186). Although *The Schoolmaster* in the end does not wholeheartedly endorse Father Vincent's original expression of nostalgic doubt about opening a school, nor does it dispense with the wistful respect of tradition it represents. The priest's own ruminations about his disagreement with Paulaine Dandrade concerning the school outline the novel's carefully uncertain attitude towards nostalgic resistance to change: 'Paulaine Dandrade when he came to see me about the school did not understand what I was trying to say. He did not know that I was not against him' (1997: 186). The strictly anti-nostalgic stance advocated in *When Gods are Falling* is shown in Lovelace's second novel to entail its own dangers.

The ending of *The Wine of Astonishment* (1986 [1982]) likewise incorporates a rather equivocal stance toward changes that displace old, traditional values. In general, the novel's narrative endorses the need to abandon a rigid attachment to the comforting familiarities of the past, and the novel's ending encapsulates precisely this point. In it, the narrator, Eva, relates her recognition of the passing of the mantle of viable community practice after the failure of her church's newly legalised service: 'I listening to the music; for the music that those boys playing on the steelband have in it that same Spirit that we miss in our church: the same Spirit; and listening to them, my heart swell and it is like resurrection morning' (1986: 146). Thus, as the novel ends, Lovelace evokes religious imagery of rebirth and daybreak in order to demonstrate the need for the villagers of Bonasse to move on, to accept the new dispensation instead of clinging nostalgically to their older folkways.[13] Eulalie, the young beauty of the village, is also used to make this point by her choice of Ivan Morton over Bolo, which serves to indicate the momentous shifts in the villagers' traditional understanding of the world's hierarchy of heroes.[14] As Eva explains to the reader, she feels that Bolo's warrior ethic is giving way to something else: 'I see that what happen with Eulalie was showing something bigger that was happening in the village right under our nose. What was happening was that the warrior was dying in the village as the chief figure. The scholar, the boy with education was taking over' (1986: 46). Eva names the warriors as no longer vital in the same way, 'just something to remember' (1986: 46), as changes continue to sweep through Bonasse.

However, Eulalie's choice is seen to be a bad one; just as Paulaine Dandrade's embrace of the schoolmaster is seen to be disastrous, Eulalie's (more literal) embrace of Ivan Morton, who betrays the hopes of the community for his own political and material advancement, calls into question any simple, unproblematic rejection of the traditional ways that Ivan's rival, Bolo, upholds. Although the primary message of the narrative in *The Wine of Astonishment* seems plain — that the old ways are being relegated to memory and rigidly preserving them cannot be a meaningful way forward — there is a sense that many of the changes are far from beneficial in that they have lost sight of important values embodied in more traditional behaviours. Eva expresses a sense of the new dispensation as somehow empty and ineffectual when discussing her son Reggie's preparation for college entrance examinations: 'I look at the boy. And I feel sorry for all of us. We push these children to this education. We stuff them with it. And we don't know what this education doing to the heart inside of them. But what else to do?' (1986: 79). Eva's thoughts convey a strong sense of the novel's suspicion of blindly embracing the seemingly inevitable onslaught of modernisation and change. Eva's concern for the children's emotional well-being — evoked by her mention of Reggie's heart — suggests that something crucial is missing in the village's headlong rush into the modern world of education and universal suffrage, and that 'the wine of astonishment' brought on by exposure to the new could just as easily stun the village into a cowed complacency as it could provide communal spiritual sustenance.[15]

In both *The Schoolmaster* and *The Wine of Astonishment*, then, a crucial function of nostalgia for Lovelace emerges: the critical distance it provides on an often unwieldy, fast-moving present. In the books, nostalgia provides an ever-hopeful, yet sadness-laden sense of the loss of what has been good or positive in the past.[16] Standing as a critique of the present based on the good that has been destroyed, nostalgia, understood in this sense, provides a benchmark against which to measure the competing claims of the new. The most prominent marker of this aspect of nostalgia is seen in the proliferation of reprehensible characters who self-servingly advocate change for its own sake by using an anti-nostalgic argument. For example, in *The Wine of Astonishment*, Mitchell rebukes Bolo for living in the past, telling him:

> You know what wrong with you? You don't know how to change. You don't know how to use your brains. You sit down here thinking you is king, holding on to your stickfight fame, and don't realise that things ain't the same and the days you waiting on not coming back again. Why you don't do like everybody and have a good time and try to make some money now that the Yankees giving it away on the Base? (1986: 27)

Mitchell, a grasping ally of the novel's arch-villain Ivan Morton, attacks nostalgia merely to justify his own profiteering; Mitchell's outright dismissal of anything valuable about Bolo's stickfighting (a clearly valorised, if increasingly outmoded, activity in the novel) leads to a crass material ethic that Lovelace's novels consistently decry. In *Salt* (1996), the wry depiction of the People's National Movement (PNM) suggests a critique of the unproblematic assumption that the past has been fully broken with. The stump speech assertions that the crimes of colonialism 'were done in the dark ages of our past' and that 'today we have Democracy, Brotherhood, Unity' (1996: 154) are belied by the novel's depictions of social separation and neocolonial economic relations, implying again that an argument about changed times overlooks something of value in the past.[17] Clearly for Lovelace, in the postcolonial Caribbean context, a facile replacement of nostalgic memory by the uncritical embrace of change poses its own problems, not least a failure to appreciate the past and thus address its injustices.

Lovelace's most discussed novel, *The Dragon Can't Dance* (1979) also problematises the resolutely anti-nostalgic message of *While Gods are Falling* and brings to light some more ameliorative qualities in nostalgia. Returning to modernity in an urban setting, the novel is overtly concerned with facing up to the changing nature and effectiveness of social protest, articulating an anxiety about the seemingly inevitable obsolescence of the steelband and Carnival as valid political activities.[18] Fisheye is the figure in the novel most demonstrably unable to adjust to the present, someone who insistently clings to a vision of past glories and the vanished social structures that underwrote them instead of facing up to the changing contemporary dynamics. Victor Chang (1992) notes how, by the end of the novel, Fisheye takes on the role of mock hero, pitiably unable to extract himself from a life based on nostalgia. Chang cites the novel's assessment that 'it was as if [Fisheye] had decided to live on those memories alone, not so much to learn from them, but to recall them so that they would celebrate himself' (1979: 190) in illustrating the novel's critique of living in the past. Another critic, John Stewart, describes Fisheye as 'an anachronism ... a throwback to simpler times and ill-equipped to deal with the subtleties of the new system' (Stewart, 1989: 107). In contrasting Fisheye to the true hero of the novel — Aldrick, whose hard-won realisation of the essential ineffectiveness and disengagement of his Carnival role as the dragon gives the novel its title — Lovelace again critiques a nostalgic adherence to past practice as a counterproductive, perhaps even self-deluding, exercise in futility.[19] Aldrick makes this view clear when he notes the Yard's unthinking adherence to traditional ways as a dangerous state of ignorance, ruminating that with regard to their life struggle, people in the Yard 'could not explain it to themselves, since it was something lived for generations, lived so long that it had become a life, beyond explanation' (1979: 204). Thus the novel critiques a dull, unthinking adherence to past forms and suggests in some sense that the people need to separate themselves from the easy, nostalgic embrace of long-lived patterns of behaviour.

Nevertheless, *The Dragon Can't Dance* does not merely advocate a complete abandonment of the past, and indeed places a productive nostalgia at the centre of one of its most redemptive moments. This occurs near the very end of the novel when Philo listens to old calypso music, having 'begun a ceremony geared not to stop his nostalgia but to encourage it' (1979: 221). In this scene, Philo thinks back over his life, coming to a variety of important conclusions, but his main realisation is a recognition of what he has lost by moving on to Diego Martin from the Hill. Instead of apologising for being a traitor to his people, however, Philo maintains that 'the thing is to live and to grow on, not even to think that you could right wrongs, but grow on take it from here' (1979: 238), and composes a heartfelt calypso to the Hill people on the spot. This is subtly different from quietism or acceptance of past injustice: it is something closer to a pained, wisdom-infused acknowledgement of loss coupled with the desire to, as Philo's song puts it, 'remember,' 'hold' and 'love' anyway (1979: 239). Crucially, Philo's calypso, though it springs from his personal concern with being considered a traitor, is 'not a selfish thought', and it was 'not for himself alone' that the calypso was composed (1979: 238).[20] Instead, Philo's lyrical outpouring is expressly designed to signal his recognition to the Calvary Hill community of their shared loss and, consequently, a legitimate basis for their mutual solidarity. Thus, although the novel clearly critiques the Hill's misplaced (nostalgic) dependence solely on Carnival as its mode of political protests, it also names nostalgia as a crucial factor in the Hill's potential for awakening to the need for new forms and practices.

This ending section of *The Dragon Can't Dance* thus suggests another key to the useful social function of nostalgia for Lovelace: its ability to foster a sense of community, which is one of Lovelace's most recurrent political and moral concerns. For Lovelace, an indispensable prerequisite for a successful Caribbean society is a sense of rooted belonging and togetherness: 'When we begin to think of living, we must begin to think about community, for community is the framework in which people grow and have being. Community is that area which provides people physical and psychological protection' (2003: 155). In Lovelace's later works, nostalgia seems to help in the creation of such secure, protecting collective identities.[21] For example, in the novels the enchantment associated with a feeling of community is often illustrated through romantic love, as older characters wax poetic in their minds about past love while admiring and empathising with younger characters, such as when Paulaine Dandrade gets the letter from Pedro, Christiana's suitor, asking for her hand in marriage in *The Schoolmaster*. As he ruminates on the situation, Dandrade is shown thinking of his own romantic past and getting emotional: 'he thought of his wife, and he turned, looked through the window where the greenness was turning to grey as the last sunshine died, and his eyes clouded a little and he blinked rather quickly' (1997: 109). Such reminiscence is directly linked to Dandrade's selfless recognition that, despite his own needs and desires, he must consent to the marriage for the greater good. Likewise, the female solidarity on the hill for Eulalie in *The Dragon Can't Dance* is inspired by others' nostalgic reminiscences of their own youth, as 'the women, the older women who had eyes, who had felt the burnings of this living ... would want to take [Eulalie] in their arms to protect her, would want to wish a magic guard over her so that she would not be trampled' (1979: 26). At many points, Lovelace's characters are driven to unite, protect, share and help their neighbours via an emotional connection fostered through nostalgia; indeed, Lovelace suggests that the emotions surrounding a sense of shared experience — at some level nostalgic — are an important element in the formation of communal solidarity.

A crucial example of the unifying nature of nostalgia can be found in Bolo's stickfighting in *The Wine of Astonishment*. His enactment of this traditional form communicates a shared sense of beauty, his performance given 'as if what he really want was for people to see in him a beauty that wasn't his alone, was theirs, was ours to let us know that we in this wilderness country was people too' (1986: 22). The pronouns shifting from 'his' to 'theirs' to 'ours' emphasise the unifying work of Bolo's evocation of the past. In the rum shop, Bolo's stickfight dance is performed 'with a sadness and a loss too, and a smooth tallness that bring water to the eyes of those who remember him in a real battle', again illustrating the collective emotions unleashed by nostalgic reflection (1986: 24). Bolo's friend Clem, the chantwell, also serves to unify the village, playing old stickfighting songs or even 'taking the old music, stickfight tunes, and bongo songs and putting words to them and singing them as calypso' (1986: 28).[22] Clem plays old stickfight tunes in the rum shop with so much emotion 'that men playing draughts — and Bee was one of them too — stop their game and listen' (1986: 24) while, as Eva remarks regarding Clem, 'when he was in Bonasse singing, with all the changes, we had a feeling that the village was still our own' (1986: 29). These evocations of the past clearly serve to unify the villagers and give them a shared sense of responsibility and belonging.

In addition to pointing out how Clem's refashioned old school songs serve as a focal point for everybody in the village, Eva's assessment highlights another important function of the nostalgic in community building that Lovelace suggests — the sense of comfortable familiarity and stability it provides.[23] Clem's songs are specifically credited with providing a sense of unity and stability in a quickly changing world. Thus, although wary of the torpor inspired by approaches that try to freeze the past into place, Lovelace's novels also evince, invariably, both a recognition of the emotional upheaval fostered by change and an acknowledgement of the inevitably slow pace of such change. The suspicion of the National Party that propagandises an already extant, wholesale change in the country — while covering over the neocolonial relations that still prevail — is palpable in *Salt*. Indeed, as Lovelace relates in a 1997 address, the long history of enslavement and oppression in the region will require a steady, long-term effort to counteract:

> The period of enslavement took, in the Caribbean, from 1492 (and here we have to include the Native Americans) to 1834. That is about more than 300 years and the propaganda of second-classness inflicted upon Africans has been going on for another 100 and more years ... A process that has taken 500 years will take a little more time to counter. (Lovelace 2003: 203)[24]

Instead of the naïve belief in 'the propaganda that Independence by itself has brought the previously colonised to a state of perfection' (2003: 209), Lovelace holds up small, but meaningful incremental changes as the most realistic hope for social change in the post-Independence period.

The very ending of *While Gods are Falling*, for example, underscores Lovelace's gradualist view. After Walter's epiphany, which initially takes on the trappings of a world-shaking shift in the context of his own life, he goes to the office where 'there is nothing here to indicate any change. Nothing in the office changed. It is he that has changed' (1965: 249). Adding to this sense of the comparatively small, personal scale of the change that Walter has wrought is the description of Walter's thoughts at the final, climactic meeting reflecting on the necessity for much more involvement and participation: 'There are still too many people at their windows; there are still too many of them hurrying to the cinema or God knows where. He wishes he were bold enough to shout like a madman so that they would hear him up and down Webber Street ... But he is not so bold. Not yet' (1965: 255). What has been figured as an emotional, spirit-giving breakthrough of great consequence has been put into a much more humble perspective: Walter's change is important, but there is much to be done, many more hard-fought, individual changes and recognitions that lie ahead.[25] Nostalgia, and the sense of comforting familiarity it provides, seem important in the novels because they, like Clem's song, can provide a sense of unifying permanence, without which society is unlikely to have the strength to accept or catalyse change of any kind.[26] As attractive as sweeping revolutionary change may appear to be, politics in Lovelace take on a much more personal, intimate and incremental character, facilitated at least in part by the comforting communal security created by nostalgic reminiscence.[27]

The double-edged nature of this aspect of nostalgia — basing present-day communal security on a reverence for the past — is taken up in *Salt*. On one hand, nostalgia is linked to colonial rule in the novel, as Lovelace portrays Andre Carabon's insistence on sticking to the customary plantation style of agriculture for export as a deeply unfortunate inability to change course. In refusing Jo-Jo's initial request for meaningful reparation, Carabon insists, 'we are organized for plantation, for export crops. We need plantations, large plots, not little peasant plots' (1996: 210). Lovelace emphasises the regressive nature of these fears by contrasting them with Jo-Jo's optimism: in response to Andre Carabon's fears about a ruinous end to the plantation system, Jo-Jo retorts that this ending could also be seen as 'the beginning of something new' (1996: 210). Carabon's grandson Adolphe's maintenance of the plantation system despite his own inclinations — 'he kept things going as they used to go, making a little change here and there but nothing on the scale he knew would bring success' (1996: 204) — is another of the book's representations of the crucial moment of potential change squandered by an over-investment in preserving past ways. The stasis of the planter class is emphasised in the novel as a product of its clinging stubbornly to old ways, nostalgically trying to relive the easier times of their past dominance. What Adolphe Carabon observes in social rituals such as his daughter's dance recital is precisely this stagnation: 'he met there the people from down the islands, the old lime, Whitepeople from his youth, the gathering of a withering species who got together at these events to talk about the same things' (1996: 205). In this version of nostalgic practice — in which the habitual ways of the past repeat themselves in a desiccated present — the yearning to live as long ago is depicted as a spiritually stifling attempt to revive lost glory and cling to power.[28]

On the other hand, a different inflection of nostalgic recollection — a recognition of the shattered ideals of the past, combined with a resolute effort to continue to do them justice in the future — also appears as the most important lesson of *Salt*.[29] The narrator sadly declares that 'the tragedy of our time is to have lost the ability to feel loss, the inability of power to rise to its responsibility for human decency' (1996: 259), suggesting the salutary consequences of nostalgic reflection. Alford's final redemption in the novel springs from his ability, finally, to feel loss and mourn it. In the novel's concluding scenes, Alford registers the loss of his Africanness, despite its seeming impossibility. Addressing his own puzzlement, Alford thinks: 'But how do you feel the loss of a self that you did not have to lose? How can you lose an Africa you did not know? But that was what he felt: the loss of not having had that loss to lose' (1996: 256). By no means coincidentally, when Alford is flooded by this sense of loss on the podium later in the day, it brings out feelings of yearning for community: 'he felt for home, for family, for the people he had never really got close to. He looked out among the crowd, hoping to see Carabon and Lochan coming. He looked out among the crowd to see if any of his brothers was there' (1996: 257). Thus this sense of nostalgic loss ultimately manifests itself in a productive renewal of community awareness and longing.[30]

This paradox of missing what one never actually had hints at the valorised potential of nostalgia that Lovelace's *oeuvre* eventually posits.[31] While clearly on guard against the paralysing effects of what could be called a melancholic nostalgia

— an unhealthy fixation on past (and largely imaginary) beauties and advantages that the present state of affairs can only succeed in corrupting — Lovelace's novels seem equally ill-disposed to the dismissing of nostalgia out of hand merely because of 'the ideological uses to which it is ordinarily put' (Jameson 1974: 63). Instead, the novels gradually work towards distinguishing a healthier type of mournful nostalgia, which acknowledges that times have changed while still providing a polemical platform from which to call the present to account for its demolition of something valuable in the past, all in an effort to build something better for the future.[32] Although, at the outset of his novelistic career, Lovelace seems to conceive of nostalgia as counterproductively melancholic, his subsequent fiction portrays nostalgia in a more multifaceted light, acknowledging the important, if never clear-cut, usefulness of a nostalgia more akin to the mourning process. This nostalgia is important not only in helping to establish and maintain a sense of continuity and community anchored in the slowly changing processes of a shared history, but also in its resolute critique of the present based on perceived communal values of the past. Lovelace's novels thus seem to embrace the paradox of an affective allegiance to a past that can no longer manifest itself, in the interests of constructing a better national future; in a similar manner, this future can never truly be realised, as nationhood, for Lovelace, is 'not something to be achieved but something to strive for constantly' (Lovelace 2003: 159). Far from the intellectual abstractions of freedom, independence and unity emptily employed by various political economic actors depicted in Lovelace's novels, this nostalgia is a real, felt experience of loss that can be used, if only hesitantly and with great care, to mark out the contours of the ground on which the post-Independence future of Caribbean society could most satisfyingly be built.

Notes

[1] Interestingly, Stewart's formulation of 'social disease' in some ways echoes the standard rhetoric of nostalgia in suggesting a corrupting influence affecting the holistic health of the social body.

[2] In this respect, Jameson's critical move finds a parallel in the editors of a collection of essays arising from a history symposium on nostalgia at Leeds University, who confess that their original conception of nostalgia considered it to be a social malaise, but that the workshop in fact 'showed that nostalgia was ... a phenomenon more manifold and various than had been initially assumed' (Shaw and Chase 1989: 1).

[3] There are also several instances in the novels of fathers stubbornly clinging to small, unproductive plots of exhausted land, including Aldrick's grandfather

in *The Dragon Can't Dance*, Alford's father in *Salt* and Bee in *The Wine of Astonishment*; all are characterised by their vain insistence that their sons continue to live the ways of their forebears, a stagnant and domineering attitude emphatically critiqued by the novels.

4   Indeed, Lovelace has consistently emphasised his humanistic view of the role of the artist, which he formulates as the responsibility to 'call us to account as humans and, with tenacity, to insist that we honour the idea of what it means to be human' (Lovelace 2003: 49).

5   Lovelace's essays are adamant in advocating a recognition of the importance of feeling and emotion to an understanding of people's social, cultural and political endeavours. For instance, Lovelace criticises the modern state of society in the way that 'logic, argument [holds] precedence over feeling' (2003: 131). Elsewhere, Lovelace valorises the sensuous, non-linear meaning inherent in rhythm, as well as local religious practices, and considers the artist's role intimately bound up with this important level of communication — 'we have to try to communicate to people, not necessarily in ordinary logic, but to try to make them feel; I mean, to present how we feel about things as well as the ideas surrounding things' (2003: 8).

6   This lack of loquacity is repeated consistently in Walter's disagreements with Stephanie at the beginning of the novel, emphasising his hopeless state. The beginning of his re-engagement with the world, tellingly, involves him speaking out and with various people in a public forum, suggesting the importance of words (and the danger of silence) in the face of injustice.

7   Both Stephanie and Walter's brother-in-law point up the unrealistic, otherworldly quality of Walter's half-cocked plans of retiring to the countryside to become a yeoman farmer. Stephanie perceptively points out that if Walter is really intent on escaping the world, there's nowhere on earth he could really go, while Lester tells Walter: 'you want life, as you put it, to mean something — really mean something. You'll fall far short of your expectations if you leave and go like a hermit in the country' (Lovelace 1965: 189).

8   Evelyn O'Callaghan has argued for the anti-nostalgic nature of both *The Schoolmaster* and *While Gods are Falling*, noting that the former's structural parallels with Milton's *Paradise Lost* suggest 'the corruption of innocence, the loss of paradise', while the latter 'demonstrates the impossibility of trying to regain [paradise]' (O'Callaghan 1989: 45).

9   Examples of this more redemptive, mentally active narrative technique of stream of consciousness include Walter's initial journey out to hear the preacher (Lovelace 1965: 191ff.) — a sign of openness in contrast to his previous cynical quietism — and when he is walking home with Mrs Walls, concentrating carefully on her predicament (1965: 211–12).

10 The ending is, in fact, considerably more nuanced than this broad reading suggests, of course: not *too* much has actually changed. The cautionary note of this and most of Lovelace's other endings, as well as their interpretive implications, will be discussed below; nevertheless, the overall optimism and sense of change at the end of *While Gods are Falling* is a palpable contrast to the stultification and despair of the book's beginning.

11 If Nuggles is depicted as an idealised Eden (and thus devalued in relation to Walter's present) in the first novel, Kumaca is the very real, very important setting of all the action in the second novel, suggestively moving Lovelace's examination away from a metropolitan location, in which the rural can conveniently be figured as imaginary, to a location in which the value of the rural cannot be relegated to the merely symbolic.

12 Of course, the violence of his response — which has the characteristics, however justified, of an almost atavistic act of vengeful 'frontier justice' — problematises any outright valorisation of tradition at the expense of modernity.

13 This scene, of course, although illustrating the importance of accepting change, is also infused with a sense of sadness at the loss of potency of the old Shouter rituals.

14 It is also noteworthy that Eulalie, an archetypal Lovelace character symbolising youthful female promise and beauty, is the person making such a significant decision. Eulalie is different from the normal girls, described as 'brisk, bright-eyed, her black smooth-skin body carrying a warm woman aliveness and rhythm of joy' (Lovelace 1986: 44). Eulalie, more than almost anyone else in the novel, is in touch with life energies, making her decisions more meaningful than most, and the negative consequences of them that are much more ominous as well.

15 Lovelace notes the hollowness of what passes for progress when he has Eva comment that, although Ivan Morton embodied the hopes of the village with his initial longing for education, the conditions for his success were missing: 'I mean, we wasn't the trunk of a tree that grow out from roots to make him a branch that grow out of our body' (Lovelace 1986: 136). The image suggests a need for something solidly rooted in the community and its history in order for the political process to work for the island's black underclass.

16 In the article 'The Ongoing Value of Our Indigenous Traditions', Lovelace maintains the importance of recognising 'the persistence of the best of the values of an ancient civilization' discernible in Caribbean culture, postulating that 'it is only when we look at our own creativity and achievements that we will discover the true value of our traditions and begin a new respect for our ancestors and ourselves and find a clearer vision of our future' (2003: 36).

[17] Lovelace does seem to respect the National Party's mission of historical education; it is its sanguine claim to have moved completely on from history's effects that takes on a sinister cast. In an essay elsewhere, Lovelace, speaking to a Caribbean audience, pointedly notes his negative view of any such claims: 'Perhaps what blinds us most is that we have bought the propaganda that Independence by itself has brought the previously colonised to a state of perfection' (2003: 209.)

[18] As Grant Farred notes in a review essay on Gerard Aching's *Masking and Power: Carnival and Popular Culture in the Caribbean*, Lovelace uses *The Dragon Can't Dance* to articulate a view that Carnival 'has been policed into ineffectiveness, so denuded of its unruliness that it can no longer claim not to be owned — economically and ideologically — by the postcolonial state' (Farred 2004: 210).

[19] Aldrick himself notes the Yard's unthinking adherence to traditional ways as a dangerous state of ignorance, ruminating that with regard to their life struggle, people in the Yard 'could not explain it to themselves, since it was something lived for generations, lived so long that it had become a life, beyond explanation' (Lovelace 1979: 204).

[20] Interestingly, Lovelace also emphasises that Philo's calypso might better be described as poetry, 'to be understood by being felt' (1979: 238), underscoring the importance of a type of emotional comprehension (as opposed to strictly an intellectual one).

[21] Davis's (1979) sociological account puts a good deal of emphasis on this particular attribute of nostalgia.

[22] Clem seems to represent a version of Lovelace's ideal relationship to the past: holding on to what is meaningful about it without fetishising it, but instead being open to changes. As Eva observes, Clem 'was seeing a new time coming. New times didn't frighten him. Everything had to move on. Things had to change' (Lovelace 1986: 28). The difference between Clem and somebody like Ivan Morton in the novel, of course, is that Clem integrates the values of the old with the modalities of the new, while Ivan symbolically rejects his entire past and all the hard work of his ancestors by leaving every bit of his parents' furnishings behind in his move to the big house.

[23] Clem's songs even bring the older, more traditional men into contact with the newer, more materialist ones, who 'hear the music, something new, something that touch them in some way and they start to crowd around'; there is a strong suggestion that although these younger men are hearing something new, the 'something that touch them' arises from Clem's use of older forms and methods, in the way that he is only 'slowing them down to

bring out the sound, the cry, the tall sorrow that was flowing in that time' (Lovelace 1986: 24).

[24] In a 1993 speech, Lovelace explicitly critiques the empty, forward-looking nature of political life after Independence, complaining that: 'Independence had brought not a confrontation with the prejudices, privileges persisting from the past, but proposed the education of the people as the way forward as if once you had this certificate, that you could qualify for citizenship' (Lovelace 2003: 5).

[25] Indeed, all of Lovelace's novels end in some sense on a similar note of ambiguity, normally consisting of a forward-looking hopefulness tempered by a sadness-tinged realisation of past loss, suggesting the complexity of his stance towards nostalgia and other ideological uses of the past.

[26] Davis (1979) considers this important balance that nostalgia provides in response to a sense of constant change as another one of its useful social functions.

[27] There is some sense of the illusory nature of simplistic grand narratives of liberation in the dramatic mural that appears several places in *Salt*. Although it does have some pedagogic and inspirational value, the mural's fundamentally facile nature is represented by 'its easy, its simple resolution' of the four racialised foreground figures, and its power is further deflated by the fact that it has been 'done by an artist selected as a result of a Caribbean-wide contest, the winner a West Indian living in London', whose murals for all the separate Caribbean islands upon Independence are exactly the same, just with a new title (1996: 126). Thus, Lovelace suggests, political change is much messier, much more local. As Cleothilda responds to the pie in the sky dreams of Talbot, the self-proclaimed revolutionary who courts Sylvia: 'people does live life every day, today and today and today, and they have to live it somewhere' (Lovelace., 1979: 218).

[28] Indeed, Adolphe's longing to catalyse 'the beginning that was waiting' (Lovelace., 1996: 214) is countered by his more successful brother Michael's insistence that his only chance in politics is 'representing the interests of the old elite' (1996: 207), and within the family setting, this traditional allegiance maintains supremacy despite both Adolphe and Andre's more progressive longings for fundamental change, which are actually anchored in a more thoughtful reckoning with the past, 'the old world, with the old hope', rather than the fatuous 'modern' commercial (and self-serving) attitude of Michael (1996: 216).

[29] This lesson seems to be a reiteration of the moral extracted from Philo's nostalgic musings in *The Dragon Can't Dance*.

[30] Lovelace generally emphasises this positive side of the awareness of loss, while allowing that, due to the overwhelming nature of the suffering resulting from imperialism, 'it is easy to understand how the experiences of loss have come to obscure for us the fact that loss has often meant a corresponding gain' (2003: 25).

[31] Something of the paradoxical nature of this approach is suggested in Myrtle's simultaneous perception of Bango both as he was long ago and in a completely new, more understanding light (Lovelace 1996: 165), as well as in Aldrick's tortuous explanations of the Hill's relation to time and tradition and how 'they were unable to hold in their minds the two contradictory ideas — their resistance and surviving, their rebellion and their decency' (Lovelace 1979: 164).

[32] The terms 'melancholic' and 'mournful' are intended to evoke Freud's useful distinction between, respectively, the debilitating and productive modes of processing the loss of a love object.

References

Chang, Victor (1992) 'Elements of the Mock-Heroic in West Indian Fiction: Samuel Selvon's *Moses Ascending* and Earl Lovelace's *The Dragon Can't Dance*', in Gillian Whitlock and Helen Tiffin (eds), *Re-Siting Queen's English: Text and Tradition in Post-Colonial Literatures* (Amsterdam: Rodolpi).

Davis, Fred (1979) *Yearning for Yesterday: A Sociology of Nostalgia* (New York: The Free Press).

Farred, Grant (2004) 'The Ellisonian Injunction: Discourse on a Lower Frequency', *Small Axe*, vol. 16.

Fanon, Frantz (2004 [1963]) *The Wretched of the Earth* (New York: Grove Press).

Jameson, Fredric (1974) *Marxism and Form: Twentieth-Century Dialectical Theories of Literature* (Princeton: Princeton University Press).

—— (2004) 'The Politics of Utopia', *New Left Review* (second series), vol. 25.

Lovelace, Earl (1965) *While Gods are Falling* (Chicago: Henry Regnery).

—— (1979) *The Dragon Can't Dance* (London: André Deutsch).

—— (1986 [1982]) *The Wine of Astonishment* (Oxford: Heinemann).

—— (1996) *Salt* (London: Faber and Faber).

—— (1997 [1968]) *The Schoolmaster* (Oxford: Heinemann).

—— (2003) *Growing in the Dark. Selected Essays*, ed. Funso Aiyejina (San Juan, Trinidad: Lexicon).

O'Callaghan, Evelyn (1989) 'The Modernization of the Trinidadian Landscape in the Novels of Earl Lovelace' *ARIEL*, vol. 20, no. 1.

Shaw, Christopher and Chase, Malcolm (eds) (1989) *The Imagined Past: History and Nostalgia* (Manchester: Manchester University Press).

Stewart, John (1989) 'The Literary Work as Cultural Document: A Caribbean Case', in Philip A. Denis and Wendell Aycock (eds), *Literature and Anthropology* (Lubbock, TX: Texas Tech University Press).

Stewart, Susan (1984) *On Longing: Narratives of the Miniature, the Gigantic, the Souvenir, the Collection* (Baltimore: Johns Hopkins University Press).

4
ILLUSIONS OF PARADISE AND PROGRESS: AN ECOCRITICAL PERSPECTIVE ON EARL LOVELACE

Chris Campbell

> There is the theme of annihilation (earthquakes, atomic power, tidal disasters, the psychological and cosmic peril to which man is subject) ... The concern with annihilation brings out sharply the masses and materials of the world piled into overwhelming structures. What sort of art is the outcome of this environment?
> — Harris (1967: 13)

> Those who have endured the land's constraint who are perhaps mistrustful of it, who have perhaps attempted to escape it to forget their slavery, have also begun to foster these new connections with it, in which the sacred intolerance of the root, with its sectarian exclusiveness, has no longer any share.
> — Glissant (1997: 147)

As early as 1952, in his essay 'The Question of Form and Realism in the West Indian Artist', Wilson Harris identified the history of the Americas as one of twin trial. As a location prone to intense environmental activity, he argued, it is frequently beset by 'natural disaster' — geological or meteorological — and those 'avoidable' errors of human-inspired catastrophe, often the result of a multi-faceted colonial inheritance. It is certainly the case that, to continue Harris's apocalyptic tone, annual hurricanes, tropical storms, floods and a history of environmental degradation and of social and political dispossession leave the region ecologically and economically vulnerable.[1]

This ecological volatility and vulnerability have consequences for economic stability and sustainability, and for the national economic growth in the Caribbean, where agriculture and tourism — both industries dependent on realities and conceptions of the environment — are the main foreign exchange earners. Across the contemporary Caribbean, increased migration to coastal urban centres, continuing poverty and inadequate environmental protection policies have become issues of pressing and immediate concern for communities.

Alongside the Harrisian apocalyptic vision of ecological and political tectonic shifts and upheavals, Édouard Glissant envisages the possibilities for a transformative comprehension from understandings of the ecological history and reality of the Caribbean. A refiguring of the relationships between peoples and landscapes can reveal a transformed understanding of communality and the opportunity for revisioning the exacting and problematic historical contract of enslaved existence on the land. Such 'new connections' could form a new phase in the continued pursuit for emancipation in cultural, economic and political spheres:

> Gradually, premonitions of the interdependence at work in the world today have replaced the ideologies of national independence that drove the struggles for decolonization. But the absolute presupposition of this interdependence is that instances of independence will be defined as closely as possible and actually won or sustained. (Glissant 1997: 143)

Glissant and Harris question the role of the artist in the process of understanding 'environmentality', and see that implicit in a successful Caribbean ecologism is the development of a new relational, cultural vocabulary which recognises *inter*dependence as continued liberation and *in*dependence.[2]

Over the past decade or so, negotiating between these perspectives of an awareness of ecological vulnerability and possibilities for renewal, and under the pressure of the perceived incompatibility of environmental focus with the postcolonial politically resistive and reparative analyses, a critical area of Caribbean ecocriticism has sought to define itself. Such critical investigations carried out and discursively aired at conferences in the Caribbean and Britain have contributed to what can be seen as a 'second phase' of cultural ecocriticism. This 'second phase' constitutes a corrective which rethinks issues of environmentality, which progresses beyond an Anglo-American preoccupation and emphasises the 'de-naturing' of ecological thought, and which brings into full focus the philosophy and political actualities of 'environmental justice'.[3]

The collection *Caribbean Literature and the Environment: Between Nature and Culture* marks the first truly significant engagement with issues of cultural ecology in the Caribbean, and has been important in setting some initial parameters for the scope and direction of Caribbean ecocriticism. A comprehensive selection, which profitably addresses not just the Anglophone but the Francophone and Hispanophone Caribbean as well, it articulates many overlapping themes, including the ways that Caribbean texts 'inscribe the environmental impact of colonial and plantation economies'; a revision of Edenic pastoral mythology of the region; and also how Caribbean literature might 'usefully articulate a means to preserve sustainability in the wake of tourism and globalisation' (De Loughrey, Gosson and Handley 2005: 2). Despite its impressive breadth and depth of analysis, any assessment of the role of Earl Lovelace's work in coming to such conclusions is conspicuous only by its absence. Given these concerns with continued resistance and reaction to continuing forms of global imperialism, and the revisioning of the old colonialist Edenic excitement, Lovelace's novels mark a desirable — if not requisite — addition to the debates raised in the collection.

The critical quiet over Lovelace as ecoliterary figure may be due in part to the misperception of him as a writer with exclusively anthropocentric concerns. This, I think, is a misperception — not in the sense that Lovelace does not have the cares and interests of his human communities at the heart of his writing, but rather that such a focus is not, or could not possibly be, imbricated with a comparable consideration of and for the non-human world. Indeed, this overlapping of authorial attention, a figuring of the natural world with a careful, caring situation of humans within it, is precisely the reason why Lovelace's vision is valuable to the development of Caribbean ecoliterary discourse.

In this chapter, I aim to examine how his art establishes an ecological concern for the intrinsic worth of the 'natural world' *and* highlights a pressing need to see nature in instrumental terms — as a cultural, political resource to be repossessed and reclaimed. In this way, Lovelace is able to articulate a vision of postcolonial ecologism. He provides a corrective response to the perceived misanthropy of much environmentalism through a refusal to decentre issues of social and racial dispossession, while simultaneously demonstrating the essential value of nature itself.

Lovelace reveals the possibilities of political independence through a vision of ecological interdependence: through his belief in the ability of the creative artist to 'heal the wounds of history', he can be seen to articulate novel variations of Glissant's characteristic determination to centre in his imagination his concern with the ecologies of the Caribbean region.

Through an ecocritical reading of *The Schoolmaster* (1997 [1968]) and *Salt* (1996), it is possible to trace Lovelace's critique of facile notions of 'paradise' — an unfortunate tradition which seems to start from colonial travelogues and is endlessly reinvigorated into contemporary guises: a way of seeing the Caribbean which begins perhaps with early modern European observation and ends up with the fantasies of tourist brochures. Similarly, Lovelace's fiction works to detect a tradition of empty promises of political progress which, in actuality, serve to undermine independence by furthering the poverty gap and continuing the disenfranchisement of the Caribbean peoples. Each novel seems, in its own way, actively to interrogate the assertion of Derek Walcott's mariner Shabine that 'progress is history's dirty joke' (Walcott 1979: 14).

Louis James has argued that 'the real hero' of the novel *The Schoolmaster* is the village of Kumaca itself, and that the novel is constructed around the revolution of one year (James 1995: 224). This presciently engages with Lawrence Buell's initial criteria of what might constitute an ecoliterary work: a text which figures the natural world as more than backdrop or framing device for a description of human affairs and an awareness of the environment — not as an icon of timeless constant or landscape portrait of fixed (and false) naturalness but, on the contrary, as a properly historical relation which remains unfinished (Buell 1995: 7–8).

Indeed, the putatively natural world provides a narrative which demonstrates, above all else, how history is implicated in nature. The non-human world, while acting as witness to the evolution of human tragedy, is simultaneously and equally laid open, and thus becomes vulnerable, to exploitation. Nowhere is this more evident than in the portrayal of the couple who throughout *The Schoolmaster* seem to represent hope in the face of the pressures of economic and political impoverishment, and who encapsulate instead the ultimate betrayal of the hopes of youth and the future aspirations of the community.

Pedro's urgent return from labouring on the new road, ironically removed from Christiana by the symbol for a supposed improvement, is attended by the chorus of the forest. It is here that the awareness of natural activity — the flora and fauna present at the opening of the novel and integral throughout, and which seem to have operated as standard framing devices — become complicated in Lovelace's portrayal of the fate of the village. 'The doleful notes of the poll-poll ... the frog voices, and the long shrill, piercing screams of the cigales' accompany Pedro in a passage that moves significantly and symbiotically beyond pathetic fallacy, as Lovelace reveals the interrelation and inextricability of imminent human tragedy *and* the consequences of deforestation of the landscape (Lovelace 1997: 162). The seeming backdrop of the ecology of forest serves to remind us of what is at stake, what is to be lost in both human and natural terms. Here Christiana and Pedro parallel Wilson Harris's landmark and land-marked couple, Cristo and Sharon, in the third novel of the Guyana Quartet, *The Whole Armour*. Here the young couple is also positioned to represent an environmentally attuned state of dwelling which is to be frustrated and thwarted by spectres of supposed progress in the Guyanese forest. Cristo urges comprehension of their privileged position:

> what we possess comes from the ground up — coconut, copra, plantain, banana, wood-grant, sawmill ... There's a whole world of branches and sensation we've missed, and we've got to start again from the roots up even if they look like nothing. Blood, sap, flesh, veins, arteries, lungs, heart, the heartland, Sharon. We're the first potential parents who can contain the ancestral house. (Harris 1985: 333–5)

C.L.R. James brings this passage back into focus to conclude his essay on Caribbean sovereignty which forms the appendix to the 1963 edition of *The Black Jacobins*, reaffirming the centrality of independence through environmental interdependence: 'Harris sets the final seal on the West Indian conception of itself as a national identity' (2001: 325). It is difficult not to see Lovelace's Christiana as the female mirror of Harris's Cristo. Indeed, *The Schoolmaster* reveals, in Christiana's drowning, an altogether more painful realisation of the mixing of blood, sap, heart and heartland: 'She was sticking in the bamboo roots in the big river' (1997: 168). All the urgent potential of Cristo's comprehending speech becomes submerged by the narration of Christiana's death: his manifesto for organic community and repossession of natural resources seems to be dissipated and carried away by the river that takes her life. Lovelace offers a conclusion that provides a more pessimistic view, perhaps, of the Jamesian hopes for nationhood that reside in the younger generation.

William Clemente (1999) has similarly identified Christiana and Pedro as a hope-filled, hopeful 'nature-bound' couple, and offers a detailed assessment of the pastoral contours of the novel. He also communicates effectively how the novel contemplates visions of paradise and conceptions of retreat and regeneration which are, arguably, inherent in the pastoral mode. It is worth considering, however, the extent to which the novel actually problematises these notions of contemplative and redemptive retreat in rurality by attempting to assess the way in which Lovelace interacts with the history of the pastoral in the Caribbean.

Lovelace's problematic pastoral functions to disabuse readers of the illusions inherent in seeing visions of 'paradise' in the landscapes of Trinidad. The novel serves as a necessary textual corrective to two intertwined Edenic epistemologies, both of which are expressly imperialistic. At once, the novel highlights the perils of venerating a state of innocence in paradise, an assumed state which, for self-serving ends, is then imposed upon the village, its surroundings and its inhabitants. At the same time, painfully aware of the colonial legacy of 'discovery', the novel reveals the economically inflected understanding of 'paradise' as a location ripe for harvesting.

The priest Vincent typifies the first strand of the imposition of Edenic wish-fulfilment through his exhortation to Paulaine that there is a spiritual virtue in the poverty of agrarian existence: 'Your people are different, Mr Dandrade. They are ... well ... simple ... yes, unsophisticated ... I have seen your beautiful festival at the time of Easter' (1997: 35). In his enshrined conception of the 'beautiful' and 'simple', the priest reinscribes a historiography, bolstered by overtones of racial superiority and hierarchy, that erases the realities of the painful contracts of land-bondage. The connotations of this philosophy almost seem to hang, suspended in the air in front of Paulaine and correspondingly on the page for the reader: you are 'beautiful' and 'simple' ... 'beautiful' *because* you are 'simple' ... the 'beautiful simplicity' of working the land. Such connotations might easily be considered, in another incarnation, to be the underpinnings or justification for a politics of underdevelopment. As well as sustaining a wilful ignorance of the human cost of agricultural production and plantation economics in the Caribbean, Vincent's investment in ideas of beauty and simplicity also replicates, at best, a poetics of euphemism, and more probably one of attempted erasure. The descriptions of enslaved Africans as labourer 'swains' in James Grainger's 1764 West Indian georgic 'The Sugar Cane: A Poem' would appear to be the forerunner of Vincent's pastoral dreams. If Grainger sought to redefine black identity through a poem of refinement and sought to distil an essence of plantation processes at odds with the lived experience of the enslaved, the priest in *The Schoolmaster* appears to be suffering the legacy of a hangover.[4]

The connection of visions of paradise and history of landscapes laid open for colonial consumption is a well-documented one. We can think of the vision of a tropical abundance which fired the imagination of Marvell and inflamed the mercantile acumen of Raleigh writing of the landscape of Guyana, or of the lengthy subtitles to many eighteenth- and nineteenth-century histories and accounts of travels to and through the Caribbean which read like a shop inventory of natural resources up for grabs (see, amongst others, Schomburgk, 1840; Stedman, 1796; Waterton, 1903). The economics of global capital (in its historic and contemporary guises) are fully recognised in Lovelace's narrative, where virtually every mention of the landscapes of Kumaca is imbued with its instrumental value. In what appear to be unproblematic visions of the world of the novel, Lovelace demonstrates that the history of Caribbean lands cannot be expressed without recourse to awareness of the economic and ecological issue of resource: 'Sunlight blazes the hills; and scattered between the hills' valuable timber trees — the cedar, angelin, laurier-matak, galba and manhoe — the poui is dropping rich yellow flowers like a madman throwing away gold' (1997: 1). In an inversion of Marvell's and Raleigh's desires (one which more accurately and appropriately echoes the actuality of Raleigh's experience in the New World), Lovelace's vision is one of elusive and disappearing wealth. 'The gold' of the harvest flows all too quickly away from the community and the sense of the economic imperative underpinning agricultural process is echoed in the following description of the processes of cocoa harvesting. The control of the crop, and whatever wealth there is to be made, flows through the hands of avaricious shopkeeper Dardain, 'who has a licence from the government to deal in cocoa' (1997: 18), and it is wealth that seems destined never to return and never to 'trickle down' to others in the community. The lands of the village which have sustained the community and upon which the people of Kumaca are dependent for a degree of autonomy become refigured as a self-serving spiritual paradise for the priest, a personal commercial heaven for the merchant shopkeeper, and indulge the neocolonial fantasies of sexual and political domination for the schoolmaster, Winston Warwick. The schoolmaster himself replicates modes of domination that identify him more closely with colonial mastery than with the people of the village, with whom he might have been expected to claim kinship; indeed, the terminology of colonial administration is invoked explicitly, as he is proclaimed 'governor' and 'ruler' in the village (1997: 135).

If the pastoral is, in part, a discourse of 'retreat, renewal and return' (Gifford 1999: 174), *The Schoolmaster* forcefully exemplifies a revisioned version of the mode. Rather than simply celebrating 'the regenerative powers of the pastoral' (Clemente, 1999), the novel offers up a reimagining of Caribbean pastoral which acknowledges the brutalising systemic violence that followed the fallacy of 'discovery'. Pastoral notions of retreat, return, renewal and regeneration are complicated by a legacy of conquest and colonisation — a legacy still experienced and endured by the Kumaca community. Lovelace demonstrates, in a Caribbean context, that a discourse privileging personal or communal regeneration (supposedly brought about through a harmonic relationship with a particular landscape) is undoubtedly problematical and is arguably an ideological fallacy. Here, the novel echoes and even prefigures the current ecocritical and postcolonial debate about the status of the pastoral in contemporary literary studies. Lawrence Buell's (1995, 2005) understanding of an 'indigene pastoral' and Terry Gifford's (1999) proposal for 'post-pastoral' are both arguments which demand a reappraisal of the pastoral in the light of postcolonial critique. Graham Huggan (2005) has recently outlined what such a postcolonial recasting of the pastoral — or, more specifically, what a peculiarly *Caribbean*-postcolonial recasting of the pastoral — versions might require: most of all, the urgent task of addressing the question of how viable it is to celebrate 'nature' when nature itself has been so systematically alienated from its peoples, and when its very beauty has become a vehicle for mystification, concealing its own history of dispossession. Furthermore, Huggan suggests that we need to learn to hate the pastoral properly, to inhabit it imaginatively and to eviscerate it intellectually, in the hope that it might be restored in a properly 'critical' mode. Lovelace's novel of 1968, I argue, offers the reader the opportunity of doing just that.

As the novel investigates long-standing assumptions about pastoralism, it also provides a sensitive analysis of debates about progress and development. While the tragic mood of the novel largely dominates, the author complicates the issue of economic development in a number of ways. Lovelace's exploration of the painful complexities of a community attempting to construct a sustainable and educationally enriched future frustrates any simplistic eco-binary thinking in regard to issues of development. The novel simply will not allow us to assume that the 'road of progress' is wholly without potential or actual benefit. Nor does it attempt to persuade the reader that the state of the village is a satisfactory resolution. Indeed, Lovelace invites us to consider the fact that to do so would be to replicate, in ecocritical terms, the self-serving viewpoint of Vincent. Lovelace's presentation of the tension between destruction of what was, and the idea of personal and communal progression, relates interestingly to other ecoliterary representations of road programmes in Trinidad. One might think of Samuel Selvon's *A Brighter Sun* (1952), where road-building is envisaged as *Bildungsroman*, and also Walcott's play, *Beef, No Chicken* (1986), where the highway as symbol is figured in a wonderfully perverse, farcical tragi-comedy of social change and environmental destruction. For Lovelace, Paulaine's argument for the necessity of progress, through school and road, in order to secure a better future for the younger generations of the village, is sincere and persuasive to the point of compulsion. Conversely, Vincent's fears for the destructive effects on the people are partial and expedient to the point of delusion. And yet, as the novel unfolds, Paulaine's principled hopes are disappointed and Vincent's anxieties tragically fulfilled. In *The Schoolmaster*, Lovelace provides a modulated, reasoned and understanding response to the discomforting complexities of the issues of development in the post-independence Caribbean.

The very title of Lovelace's later novel, *Salt* (1996), immediately brings to the fore ideas of interdependence and the connection of human life to the environment. It implicitly connects the people and the earth, and establishes a delicate balance between that which is sterile, or results in an emptiness of being, and that which is life-sustaining, productive and affirming. Furthermore, it also posits a link between the history of the sweat of enslaved human labour and the environment through the salt water of the surrounding seas. The salt of the novel is transcribed as the life-force and the pain of human existence in the Caribbean, and this is then — essentially and chemically — connected to the extra-human world. Lovelace here echoes Glissant, whose poem *Le Sel Noir* (1960) similarly explores the balance between negation and growth in the Caribbean and conjures metaphors of resolve and resistance from the biological building blocks of life collecting on the shorelines of the New World. In connecting the sweat of slave labour with the ocean, *Salt* can also be seen to echo Walcott's reading of a human history which is implicated in natural history — all history held in saline suspension under the waves that seal up 'that gray vault' Atlantic:

> Exodus
> Bone soldered by coral to bone,
> Mosaics
> Mantled by the benediction of the shark's shadow,

> ...
> and in the salt chuckle or rocks
> with their sea pools, there was the sound
> like a rumour without any echo
> of History, really beginning. (Walcott 1979)

Lovelace takes up this idea that the locus for an understanding of Caribbean history is fundamentally environmentally oriented, that 'the sea is history'. He employs it to interrogate not only the history of the Middle Passage but also to explore the diasporas of the contemporary Caribbean. The story of Guinea John and the story of the Rastafarians become interwoven: 'You hear any of them talking about Africa? You see any of them going back? Eh? Salt. Too much salt. Rastas don't eat salt. Too much salt meat' (Lovelace 1996: 213).

The residue of salt which covers the narrative is then the metaphorical point of departure for the discussion of emancipation in all its forms, and provides Lovelace's most sustained, caustic examination of the vagaries of many neocolonial promises of 'progress'. If the promise of progress in *The Schoolmaster* is shown to be, for the character Christiana, a particularly brutal and dirty joke, *Salt* traces the potential for similar fractures between promises of office and the actual results of policy, through the course of Alford George's perceptions and accomplishments. His growing understanding of the education system, the precarious potentiality of tourism and his own complicity in governance all combine to force George — and us as readers — to reinvestigate the representation of progress in 'paradise'. Alford's time in power results in his reassessing all areas of authority and, as his awareness of the political and social situations grows, so does his understanding of the true 'trappings' of office.

Just as one manifestation of the promise of education fails the village of Kumaca, so Alford comes to comprehend and to question the inheritance of a colonial education system which is predicated on individual success at the expense of the majority: 'Failure was to not escape. To fail to escape was defeat; defeat even before you began ... He realized that saving the two or three, if you could call it saving, was not enough for his life's vocation. If he was to go on, he would begin afresh to prepare children for living in the island' (1996: 76). Moreover, he becomes aware that there was a need for action: 'What we need to counteract the three, four hundred years of colonial propaganda is a tourism thrust of our own. We need to look at ourselves afresh' (1996: 122). Here Alford, the budding politician, echoes the words of Jamaican Prime Minister Michael Manley as he has warned of the need to take stock of the history of the region in order to address new the challenges brought about by the emerging global economic system:

The vacation industry is clearly here to stay. But the question which we dare not ignore is whether we, the Caribbean people, are going to have the wit and the will to make it the servant of our needs. If we do not, it will become our master, dispensing pleasure on a curve of diminishing returns while it exacerbates social divisions and widens that legacy of colonialism. (Cited in Pattullo 1996: ix–x)

In order to look 'afresh', *Salt* directs us again to Glissant's imperative of a refigured understanding of interrelational history; Glissant's conception of 'relation identity' is the basis for a renewed understanding of the interdependence between humans and environment (Glissant 1997: 144). Lovelace is able to examine this interrelational history in *Salt* primarily through his treatment of the question of land ownership. Bango articulates the most profound understanding of the double-edged concept of being connected to the land. On the one hand, the very landscape and the climate itself seem implicated — even complicit — in the enactment of domination. For the colonial rulers: 'It was so hot ... they had to get people to fan them. People to carry their swords, people to carry cushions for them to sit down on. They had to get people to beat people for them, people to dish out lashes' (1996: 6). On the other hand, the landscape in *Salt* provides a focus for articulating a history of emancipation: 'Watch the landscape of this island,' Bango explains, '... And you know that they could never hold people here surrendered to unfreedom. The sky, the sea, every green leaf and tangle of vines sing freedom' (1996: 5). In reality, as Bango himself has learnt, the landscape of the islands provided as well a very real site for the resistance of maroon societies. Through Banjo's reading of maroonage, it is perhaps possible to see an example of a valuable Caribbean refiguration of the traditional pastoral themes of retreat and regeneration.

Bango and Myrtle are the archetypal figures of a Glissant-type vision, mistrustful of the land but already figuring new connections to it. In seeing history 'afresh', Myrtle perceives the racialisation of the landscape, and its social and economic consequences: 'She saw the greed, the brutality, the people in grief, the land carved up to claimants according to their colour and the number of captives they brought to the enterprise: whiteman so many captives multiplied by thirty acres of land; mulatto and Free Coloured, so many captives multiplied by fifteen acres' (1996: 153). Both Bango and Myrtle appreciate that this dynamic of land ownership taints the contemporary and gestural politics of land donation pursued by Alford's National Party. Glissant's 'new connections' with the land must be those that fully acknowledge all that has gone before. Public, open and official recognition of dispossession must be an indivisible part of any process of reparation and reclamation. Anything short of this, Lovelace seems to be saying, amounts to a continuation of the dispossession brought about by the imperatives of colonialism, denying the people of the region 'what is their due'. Indeed, 'what is due' to Bango and Myrtle is a democratised land ethic, one that can simultaneously acknowledge the intrinsic value of the island ecology and understand that, as a matter of survival, land must cease to be an exclusive luxury and become a properly communal resource. This realisation of a revisioned land ethic is wholly compatible with Lovelace's undertaking to narrate an ideology of personhood: a vision of independence through interdependence, an eviscerating of pastoral illusion, and a searching evaluation of the costs of promised political progress. In Alford George's words:

> How can you free people? ... When every move you make is to get them to accept conditions of unfreedom, when you use the power to twist and corrupt what it is to be human, when you ask people to accept shame as triumph and indignity as progress? What is power if power is too weak to take responsibility to uphold what it is to be human? (1996: 257)

In another telling example of interconnection in the narrative, Lovelace's iconic image of freedom, the steelband, represents the attainability of personhood through cultural expression: 'a single steelband that we make from oil drums — that is the part of the oil we get: the steel' (1996: 44). The music of emancipation itself is beaten out on the empty containers of illusory economic promise. Just as the 'gold' of Kumaca's harvest was carried away from the community which produced it, so Trinidad's 'black gold' proves to be equally elusive.

The scepticism of neocolonial promises in the novel is balanced, in one sense, by an equal rejection of 'back to nature' movements, which are seen as little more than withdrawals into a state of eco-hermitage. Indeed, *Salt* suggests that adoption of such positions is evidence of an almost complete abdication of social and environmental responsibility. 'Back to nature' beliefs are shown to be synonymous with 'away from issues' politics, and are exemplified in the narrative by Mother Earth. She is depicted with revealing irony, as years earlier she had left the city to live 'naked with nature' and now returns 'wearing skirts of plantain leaves to tell [Alford] not to waste his time trying to change the system, leave it. Leave Babylon and come back to the land, to the forest, to nature, where the lion will lie down with the lamb' (1996: 82). Once more, *Salt* presents a vision that is consistent with Glissant's version of sceptical ecologism:

> A reactionary, that is to say infertile, way of thinking about the
> Earth, it would almost be akin to the 'return to land' championed by

Pétain, whose only instinct was to reactivate the forces of tradition and abdication while at the same time appealing to a withdrawal reflex. (Glissant 1997: 147)

The case of Mother Earth can be viewed as Lovelace's criticism of this 'withdrawal reflex' which, he insists, jeopardises a constructive environmental ethic in the Caribbean. However, in his rejection of this kind of ecomysticism, Lovelace does not discard all notions of the connection between human spirituality and the environment. The relation of the healing of young Alford at the hands of the Shango woman Mother Ethel makes the importance of this connection explicit. Her power to commune with the spirit world is realised through the fruits of the land acting as conduits — 'the calabash tree and the pomegranate tree with the iron for Ogun and the conch shell for Yemanja and the sugarcane plant, for Damballah, the snake' (Lovelace 1996: 22).

It is clear, then, that issues of spirituality are important to Lovelace's environmental conception as they are central to understandings of selfhood within one's community, one's interactions with the wider world and one's sense of responsibility towards it. However, what is demonstrated to be of equal importance is an understanding of the dangers of forms of spirituality which attempt to exert control by erasing the history of labour, and in doing so to romanticise the relationship between people and land (Father Vincent's spiritual gaze), or the contemplation of spiritual retreat that becomes, in effect, little more than political evasion (the cult of Mother Earth).

The incisive ecoliterary stance of the novel, then, can be seen to operate alongside those recent, 'second wave', examples of ecocritical inquiry which seek to identify and purge the 'obsolete mysticism' of some contemporary forms of environmentalism. The distrust concerning schemes of governance and corporate interest that replicate dispossession, whilst talking of emancipation, when coupled with his insistent politics of human agency, signifies Lovelace's value to a Caribbean literary ecocriticism. The novels *The Schoolmaster* and *Salt* strike up imaginative dialogue with the literary environmentalism of Wilson Harris, of Derek Walcott and of Édouard Glissant in particular, and offer revealing readings of how environmental justice can be figured as part of a struggle for a human emancipation that is truly worthy of the name. Indeed, his work provides an interrogatory and constructive response to Harris's question about what sort of art it is which emerges from under the shadow of annihilation.

If one of the significant responsibilities of a Caribbean environmentalism and, by extension, ecocriticism is to find a response to what Hilary Beckles has identified as 'the culture of plantation management which continues to prevent the majority from owning land in the countryside [and which] has alienated people from environmental issues' (1996: 193), then Earl Lovelace's fiction certainly offers a powerful vision. His writing represents a conscious counterpoint to the threat of reductive, or even misanthropic, environmentalist thought — especially that which over-privileges ideas of rootedness in landscape, a notion which Glissant argues had to evaporate with the extermination of the Caribs (1997: 146). His narratives explore, and then explode, all levels and varieties of Edenic illusion in relation to the lands of the region, and in so doing illuminate the task of articulating a new land ethic underwritten by an imaginative realigning of the historical contract with the earth.

Notes

[1] Indeed, the fact of meteorological and geological volatility has become a narrative and poetic resource for reading the history of the Caribbean region. The most notable, but by no means the only, example is the image of the hurricanes which have been used variously, and at times persuasively, to describe: the history of revolutionary, political upheavals; the innate connection between the Caribbean landscape and nation language; and the processes of twentieth-century Caribbean diasporas (see Gott 2005: 1; Braithwaite 1984: 5–12; Wambu 2000).

[2] Glissant is an author of great significant here, as is Harris, because his thinking on matters of the environmental reality of the Caribbean has evolved and deepened over the past 50 years in step with political environmental discourse, which itself has become complicated as a result of developments in ecological science. The oeuvre of both writers demonstrates an accountability to advances and shifts in scientific understanding which must be the basis for all forms of environmental thought: see Garrard (2004: 10, 23).

[3] The ecocritical panel at the conference New Approaches: Caribbean Scholarship in the New Millennium, University of the West Indies, Cave Hill Campus, June 2003 and the conference Trouble in 'Paradise'? Ecocritical Responses to the Contemporary Caribbean, University of Warwick, UK, November 2005 are both indicative of a growing ecocritical discourse within Caribbean Studies which contributes, in turn, to wider postcolonial debates of environmental justice. See especially Nixon (2005: 233–51); Young (2003); and Adamson, Evans and Stein (2002).

[4] For a comprehensive and objective assessment of Grainger's attitude to the politics and poetics of slavery, as well as a consideration of the reception to the poem from the eighteenth century to the present, see Gilmore (2000: 54–65).

References

Adamson, Joni, Evans, Mei Mei and Stein, Rachel (eds) (2002) *The Environmental Justice Reader: Politics, Poetics and Pedagogy* (Tucson: University of Arizona Press).

Beckles, Hilary (1996) *Black Masculinity in Caribbean Society* (St Michael, Barbados: Pine).

Braithwaite, Edward Kamau (1984) *History of the Voice* (London and Port of Spain: New Beacon Books).

Buell, Lawrence (1995) *The Environmental Imagination: Thoreau, Nature Writing, and the Formation of American Culture* (Cambridge, MA: Belknap Press).

—— (2005) *The Future of Environmental Criticism: Environmental Crisis and the Literary Imagination* (Oxford: Blackwell).

Clemente, William A. (1999) 'Priest and Teacher: Pastoral Conflict in Earl Lovelace's *The Schoolmaster*' *Sincronia*, Fall, http://sincronia.cucsh.udg.mx/clemente2.htm.

DeLoughrey, Elizabeth M., Gosson, Renée K. and Handley, George B. (eds) (2005) *Caribbean Literature and the Environment: Between Nature and Culture* (Charlottesville: University of Virginia Press).

Garrard, Greg (2004) *Ecocriticism* (London: Routledge).

Gifford, Terry (1999) *Pastoral* (London: Routledge).

Gilmore, John (2000) *The Poetics of Empire: A Study of James Grainger's The Sugar Cane* (London: Athlone Press).

Glissant, Édouard (1997) 'Distancing, Determining', in E. Glissant, *Poetics of Relation*, trans. Betsy Wing (Ann Arbor: University of Michigan Press).

—— (1960) *Le Sel Noir* (Paris: Editions du Seuil).

Gott, Richard (2005) *Cuba: A New History* (New Haven: Yale Nota Bene).

Harris, Wilson (1985) *The Guyana Quartet* (London: Faber and Faber).

—— (1967) 'The Question of Form and Realism in the West Indian Artist', in W. Harris, *Tradition, the Writer and Society: Critical Essays* (London and Port of Spain: New Beacon Publications).

Huggan, Graham (2005) 'Hating Nature Properly: Naipaul and the Pastoral', paper presented at the Trouble in 'Paradise'? Ecocritical Responses to the Contemporary Caribbean conference, University of Warwick, UK, November.

James, C.L.R. (2001 [1938, 1963]) 'Appendix: From Toussaint l'Ouverture to Fidel Castro', in C.L.R. James, *The Black Jacobins* (London: Penguin).

James, Louis (1995) 'Earl Lovelace', in Bruce King (ed.), *West Indian Literature* (London: Macmillan).

King, Bruce (ed.) (1995) *West Indian Literature* (London: Macmillan).

Loomba, Ania et al. (eds) (2005) *Postcolonial Studies and Beyond* (Durham: Duke University Press).

Lovelace, Earl (1996) *Salt* (London: Faber and Faber).

—— (1997 [1968]) *The Schoolmaster* (Oxford: Heinemann).

Nixon, Rob (2005) 'Environmentalism and Postcolonialism', in Ania Loomba et al. (eds), *Postcolonial Studies and Beyond* (Durham: Duke University Press).

Pattullo, Polly (1996) *Last Resorts: The Cost of Tourism in the Caribbean* (London: Latin American Bureau/Cassell).

Schomburgk, Robert H. (1840) *A Description of British Guiana* (London: Simpkin, Marshall and Co.).

Selvon, Sam (1952) *A Brighter Sun* (London: Wingate).

Stedman, John Gabriel (1796) *Narrative of a Five Years Expedition against the Revolted Negroes of Surinam in Guiana on the Wild Coast of South America from the Year 1772 to 1777* (London: Johnson and Edwards).

Young, Robert (2003) *Postcolonialism: A Very Short Introduction* (Oxford: Oxford University Press).

Wambu, Onyekachi (ed.) (2000) *Hurricane Hits England: An Anthology of Writing About Black Britain* (New York: Continuum).

5
THE CRISIS OF CARIBBEAN HISTORY: SOCIETY AND SELF IN C.L.R. JAMES AND EARL LOVELACE

Aaron Love

C.L.R. James and Earl Lovelace have perhaps been most associated through James's critical praise of Lovelace as 'a new type of West Indian writer' who, unlike the previous generation of novelists, 'with all the echoes and traditions of English literature in their minds', is a 'native writer ... in the sense that [his] prose and the things that [he is] dealing with spring from below' (cited in Walmsley 1992: 102). James saw parallels between Lovelace's work and his own, especially in their shared concern with addressing the political and social realities of post-Independence Trinidad. The work of both exhibits an awareness that historical conditions had shifted in the post-Independence period, revealing social antagonisms that had remained hidden during the national struggle against colonial rule. James differentiated the older political generation of novelists from Lovelace (the 'native' writer) due to the fact that many of the former, in departing their native islands, were removed from the immediate impact of the class and cultural conflicts of the newly independent nations. Lovelace, and others who made the decision to stay, confronted more starkly the contradictions that were generated by a nationalist politics that had promised so much but that in reality was delivering so little. *The Dragon Can't Dance* (1998), for example, can be read as a remarkable distillation of precisely this historical reality. Responding to the cultural and political sensibilities of the Black Power era, *Dragon* addresses the overwhelming imperative to search for solutions to the crisis of the post-Independence nation in the Caribbean, and to transcend what increasingly came to be perceived as the failure of the nationalist project. This imperative gave rise to a series of important cultural and political movements, from the later 1960s to the early 1980s, in which both Lovelace and James were active.

A defining issue that emerges from a comparative reading of *The Dragon Can't Dance* and James's work is the problem of the politics of subjectivity. In Trinidad and Tobago, as elsewhere in the Caribbean, the mass of the people found themselves excluded by the nationalist politics which had been bequeathed by the end of the colonial period. Critical to both Lovelace and James was the project of imagining a politics in which those who had been excluded could move to the centre of things, in which their lives and their subjective sense of the world would become the vehicle by which a new social order could be imagined, and brought into realisation. It is with this aspect of Lovelace and James — their engagement with the dialectic between self and society, between subjectivity and history — that I am most concerned in this chapter. But although both took this issue to be a significant component in the crisis of the emergent new nations in the Caribbean, and a matter of political urgency, they brought to the problem distinct conceptual strategies.

In reading *The Dragon Can't Dance* and James's writings of this period through a single optic, I hope to demonstrate that, if the question of the subjective dimensions of politics is common to both, Lovelace succeeds in overcoming certain limitations in James's positions — succeeds, indeed, in overcoming a certain formalism to be found in James. James, I suggest, espoused theoretical positions which were inherently contradictory. As I will show, this is a complex matter. In his years in the United States (1938–53), James produced a body of work of great originality, much of which turned on the question of the politics of subjectivity. This work was driven by his prolonged engagement with Americanised mass culture, and formed within the crucible of US politics. Yet what James was able to think through in terms of the United States, carrying with it many daring theoretical advances, he seemed later, in the 1960s and 1970s, unable to translate into an effective *Caribbean* politics. Lovelace, on the other hand, although sharing many of C.L.R. James's concerns, demonstrated a more intimate grasp of the dialectic between self and society in Trinidadian society.

James and the Post-Independence Caribbean

On the invitation of Eric Williams, the dominating personality of the People's National Movement (PNM) that led Trinidad and Tobago to Independence, James returned to his homeland in 1958, after more than a 25-year absence. Williams proposed that he become editor of the party paper, the *PNM Weekly*, which James renamed *The Nation*. This presented an extraordinary opportunity for James, since he was isolated and almost unknown in Britain after his deportation from America in 1953, and his connections to his old political allies in the United States were, for a variety of reasons — the passage of time, continuing sectarian disputes, political exhaustion — rapidly weakening (for a sense of this, see Lamming 1992: 196). However what initially held much promise soon turned in on itself, the relationship between James and Williams quickly descending into a spectacular collapse. In 1960, James was purged from the PNM, and shortly after headed back for Britain. He returned briefly to Trinidad in 1964, challenged Williams in the 1966 elections and faced a brief period of house arrest. Thereafter he became a mentor to the various groupuscules of the Caribbean New Left through the 1970s and early 1980s. It was in this period of his life, from the late 1950s to the early 1980s, that James renewed his engagement with the political movements of the Caribbean.

It is difficult to reconstruct the intention of his political-cultural thought at this time, partly because of an apparent lack of continuity between his American and Caribbean years. The move back from metropole to 'periphery' generated for James a host of new strategic questions. As Denis Benn has noted, 'it must be concluded that James' prescription for party organisation in underdeveloped countries is inconsistent with, and indeed contradicts, his more general theoretical principles concerning social and political change' (Benn 1987: 122). One of the puzzles about James in these years in the West Indies concerns the degree to which his actual political practice drew him away from the maxims he had previously advocated. In Trinidad and Tobago, he proclaimed the virtues of the mass party and was willing to work with the trade unions, seemingly distancing himself from his earlier commitments to a radical anti-statism and to direct-democracy. Although the extent of James's break with his previous positions can be over-emphasised, the problem it presents is real enough. Much as he had attempted in *American Civilization* (1993 [1950]), James sought to recast what he had called the 'invading socialist society' in the specific national terms and conditions of the Caribbean. Like his work in America, this was a project that was never fully completed. In his revisionist historical narrative, he centred national purpose within the unfolding drama of Caribbean workers' history, and in doing so he hoped to establish the conceptual and historical foundations for a direct democracy of workers' self-government.

Yet in one respect James's analyses of the post-Independence period does differ significantly from that of his years in the United States and Britain. In his writings on the Caribbean, his conception of the politics of the subject is less assured, demonstrating less resolution in his own mind about the place of popular subjectivity. This ambiguity arose at least partially from his assessment of the post-Independence period as not only a crisis of the national bourgeoisie, but also of the self-conceptions of the mass of Caribbean people. There is evidence to suggest that he was aware of this, and that he was keen to address it, as we can see for example in his 1971 reflections on *The Black Jacobins*. It is true also that, even in his own earlier writings, there were fruitful models to hand where the relations between subjective life and social process lay at the very centre of things, as in his 1936 novel, *Minty Alley* and, more recently, in *Beyond a Boundary*, which although published only in 1963 had largely been completed before he had returned to Trinidad in 1958.

When he had been in the United States, alongside his re-theorisations of direct democracy and state capitalism, James had returned to his preoccupation with literary and symbolic methods, to give great emphasis in his politics to a conception of the *self-activity* of the working class, in order to grasp the hidden struggle of the social personality within the interstices of everyday life under capitalism. This was part and parcel of his very early encounter (in the Anglophone world) with Marx's concept of alienation, organised in the philosophical anthropology of the modern self found in Marx's *Early Philosophical and Economic Manuscripts*. Sections of this work were translated by Grace Lee of the Johnson-Forest Tendency, the James and Raya Dunayevskaya-led faction in the American Socialist Workers' Party and the Workers' Party through the 1940s. This understanding of the modern self was coupled with critiques not only of Stalinism but also of orthodox Trotskyism. Decisive in their critiques of these Marxist orthodoxies was their conviction that 'all development takes place as a result of *self*-movement' in overcoming contradictions in the self that have developed within as 'an alien power that he has himself created' (James 1986: 117). In its drive toward freedom from alienation the modern self was compelled to resolve 'the complexity and antagonisms of society' (1986: 151) as what he called in *American Civilization* 'a world movement towards the creation of man as an integral human being, a full and complete individuality' (James 1993: 119). This was the theoretical foundation upon which James would think through the relations between subjectivity and history. More concretely, it was from this perspective that he came to imagine the everyday life of working people, as constituted in their deepest desires and frustrations, compelled all the while — as a matter of survival — to overcome the social contradictions which daily threatened to tear them asunder. In *American Civilization*, James aimed to give substance to these philosophical reflections by locating his interpretation of American culture in the subjective lives of the masses. He analysed the motifs and metaphors found in popular movies, in newspapers and in mass-produced fiction as spectres of the struggling self-formation of the working class, thereby illuminating the abstractions of conventional political theories (much Marxism included) for which such questions remained of little concern.

However, this intimate portrait of the self that emerges in James's work during these American years does not appear as clearly in his later analysis of the Caribbean. James believed that the objective conditions of state-capitalism in the industrialised countries made possible the leap to direct democracy by the working class. For the 'peripheral' nations in global capitalism, he had other ideas. His formal commitments to the centrality of the Caribbean worker-self remained as powerful as ever, but in substance his thought could never quite deliver what he wished it to do. The difficulties that led to this were political and theoretical, though perhaps surprising given James's characteristically heterodox cast of thought. In the United States, James had argued that the process of the self-formation of the American worker was the key to the transition from the old society to the new. The semi-proletarian character of Trinidad led him to conclude that the subjectivity of the popular classes was fractured to an unusual degree, and that it was sections of the radical *middle class* that would create the political forms in which a more resolute, democratic popular consciousness would cohere. Within this scenario, the subjective self-formation of the people, by which in *making themselves* they would make the new society, assumes a more subsidiary place in his theorisation. As a consequence, the Caribbean subject, on which so much hangs for James, becomes something of a gestural, rhetorical figure.

By renaming *The Nation*, James signalled his intention to advocate moving the PNM from a parliamentary party administering the political conditions for capital to a mass party that would be educative, in the largest sense of the world, and that would eventually lead to popular self-government. In 1960 he told a public audience that the new society would be predicated on 'a close and intimate relation of the ordinary man in his labor and on the basis of his labor creating a social and political form over which he has immediate and constant control' (1973: 92). This form of self-government had, he explained, recently arisen in the Hungarian Revolution, where assemblies and councils emerged to govern production and to constitute a new government. Yet he emphasised that in different social conditions different political desiderata pertained, and that the mass party 'is still valid for countries which are underdeveloped, that is to say, where industry and therefore the proletariat is not dominant' (1973: 92). While being clear that it was the people who 'were teachers of the Colonial Office' when it came to democracy, they were not yet ready, he insisted, to make the revolutionary leap into the future. Nor could the vehicle for attaining this simply be created by revolutionaries. This had to be, he claimed, a mass event: 'You cannot appoint "the people" overnight to this committee or that board. But you encourage them, you insist that they practise self-government, that is to say, to govern themselves, in their own organizations' (James 1962: 125). On occasion, James seemed to be suggesting that the mass party would function not simply as a centre, but literally as *the vanguard*, of a coherent cultural self not yet in existence.

The party:

> must see itself as first of all a social as well as a political organization operating in the community, as the vanguard of a new regime. While India, Burma, Ceylon and Africa have an indigenous civilization and culture, they adapt and modernise this, but in the period of transition this civilization serves as a rallying-point and basis of solidarity. West Indians have nothing of the kind. Politics, economic development, art, literature, history, even social behavior, they have to be recreated. Everything. What is to be preserved, what rejected? In an underdeveloped country, particularly the West Indies, only the mass popular democratic party can be the centre of the instinctive movement and needs to fill the vacuum. (1962: 13–14)

These are, surprisingly, Naipaul-like sentiments that seem to undermine James's desire to centre West Indian self-formation as a creative historical process in his political narrative, the power of *American Civilization* derived from James's capacity to identify in US life an autonomous history of working-class self-becoming. In the Caribbean, he insisted, such a process could only lie in the future. Thus, too, his conviction in the need for a mass party. But the political party for James was caught in the tension where it functioned both as a 'centre of the instinctive movement' and as *the creator* of that instinct. In asking 'Why the organization of a mass party is a matter of life and death for an emerging West Indian society?' he insisted that 'for the people democracy is not a carefully doled out concession that rulers make to people but an inherent part of their conceptions of themselves, a possession, which they exercise and defend because they cannot conceive of existence without it' (1962: 121). Yet the party, he maintained, must also create 'everything' — not only the political institutions of the transitional society but also the very self-formation of the people as well. Thus it seems here as if the mass party is not 'adapting and modernising' an already existing set of 'self-conceptions' and 'instinctive movements' toward direct democracy, but on the contrary intervening *from the outside* in order to create these new forms of selfhood.

James attempted to explain this further in *Nkrumah and the Ghana Revolution* (1977b), parts of which were written through the 1960s, although not published in book form until 1977. Writing about 'Lenin and the Problem' of underdevelopment, James put forward a comparative examination of the difficulties in the Russian Revolution and the contemporary Third World in reconstructing society on the basis of the self-governing councils and popular assemblies. James put the following argument:

> Now in the face of the threatening catastrophe of all [Lenin] had worked for, he faced the fact that what was required the proletariat could not do. What elements, he asked, do they have for building this new apparatus instead of the pre-bourgeois, bureaucratic serf-culture which they had?

He then quoted directly from Lenin: 'They cannot do it. They have not yet developed the culture that is required for this; and it is precisely culture that is required for this.' James himself then added:

> That was for Lenin the end of the road. The workers on whom he depended for everything creative, everything new, were incapable of initiating this mighty reorganisation. He had indicated in what way the energies of peasants could be channelled into the social reconstruction of Russia. But neither peasant nor proletariat could reconstruct, reorganise the pre-bourgeois, bureaucratic, serf-culture with which Soviet Russia was still saddled.

Here James understood the very basis of the new society in terms of what he called 'dependence on the subjective element' (1977b: 209–10).

It was with these issues in mind that James came, at the end of the 1960s, to envision a role for Trinidad's Oil-field Workers' Trade Union (OWTU) and its paper *The Vanguard*: 'Once *The Nation* did it. Today *We the People* is doing all that it can. But *The Vanguard* is in a position today to undertake the responsibility on a widening scale.' Comparing the Caribbean situation to pre-1917 Russia, he declared that the West Indian intellectual establishment could not 'penetrate the aristocracy of colonialism', just as the Russian intellectuals were not able to combat Tsarism. Therefore:

> the Oilfield Workers' Trade Union has the responsibility to lead the struggle for parliamentary democracy and the defense of democratic rights. In fact it had better do so. Our West Indian history, the principles of political thought, sociological analysis, biographies of our important men, arts and letters, these are the intellectual foundations of a modern community, our pressing need. *The Vanguard* must do it. (1969: 6)

Nevertheless, he still spoke *in general* of the autonomous self-constitution of the subject in its self-movement towards freedom. Speaking at the public library in Port of Spain earlier in the decade, James had asked: 'What is the good life?'

(1973: 103). In answering, he contrasted two competing visions of freedom for the modern self: 'What, in Washington, in London, in Moscow, what is their conception of the good life for society?' answering that it was the 'Welfare state ... [but] Men are not pigs to be fattened' (1973: 105). Instead, the good life would only be possible 'when the masses of men and women are in control of society' (1973: 104). This explains his use of direct democratic Athens as a historical model for Caribbean nations. He saw in ancient Athens an overcoming of alienation — producing 'the enormous force and the enormous freedom of his personality' — in which the self had achieved a harmony through a complete integration of all spheres of human activity (1956: 20).

Yet in 1971, James re-examined his *The Black Jacobins*, originally published in 1938, arguing that, in an effort to prove that black people had been world historical leaders, he had concentrated too much on the personality of Toussaint l'Ouverture and not enough on the activity of the self-emancipated Africans. 'I would write descriptions in which the black slaves themselves, or people very close to them, describe what they were doing and how they felt about the work they were forced to carry on,' James asserted. 'I would write the actual statements of the slaves telling *what they were doing*' (2000: 99–100). In a second edition, published in 1963, he had gone some way towards this, by drawing from the French historian of popular Jacobinism, Georges Lefebvre, in order to highlight this as an important theme. By 1971, when he compared negatively his own *The Black Jacobins* to W.E.B. Du Bois's *Black Reconstruction* (published three years earlier in 1935), he showed how he had failed to integrate into his study the self-conceptions of the slaves who had made the revolution in Santo Domingo. 'Du Bois was aware of why the blacks *fought* and what they *thought*,' he wrote, implying that this was something that he himself had failed to convey (2000: 93). These reappraisals of *The Black Jacobins*, of 1963 and 1971, coincide with his political involvement in the Caribbean: the shortcomings of which he was aware in his own historiography, I suggest, had a wider provenance.

For James, art represented a privileged means by which the hidden conflicts of the alienated social personality could be revealed; indeed, the aesthetic domain also represented for him an arena in which the social resolution to human alienation could be prefigured. Much twentieth-century Western art he found lacking in this respect:

> In previous periods of transition, the new society always announced itself in innumerable ways, not least in the literature and art of the day ... But whereas for a century the finest minds in the arts have devoted themselves to destroying the intellectual and moral

foundations of bourgeois society, they have been incapable of putting into the concentrated, illuminating, and exhilarating forms of art, either the general contours or the individual personalities of the new society. (1974: 83)

However, he identified in a younger generation of Caribbean writers a powerful exception to this tendency. In their work he saw emerging a coherent conception of the 'transition in national life', an apprehension of the peculiarly Caribbean dispositions of the self, and also a sense of grasping the 'general contours' of the new society (1990: 49). As with Shakespeare, 'for whom thought and feeling were always experienced in terms of nature, the physical responses of human beings and the elemental categories of life and labour', Caribbean novelists understood the life experiences of the masses, both collectively and in the study of individual personalities (1977a: 184).

What made Shakespeare a critical model for him was his belief that Shakespeare had the capacity to articulate the popular voice at decisive, epochal moments of historical transition, in which the larger historical contradictions were played out in his dramatisations of the inner self:

> Shakespeare's audience understood him instinctively [sic] in the individual passions he portrayed and violent conflicts with the established order ... Shakespeare is the outstanding example of the strength a great artist derives from a living communion with the class or classes whose destiny is his subject matter. (1955: 8)

In much the same way, he thought, the Caribbean novelist of the mid-twentieth century, through 'a combination of learning (in his own particular sphere), observation, imagination and creative logic' could 'construct the personalities and relations of the future, rooting them in the past and the present' (1977: 185). If 'creative originality in literature is a sign, a portent, evidence of creative originality in politics, and in social life', then the vision of Caribbean writers was crucial for revealing these 'portents' of the future (1967: 73). One such novelist that James often spoke of in these terms was Earl Lovelace. In a review of *The Dragon Can't Dance*, James commented that 'nowhere have I seen more of the realities of a whole country disciplined into one imaginative volume' (1980–81: 84). Indeed, I would argue that Lovelace enabled James to grasp the 'subjective element' that was so significant for his own narrative of Caribbean history, but which had come to be obscured by his anxieties about the 'underdevelopment' of Caribbean societies.

Society and Self in The Dragon Can't Dance

Wilson Harris has written about the 'creative phenomenon of the first importance in the imagination of a people violated by economic fates' (Harris 1999: 159). In his view, the ignorance of the intellectual elite about the everyday institutions and cultural forms of the people is indicative of a philosophical impasse and a parallel 'political deterioration' (1999: 161). The impasse, he adds, is located in methodological assumptions that empty historical forces of the structuring agency of the Caribbean peoples themselves. It is an error, Harris believes, repeated by radical historians who, 'militant and critical of imperialism as they are, have fallen victim, in another sense, to the very imperialism they appear to denounce. They have no criteria for arts of originality springing out of an age of limbo and the history they write is without an inner time', a problem rooted in their 'historical refusal to see' (1999: 159). This could well illuminate the conjuncture between the problematic status of the subject in James's thought and the urgent foregrounding in *The Dragon Can't Dance* of the cultural self-conceptions that led Lovelace to the 'inner time' of the Trinidadian oppressed.

From its first pages, the novel establishes the origins of Calvary Hill in the desires of Africans who, continuing 'the most wonderful acts of sabotage' after emancipation, left the plantations, 'refusing to be grist for the mill of the colonial machinery that kept on grinding in its belly people to spit out sugar and cocoa and copra'. Lovelace poses against this a narrowly sociological perspective in which the Hill is simply a place 'where the sun set on starvation and rise on potholed roads, thrones for stray dogs that you could play banjo on their rib bones, holding garbage piled high like a cathedral spire'. The novel connects the observing, objectifying empirical eye with the operations of the state, whose operations by the police against the men on the corner move 'them to strain all the harder to hold their poses on the walls, to keep alive the visibility and aliveness'. It is an 'aliveness' institutionalised during Carnival, when 'the steelband tent will become a cathedral, and these young men priests' (Lovelace, 1998: 1–4). However, the idea of a 'pose' already suggests the complex double meaning of masking and Carnival that underscores Lovelace's notions of 'selfhood', and the desire for 'visibility and aliveness'. It is a term that implies there is in play a process of reification in which, for example, Carnival ceases to offer an authentic form of self-determination, but rather masks contemporary social oppression, and in which the philosophy of 'all o' we is one' becomes incoherent in the face of new historical realities. It suggests an increasingly incoherent social relation between 'visibility and aliveness', which triggers a corresponding disorientation in the characters. *Dragon* foregrounds the historical consciousness of the Caribbean worker-subject whose search for a new authenticity — for a selfhood that can be *recognised* — is trapped in a social situation in which, in the words of Walton Look Lai, 'the old order is dead, but not yet gone. The new order is alive all around us, but it has yet to establish itself firmly upon the stage of history' (1972: 9). If James's assumptions — to borrow his own metaphors — of 'a bureaucratic serf culture' and its relationship to the continuing hold of 'Tsarism' in the Caribbean blinded him to the hidden reality of an autonomous worker-agency, leaving him trapped in the flatness of a gestural, rhetorical mode, then *Dragon* apprehends that autonomous agency in dynamic tension with the historical forces that would reify it. Lovelace completes James's philosophical endeavour by illuminating the manner in which history *moves through* the self-conceptions of the Caribbean dispossessed. In this way, the writer becomes the eye that sees through the aporia in James's own thought.

The connection between 'visibility and aliveness', and the dialectic between the old society and the new, is partially presented in the relationship between Aldrick and Sylvia within the social dynamics of the metaphorical polity of the Yard, in its movement from the old to the new. Sylvia's 'aliveness' is 'too quick' to be trapped by the determining poverty or by the 'fumbling hands' on the Hill, which is tied to Sylvia's potential as a single, young woman who 'ain't have no man' (1998: 16–17). Aldrick must disassociate his own desire for her from Guy, as the symbol of 'economic fates' (and 'fumbling hands' as well) on the Hill. However, Aldrick's desire is kept invisible both to Sylvia and to himself so as not to undermine his philosophy of non-attachment to those around him. The growing disconnection which emerges in the novel between the meaning of the dragon and the social realities of the Yard are reassessed in relation to the symbolic significance of Sylvia as the promise of a new order, whose visibility is felt as a desire, but not yet revealed in historical form.

Sylvia's symbolic location as representative of the 'new yard' is revealed in her proximity to the forces of the old in the figures of Cleothilda — the light-skinned former Carnival Queen and local shopkeeper — and Guy, the rent-collector. Both attempt to cannibalise Sylvia's energy under the old, symbolic order, in order to shore up their own social authority. Cleothilda's vendetta to enforce petty, ethnic loyalty against the Indian Pariag — who has also left the stifling past in the countryside to join the community on the Hill, where 'He wanted to be a man, to join the world, be part of something bigger something in a bigger somewhere, to stretch out, extend himself, be a man among people' — as well as encouraging Guy's relationship with Sylvia, also represents a bid to reassert the authority of the old hierarchies in the Yard (1998: 139). Aldrick's rejection of Cleothilda's endeavour to get him to intimidate Pariag and, in effect, to exclude him symbolically from the Yard, as well as his attempt to encourage Sylvia to break with Cleothilda and Guy, is not wholly successful. Aldrick fails at this point because he has yet to see not only the desires of Pariag and Sylvia, but also his own integral relationship to them. Aldrick begins to understand that the fates of Sylvia and Pariag are not individually determined, but rather are a function of the wider, historical forces that have given life to the subjective desires and social relations on the Hill. Aldrick becomes

> helpless as Sylvia surrendered herself to Guy and Cleothilda, surrendering not only her own body and time of her own, but surrendering in herself that thing in herself that was not hers alone, that others — the whole Hill — could lay claim to; that spirit, that hope that has lived in the Yard ... that belief that there was ahead a better life, a nobler life, for which they, the whole Yard, were candidates out of their steadfastness insistence on their right to humanness unlinked to the possession of any goods or property, arrived at, realized, born to, in consequence of their being.
> (1998: 143)

His 'hurting over Sylvia' makes him realise 'that he had never really lived here on this Hill, never embraced this place as home, never felt it to himself, to his bones. He had been living in the world of the dragon, avoiding and denying the full touch of the Hill.' Aldrick links this in his mind to older memories, 'thinking beyond Sylvia to his dead uncle' who used to tell him, '"Take it easy. We soon going to leave this place." He died there, with the old house falling down about him' (1998: 123). In imploring Sylvia to be true to her own 'selfhood', Aldrick questions his own. He begins to see that organising his life around a commitment only to the dragon has, ironically, blinded him to the social realities of the Hill. The dragon may have promised a continuity with the past and liberation in the future. But in fact he discovers that the dragon has become separated from the 'aliveness' of the Hill and can no longer embody its collective 'selfhood'.

The unresolved tension between the dragon as authentic and reified is closely linked to the historical crises of social compacts that the community has had to abandon, reconceptualise and then find again. Aldrick 'knitted into his dragon' the memories of his father, who 'refused to hear anything against the promise of the land'. He recalls his father's predicament:

> all the toil and time he had put in on the land with his wife and children and grandchildren, he expected as return not produce, not cocoa or coffee of bananas or oranges, but that he could say to God, who must have been the one to make him the promise: I kept my

part of the bargain. You told me to cutlass and hoe and weed and sow; well, I have done all of it. I have kept my part of the bargain. (1998: 29)

The promise of the land and his labour signifies the possibility of fulfilling the desire for 'selfhood' recognised, in this instance, not by human others but by the deity. This promise, however, cannot *not* be fulfilled, as the sustainability of peasant life collapses and the younger generation must travel to the city in order to find work. The dissolution of this promise for the father is in fact to be repeated by the son, in the new historical situation in which he finds himself. Later in the novel, with the preparations complete and the dragon costume finished, Carnival begins and Aldrick is possessed by the dragon. 'For two full days Aldrick danced the dragon in Port of Spain', embodying not only his own desires but those of the neighbourhood, of the nation, and of his larger ancestral history:

> dancing the bad-devil dance, the stickman dance, dancing Sylvia and Inez and Basil and his grandfather and the Hill and the fellars by the Corner, leaning against the wall, waiting for the police to raid them. He was Manzanilla, Calvary Hill, Congo, Dahomey, Ghana. He was Africa, the ancestral Masker, affirming the power of the warrior, prancing and bowing, breathing out fire, lunging out at his chains, threatening with his claws, saying to the city: 'I is a dragon. I have fire in my belly and claws on my hands; watch me! Note me well, for I am ready to burn down your city. I am ready to tear you apart, limb by limb.' (1998: 115–16)

The dragon embodies the accumulated history of the people, but its magic — much like the promise of the land for an aspiring independent peasantry — turns into a force altogether more oppressive. Aldrick finds himself having to question the meaning of the dragon:

> suddenly the head of the dragon on his neck weighed a ton and, stopping to rest, he watched Carnival ending. Aldrick thought: 'you know tomorrow there is no Carnival.' And he understood then what it meant when people said that they wished every day was Carnival. For the reign of kings and princesses was ending, costumes used today to display the selves of people were going to be taken off. What of those selves? What of the selves of these thousands? What of his own self? (1998: 117)

Back in the sacred space of his room-workshop after Carnival, Aldrick feels its 'small confines' and, 'surrounded by an aura of Dragon costumes', he 'felt himself a stranger in that place' (1998: 142). Cleothilda's observation that 'he must be going crazy' indicates a progressive unintelligibility of social meaning within and between the characters (1998: 142). Pariag is called a 'crazy Indian', and the 'warriors' who gather on the corner view as crazy the 'surrendered' residents of the Hill who were 'losing patience with the promise, with the hope, with the dreams, with the battle' (1998: 105). 'Outcast' and 'outsider' signal both the desire for community among the characters of the Yard and its impossibility within the present order, where Aldrick, Fisheye, Sylvia, Pariag and Philo all become outcasts whose human desires are thwarted by social forces they cannot fully see. In this way, the 'new yard' also holds out the threat of complete breakdown in social solidarity, and not only that of the promise of its renewal. Philo's succumbing to the commercialisation of calypso and his moving from the Hill comes close to destroying his friendship with Aldrick. Aldrick's 'inability to hold the two ideas in his brain — Philo as a friend, and Philo as a threat' — is indicative of a crisis in resolving emerging contradictions felt as 'a more profound betrayal of himself' which 'denied the truth of his own feelings'. 'To be rebel, to be warrior on the Corner', in these circumstances, *could* only be a pose, an 'innocence' in which 'maybe it was purer; but, it wasn't the truth' (1998: 151). Aldrick becomes an outcast to himself. Fisheye's 'warriorhood' goes through the same process of being emptied of meaning, whose own alienation is a profound indictment by Lovelace of his society. Fisheye's violent outbursts are symptomatic of a dissolution of the social personality of the 'warrior', a fact his girlfriend Yvonne readily recognises. He searches for new forms of 'warriorhood', but each is incorporated into existing social relations, allowing no possibility for realisation of the self. The coming of the united steelbands create the opportunity for the state and corporate interests to control Carnival. Listening to Eric Williams's speeches in Woodford Square — or to the speeches of a figure much like Williams — Fisheye is impelled to join the National Party, imagining it is what 'the steelband might have become, if fellars had sense, if they had vision. This was it, something joining people to people and people to dreams and dreams to hope that man would battle for more than to proclaim the strength of his arms' (1998: 57). However, Fisheye grows disappointed as the impulse behind 'all o' we is one' is used to support the national bourgeoisie, rendering hollow the hopes of Independence.

The dialectic between 'visibility and aliveness' is pushed further when Aldrick, Fisheye and assorted 'badjohns' hijack a police jeep and drive to Woodford Square, urging the people to revolt against their oppression. Aldrick shouts out over the loudspeaker:

> This is the People's Liberation Army, Shanty Town, Hill, Slum
> Army with guns and jeep coming into the city seeking power,
> making a cry for our people to rise, to rise up and take theyself over;
> take over Laventille, Calvary Hill, Belmont, take over John John,
> St James, Morvant, take power and rise to be people for our own
> self. (1998: 167)

This, it turns out, is a highly symbolic rebellion. Woodford Square is not only associated with Eric Williams's influential popular 'University' but also with the Black Power rebellion of 1970, where the National Joint Action Committee held its 'people's assembly' against the PNM government. However in the novel the episode is one fraught with ambiguity, in which the powerlessness of the advocates of Black Power is all too evident:

> The jeep passed unhindered along the street. 'What we going to do
> now?' Aldrick asked. 'How you mean, what we going to do? Ain't
> we get past the police?' 'Yes, but what we going to do?' 'I don't
> understand you,' Fisheye said. (1998: 168)

With 'the feeling of being imprisoned in a dragon costume' (1998: 169), Aldrick can only answer: 'I don't know' (1998: 171). The desire to will a new community into being fails. 'Pistach talked, Fisheye talked, Aldrick talked, Adonis made his first effort that day before an applauding crowd that stood there waiting for something else, some kind of redemption, some saving.' But Aldrick, who thought of 'his father with his hands in his pockets at his death, and … thought of his grandfather who had stuck with the promise of the land for all those years', grows weary, 'feeling an increasing impotence as they talked on, talked words that stirred the feelings but did little else' (1998: 171–2). This, indeed, is rebellion as rhetoric, and Aldrick, Fisheye and the rest have no other option than to give themselves up to the police.

This dynamic is highlighted by two interpretations of the 'rebellion'. Their defence lawyer in court, considered a radical 'on the outskirts of what called itself a Socialist Movement', who 'had read Marx and [was] grounded in Fanon and Malcolm X', calls it a 'gesture' toward the state for recognition and representation:

> The action undertaken by these men was an attempt to not even
> seize power, as we have seen, but to affirm a personhood for
> themselves, and beyond themselves, to proclaim a personhood for
> people deprived and illegitimized as they: the people of the Hill,
> of the slums and shantytowns. They came, as we have seen, without

any plan or practice for what they might have attempted, desperately, spontaneously, trying to call forth by some magic a deliverance, asking for something to happen. (189: 174–5)

After this speech to the court, Fisheye remarks to Aldrick that 'that young fellar talk good, eh?' Aldrick — perhaps remembering from their rebellion that talk has been emptied of meaning — replies only: 'he beg for us well' (1998: 176). The lawyer's interpretation echoes Williams's speech after he declared martial law during the 1970 uprising: 'The question has been raised as to why the Government waited so long to act. There was one principal consideration. The Black Power movement enlisted the sympathy of a number of people, especially young people, who bitterly resented discrimination against Black people at home and abroad' (Cited in Oxaal 1982: 268). Fisheye and his 'badjohns' concur: 'But, he say we didn't do nutten' Pistach said. 'He say is frustration and anger. We is frustration and anger' (1998: 176). However, Aldrick — rejecting this objectification of his very self by the state — replies: 'I is more than that, man ... I was serious. I wanted us to take over the town, the island. I was serious' (1998: 177). As a consequence of these divergent interpretations of the meaning and purpose of the rebellion, the idea of 'personhood' becomes not only contested, but the dominating site in which the antagonistic meanings of the rebellion are played out. What is at stake, Lovelace argues, is precisely the politics of personhood. If the court proceedings are a performance by 'official society' — to borrow a phrase from James — in a bid authoritatively to seal the rupture which has occurred in the social world, then Aldrick seeks to demystify the 'magic' of this official narrative, with its power to determine who is saviour and who victim. As Aldrick explains:

> Yes. We was speaking to them, shouting to them. We was saying to them, 'Look at us! We is people!' We wasn't ready to take over nothing for we own self. We put the responsibility on them to act, to do something. You don't see that? The way children cry, so their parents will pick them up. You don't see that? 'But,' Pistach said, 'they responsible. They is the authorities.' 'We is people. I, you, you, for we own self. For you and for you and for your own self. We is people with the responsibility for we own self. And as long as we appeal to others, to the authorities, they will do what they want. We have to act for we.' (1998: 180–1)

Addressing the failures of the 1970 movement, Lovelace echoes Aldrick's conclusions: 'what *Dragon* is saying is that the movement was still looking towards the government to change things, instead of itself providing a force capable of taking over, and addressing the issue they had raised' (Jaggi 1990: 26). Aldrick leaves prison knowing that, in the words of James, 'the old way of life can no longer be endured', and that it is necessary 'to live in a new way' (James 1962: 4). The desires of 'all o' we is one' must find a new form. As Aldrick concludes: 'We couldn't do what we didn't see to do. We couldn't enter where we had no vision to go' (1998: 179). The reader, like the character of Aldrick, can see played out new imaginative possibilities, a sense of the future which — affirmed in Aldrick's chance meeting with Sylvia — follow him back to the Hill.

If James's own vision faltered in method, if not in intent, Lovelace offers a more concrete — a more *historical* — sense of how the making of a new world might yet be imagined. Reading James and Lovelace together provides an opportunity to explore the active connections between political and artistic thought, and suggests that in the immediate decades of the post-Independence period, the social movements that engulfed the Caribbean region germinated an artistic and intellectual renaissance in which the formal boundaries between different fields of inquiry were especially porous. Placing Lovelace and James in dialogue illuminates each, and offers us a privileged perspective on the travails of the Caribbean in the years following Independence.

References

Benn, Denis (1987) *The Growth and Development of Political Ideas in the Caribbean, 1774–1983* (Kingston: Institute of Social and Economic Research, University of the West Indies).

Harris, Wilson (1999) 'History, Fable and Myth in the Caribbean and Guianas', in A.J.M. Bundy (ed.), *Selected Essays of Wilson Harris: The Unfinished Genesis of the Imagination* (New York: Routledge).

Jaggi, Maya (1990) 'Interview: Earl Lovelace', *Wasafari*, vol. 12.

James, C.L.R. (1955) 'Preface to Criticism', Martin Glaberman Collection (Detroit: Wayne State University, Walter Reuther Library, Archives of Labor and Urban Affairs).

—— (1956) *Every Cook Can Govern: A Study of Democracy in Ancient Greece* (Detroit: Correspondence Publishing).

—— (1962) *Party Politics in the West Indies* (San Juan, Trinidad: Vedic).

—— (1963 [1993]) *Beyond a Boundary* (Durham, NC: Duke University Press).

—— (1967) 'Introduction' to Wilson Harris, *Tradition and the West Indian Novel* (London and Port of Spain: New Beacon Books).

—— (1969) 'On the Vanguard' in *The Vanguard* (Trinidad), 11 October.

—— (1972) 'A Short Survey of Caribbean Literature', in Ian Munro and Reinhard Sander (eds), *Kas-Kas: Interviews with Three Caribbean Writers in Texas* (Austin, TX: Occasional Publication of the African and Afro-American Research Institute, University of Texas, Austin).

—— (1973 [1960]) *Modern Politics* (Detroit: Bewick).

—— (1974 [1958]) *Facing Reality* (Detroit: Bewick).

—— (1977a [1959]) 'The Artist in the Caribbean', in C.L.R. James, *The Future in the Present: Selected Writings* (Westport, CN: Lawrence Hill).

—— (1977b) *Nkrumah and the Ghana Revolution* (London: Allison and Busby).

—— (1980–81) 'Life on the Hill', *Race Today*, no. 84, December/January.

—— (1986 [1950]) *State Capitalism and World Revolution* (Chicago: Charles Kerr).

—— (1990 [1965]) 'A New View of West Indian History' *Caribbean Quarterly*, vol. 35, no. 4.

—— (1993 [1950]) *American Civilization* (Oxford: Blackwell).

—— (2000 [1971]) '*The Black Jacobins* and *Black Reconstruction*: A Comparative Analysis' and 'How I Would Rewrite *The Black Jacobins*', *Small Axe*, no. 8.

Lamming, George (1992) *Conversations: George Lamming — Essays, Addresses and Interviews, 1953–1990*, eds Richard Drayton and Andaiye (London: Karia Press).

Look Lai, Wally (1972) *The Caribbean Personality: A Vision* (New York: Research Institute for the Study of Man).

Lovelace, Earl (1998) *The Dragon Can't Dance* (London: Faber and Faber).

Oxaal, Ivar (1982) *Black Intellectuals and the Dilemmas of Race and Class in Trinidad* (Cambridge, MA: Schenkman).

Walmsley, Anne (1992) *The Caribbean Artists Movement, 1966–1972* (London and Port of Spain: New Beacon Books).

6
WRITING TRINIDAD: NATION AND HYBRIDITY IN *THE DRAGON CAN'T DANCE* AND *WITCHBROOM*

Patricia Murray

Trinidad occupies a special place in the Caribbean, both in terms of its cultural hybridity and its strategic location between island and mainland cultures. Its efforts to build a coherent sense of nation, while remaining alert to the competing demands of cross-culturality, have always made it a focal point in Caribbean discourse as well as a hospitable meeting ground for Caribbean travellers — a refuge for those on the move. But as the nation's leading mas man, Peter Minshall, emphasised in his stark 'Red' mas for the 1998 Carnival, Trinidad remains a wounded country, still bearing the scars of colonialism, still struggling under socio-economic tensions, though with a latent vitality that can inspire. In this context I want to explore Earl Lovelace's *The Dragon Can't Dance* (1986 [1979]) and Lawrence Scott's *Witchbroom* (1993 [1992]) as important examples of how to write Trinidad and bring into dialogue their perspectives on identity and their shared experiments with language and form. Both are searing political critiques as well as deeply reparative novels, and I will argue that both outline a process of healing that turns on the need to hybridise.

★ ★ ★

At first glance, these two novels might seem to be very different. *The Dragon Can't Dance*, Lovelace's third (and some consider his best) novel, is by now a classic of Caribbean literature. Set largely in a slum dwelling in Port of Spain over a single Carnival season, Lovelace combines a socio-historical analysis of stagnation with a celebration of the resilience of ordinary people through a powerful intimacy of characterisation. The novel's impact at the time lay in its sustained use of the language and rhythms of the oral tradition to create a new kind of narrative voice, one which narrowed the gap between realist frame and indigenous subject-matter.

Witchbroom, an ambitious debut novel, locates Trinidad in terms of its South American heritage and takes its cue from García Márquez to create a magical realist tale of the island of Kairi. Where *Dragon* focuses on the urban setting, on the tight claustrophobia of the island, *Witchbroom* brings us the sounds of the forest, haunted by the disembodied voices of the past. Where Lovelace is at home in his world, presenting the Yard in Alice Street as a microcosm of Trinidadian society, Scott tells his tale from the sill of the Demerara window, needing to confront the amnesia of the Creole planter class before he can participate in and belong to a more expansive Trinidad. *Witchbroom* is a supplement to *Dragon*, a reminder of the liminality of the nation-space; *Dragon* is an extended portrait of the kind of impoverished corner only glimpsed fleetingly in the wide-angle vision of *Witchbroom*. Despite these obvious differences, however, both novels are quintessentially Trinidadian and speak to each other in interesting ways. Their narrative styles may indicate a different point of contact (a different route through) but there are important overlaps in their reflecting upon nation and hybridity.

Both novels begin with a prologue, and their distinctive styles are immediately evident. Lovelace tells a humorous anecdote about Taffy, a man who aspires to be Christ on the cross until his followers take him too literally and pelt him with stones. He then writes:

> This is the hill, Calvary Hill, where the sun set on starvation and rise on potholed roads, thrones for stray dogs that you could play banjo on their rib bones, holding garbage piled high like a cathedral spire, sparkling with flies buzzing like torpedoes; and if you want to pass from your yard to the road you have to be a high-jumper to jump over the gutter full up with dirty water, and hold your nose. Is noise whole day. Laughter is not laughter; it is a groan coming from the bosom of these houses — no — not houses, shacks that leap out of the red dirt and stone, thin like smoke, fragile like kite paper, balancing on their rickety pillars as broomsticks on the edge of a juggler's nose. (Lovelace 1986: 23)

Scott uses his longer 'Overture' to introduce the figure of Lavren, the last of a once prosperous Creole family, whose memory is shaken up by a freak accident just as he is staring into the eyes of a scarred Indian boy. As he writes:

> Lavren entered through the black holes of those eyes, black from the black hole of Calcutta smudged with the yellow of malnutrition. He entered the white belly burnt with the pain of history. He entered

this pain into a revision of history. He entered a sea of green and yellow, coppery, silted with the refuse of the Orinoco whose mouth was crammed with wrecks, festooned with skeletons, the treasure of that far-flung folly of cross and sword whose seed was sown in Genoa. Out of the empty sockets in the algae-encrusted skulls vast processions issued, performing the liturgies of Corpus Christi, the candlelit mass of Easter. Out of one skull Las Casas swam, bearing Amerindians and welcoming black slaves from the belly of ships and baptising them. The seaweed was stained with the blood of Christ and the slaves and Amerindians had their mouths stuffed with loaves and fishes from the gospels, while archbishops and nuns copulated in confessionals to the chanting of the *Salve Regina*. (1993: 11)

A different kind of movement takes place here. Taffy is the first in a long line of characters who are craving to be seen, to be noticed, and Lovelace returns us insistently to the Hill and its claims to visibility. As Lavren identifies with the victims of history and comes adrift in a vast sea of collective memory, Scott turns history into myth: gentle irony becomes anarchic satire. But what impresses in both is the sheer intensity of the writing, the audacious use of images to convey both a fierce indignation and a heartfelt attachment to place. It is this double movement, and this rhetorical virtuosity, that energise both novels despite the difficult transitions they also outline. At the level of content, both are concerned to construct a more coherent version of nation; at the level of form, both wrestle with inherited traditions to create something more genuinely Trinidadian, a Creolised form of social (Lovelace) and magical (Scott) realism. These endeavours also converge on their particular use of Carnival to suggest new futures.

★ ★ ★

As the titles to both novels indicate, we are confronted first of all with a scrutiny of what has become static and degenerative in Trinidadian society. *The Dragon Can't Dance* is a stinging attack on slum conditions and political betrayal in post-Independence Trinidad, where the likes of Fisheye, Aldrick and Philo (the descendants of people who fought slavery and colonialism) still struggle for visibility, and where women have no choice but to drift into their 'inevitable whoredom' (1986: 44). The sadness of Fisheye's descent into violence, or Aldrick's and Philo's compromises, is as starkly told as Sylvia's sexual enslavement to Mr Guy for the price of the rent. These are people who only come alive during the two days of Carnival and, as Aldrick comments: 'That life between Ash Wednesday and Carnival Monday morning, it counted for something' (1986: 146). Even worse than this bitter alienation is the failure of the Yard and the Carnival band to effect anything more substantial than Cleothilda's trite phrase 'all o' we is one'. When Pariag and his wife arrive in the Yard, this sentiment is found to be wanting. The novel positions Aldrick (who plays the dragon) as emotional witness at two key turning points — the destruction of Pariag's bicycle and the exclusion of Philo from the Corner — and he is powerless to intervene in either.

Witchbroom is also unflinching in its attack on corruption and hypocrisy, focusing particularly on the responsibilities of the Creole planter class in the cruelties of the time. The parasite which attacks the cocoa trees (witches broom in *Dragon* 1993: 52) is here transfigured into the fungus of history that eats away at the Monagas family, causing the amnesia that Lavren's tales must now address. From the first demented military exploitation of the island to the cynical clinging to privilege post-Independence, the Monagas collude in the abuses of church and state and consistently deny the life of the people who serve in and around their houses. Obsessed with their own skin colour and with maintaining racial and social hierarchies, they are a perverse reminder of the insularity of the Creole elites who fail to hybridise. The invention of Lavren as a shape-shifting, hermaphrodite storyteller and the extravagance of his Carnival tales may lighten the tone comparatively, but there is no doubting the loneliness and alienation that also run through this novel. Having embraced the hyperbole of García Márquez and the long tales of Pierrot and Robberman to give form to his characters, Scott returns to a plainer style in the inserted 'Journal' to tell a more personal version of the same story. Here there are further gaps in the memory, further denials and betrayals, as the lonely Creole boy clings to the black housekeeper who reared him:

> She knows my pain but how do I approach hers, that double
> century of ancestral pain? How tell it? How presume to tell it? Yet
> I must not forget. I must keep the remembering.
>
> There were stories I could not tell, and I hoped their voices in
> Lavren's preposterous narratives would speak out from where they
> stood.
>
> Both stories were of pain, mine and hers, autobiography and
> herstory. They both began to merge as stories I could not go near,
> but would have to wait in this house for them to approach me.
> (1993: 96)

Part of the anxiety of *Witchbroom* is a concern with how the story gets told and the 'Journal' offers a definition of 'palimpsest' as a guide to the layers of Trinidadian history and culture that are not easily written into narrative:

> *Palin* — again
> *Psao* — to rub smooth
> ... upon each fiction another story is written, other chronicles of the new world, documents of the heart ... *palin* — again, *psao* — to rub smooth the pain from the crimes of passion on the shores of the Gulf of Sadness. (1993: 103)

Neither *Dragon* nor *Witchbroom* underestimates the challenge, the effort that is needed to rethink community and nationhood, but this desire to connect, to engage in a process of healing, is what drives them both. Amidst the many stories that collide and intersect, I want to analyse a particular movement in each to show how both novels suggest the possibility of more dynamic, inclusive futures, where the promise of Carnival forms is once more extended.

★ ★ ★

Dragon is primarily told from an Afro-Trinidadian point of view, focalised in particular through the character of Aldrick. It is his crisis of identity that triggers the central breakdown and quest for self in the novel, and his reflections often highlight its key concerns. The making of his dragon costume involves a skill and transformation that closely mirror Lovelace's method as a writer:

> Aldrick worked slowly, deliberately; and every thread he sewed, every scale he put on the body of the dragon, was a thought, a gesture, an adventure, a name that celebrated some part of his journey to and his surviving upon this hill. He worked, as it were, in a flood of memories, not trying to assemble them, to link them to get a linear meaning, but letting them soak him through and through; and his life grew before him, in the texture of his paint and the angles of his dragon's scales, as he worked. (1986: 50)

His experience of Carnival is described with religious solemnity as the novel remembers the African contexts for the ritual. Aldrick felt 'a sense of entering a sacred mask that invested him with an ancestral authority to uphold before the people of this Hill' (1986: 134) and, despite his misgivings about the loss of these rituals

> his heart grew big, and he felt a softness flow over him, and the burning of tears in his nostrils; for there before him on the street, the steelband and masqueraders were assembling ... Aldrick felt a tallness and a pride, felt his hair rise on his head, felt: 'No, this ain't no joke.

> This is warriors going to battle. This is the guts of the people, their blood; this is the self of the people that they screaming out they possess ... (1986: 136–7)

People are made visible, are given value, through Carnival, and this climaxes in Aldrick's description of Sylvia, who acts as a conduit for the spirit of the Yard that Lovelace wants to reclaim:

> Then he saw Sylvia, dancing still with all her dizzying aliveness, dancing wildly; frantically twisting her body, flinging it around her waist, jumping and moving, refusing to let go of that visibility, that self the Carnival gave her
> ... He watched her dancing into the insides of the music, into the Carnival's guts, into its every note, its soul, into every ring of the tall ringing iron; her whole self a shout, a bawl, a cry, a scream, a cyclone of tears rejoicing in a self and praying for a self to live in beyond Carnival and her slave girl costume. (1986: 141)

But this lack of a self outside of Carnival and his own ambiguous relationship to the Hill begin to haunt Aldrick so that 'Ash Wednesday' (the central chapter of the novel) brings the realisation that he needs to step away from the laughter and the banter that has protected him and confront his growing alienation:

> He felt a great distance from himself, as if he had been living elsewhere from himself, and he thought that he would like to try to come home to himself; and even though it sounded like some kind of treason, he felt that at least it was the only way he could begin to be true to even the promise of the dragon to which he felt bound in some way beyond reason, beyond explanation, and which he felt had its own truth. (1986: 146)

Aldrick's search for integrity, his attempt to make something more meaningful of his dragon dance, is shadowed by the story of Pariag. He moves to Port of Spain to become part of a wider community, part of the newly emerging nation, 'for this Trinidad was itself a new land, and he had not seen it yet, nor had it seen him' (1986: 92). But after two years Pariag is still a stranger in the Yard, no closer to his own dream of playing masquerade in a Carnival band. It is to Aldrick that he first appeals for recognition, and Lovelace is good at capturing the small moment of compassion that allows conversation to take place:

> The voice startled him, but he immediately saw the teeth in the shyly smiling face on the steps. It was the Indian fellar, Parry or Singh or something — he never could remember his name.
> 'Okay!' Aldrick said, continuing to walk, for, although the fellar lived in the Yard Aldrick did not consider him a friend.
> 'You taking a stroll?'
> Aldrick was about to walk on, but he felt tugged by the effort in the voice at friendliness, and slowed down. (1986: 88)

But Aldrick fails to act on Pariag's behalf, and stands by as the Yard's resentment culminates in the spiteful damage to his bicycle on Ash Wednesday. Despite his efforts to integrate, it is only when Pariag plays his own mas, marching solemnly out of the Yard with the bicycle in his arms, that he also claims a visibility. Lovelace stresses the tension and emotional complexity of the partial shift in relations:

> Everybody grew silent. They watched Pariag carry-push the bicycle, and in that moment they felt themselves closer to him than they ever had. It was suddenly as if he had become alive, a person to them ... Pariag, too, felt the quality of their watching ... Yet, it pained him that they had recognised him just at that moment when he was drawing away; and this pain brought a tallness to his walk, so that he was at that time both closer to them and farther from them. It would be across this distance and with this closeness that they would view each other henceforth ... (1986: 155)

This scene is typical of the way the novel stages half-moments or moments of partial reconciliation. Part of the reason why the dragon can't dance is the failure of the Yard to hybridise, but this transition in Afro/Indo-Trinidadian relations is not an easy one. Much later, as Aldrick stops outside Pariag's shop, he imagines how he could have been a friend and thinks to go in, just as Pariag sees and wants to call to him. Both move on.

But the novel does more than simply reflect on the problems of Trinidadian society; it also works to create a vision of the future. Where the characters sometimes fail in their efforts to connect, the novel is Lovelace's attempt to enter into dialogue. In three key chapters, the narrative voice shifts to include an Indo-Trinidadian perspective on events. Lovelace inhabits Pariag's voice here as intensely as he does Aldrick's, and this is an important technique for interweaving cultural hybridity in the novel. In his sustained characterisation of Pariag, Lovelace reverses the failure of the Yard and writes a more inclusive version of the nation. 'The Spectator' immediately follows Pariag's attempt at conversation with Aldrick and is a vividly rendered insight into the pain of his isolation. Lovelace contrasts the quick eagerness and innocent enthusiasm of Pariag's quest to belong with the narrowness of a city that constantly stereotypes or ignores him. 'Friends and Family' is a quieter reflection on Pariag's disappointments and feelings of estrangement, while 'The Shopkeeper' charts his growing maturity and self-awareness. This last chapter, in particular, pays tribute to Pariag's resolve and his wider vision of identity. Significantly, he rejects the consolations of the Indian talent show on TV:

> The show itself was too smooth, too easy. Its triumph was too much of a foregone conclusion ... It lacked the guts of the struggle he, Pariag, had lived and Dolly had lived and his father and his uncle Ramlochan ... It jingled with jewels, and leaves fell and there was perfume; but it didn't have bottles in it. It didn't have Balliram and Vishnu on the bottles truck at five o'clock in the morning, and Seenath, Bali and Ramjohn playing all fours in the pavilion of New Lands Recreation ground. It didn't have his struggle with the Hill in it. (1986: 223)

Though he recognises the spectacle as a part of himself, it offers too sanitised a version of Indians in Trinidad and he wants the integrity of an Indo-Trinidadian representation. As he listens to the steelband practising for Carnival, Pariag imagines how he might have arrived in the Yard:

> I wish I did walk with a flute or a sitar, and walk in right there in the middle of the steelband yard where they was making new drums, new sounds, a new music from rubbish tins and bits of steel and oil drums, bending the iron over fire, chiselling out new notes. New notes. I wish I woulda go in there where they was making their life anew in fire, with chisel and hammer, and sit down with my sitar on my knee and say: Fellars, this is me, Pariag from New Lands. Gimme the key! Give me the Do Re Mi. Run over the scale. Leh We Fa Sol La! Gimme the beat, lemme beat! Listen to these strings. And let his music cry too, and join in the crying. (1986: 224)

In Pariag's dream of a new beginning, *Dragon* embraces the Indo-Trinidadian and celebrates the power of Carnival to renew itself through hybrid forms. This is the epiphanic moment that finally links us back to the Prologue, to Lovelace's belief in Carnival and calypso as an energising force, and his invocation to get up and move:

> Dance! If the words mourn the death of a neighbour, the music insists that you dance; if it tells the trouble of a brother, the music says dance. Dance to the hurt! Dance! If you catching hell, dance, and the government don't care, dance! Your woman take your money and run away with another man, dance. Dance! Dance! Dance! It is in dancing that you ward off evil. Dancing is a chant that cuts off the power from the devil. Dance! Dance! Dance! Carnival brings this dancing to every crevice on this hill. (1986: 28)

★ ★ ★

Witchbroom is written with the benefit of *Dragon*, and is in many ways the product of the changes in Trinidadian society since 1979. The sounds of Chutney Soca ring through Scott's evocation of Carnival, and Lavren is from the outset a fantasy of hybridity. Nevertheless, 'the guts of the struggle' are still present, and *Witchbroom* carries the weight of its own racial divide. Narrated from the perspective of the white Creole, the novel is aware of the distances created by this perspective in the past and the need to bridge the gap. Looking through his aunt's paintings, for instance, the narrator of the 'Journal' comments that they are consistently empty — 'A smudge in this corner is the bandannaed black mammy' — and he recognises the insularity of the Creole class that isolated themselves in their colonial privilege:

> That was their loneliness, up on the hill, not noticing what was going on in the gully. Their loneliness was in their desire to live in large houses set on hills with beautiful views and gardens sloping away. It was part of the illusion they created, an eighteenth-century *folie*. What you see is not what is there. (1993: 125)

Though he is grateful for his aunt's landscapes, and her attachment to place, the metafictional 'I' narrator realises he must also bring the life of the wider community into focus:

> I thank her for her landscapes, but I am forced to people them. The paintings leave out everything that has happened here, except the smudge in the corner, a parody, like in the photograph: at the back the white aproned and starched cap, the black woman who holds the child. (1993: 126)

In particular, the white Creole must acknowledge blackness, the presence of Africa in their world. As Stuart Hall has argued:

> Everyone in the Caribbean, of whatever ethnic background, must
> sooner or later come to terms with this African presence. Black,
> brown, mulatto, white — all must look *Présence Africaine* in the face,
> speak its name. (1993: 231)

Witchbroom is not slow to grasp this challenge, and African voices are incorporated into Lavren's revision of history:

> S/he listened to the voice, which was a preacher's voice, a Shango
> voice, the voice of Africa lodging itself in the tongue of the
> conqueror to crack it, listened to the voice in the whips on the backs,
> the murmur of the trapped tongue, bitten lips, the tongue trapped in
> a bit like a horse with its head caged and mouth gagged, tongue
> entrapped. Lavren listened to the unmuzzled voice. (1993: 65)

Lavren's desire to learn, and Scott's reconstruction of African histories at these points, are part of the process of healing that takes place. But it is the figure of the black woman, hidden at the back of the photograph, to which the novel returns most powerfully. The black nanny/housekeeper has been a common feature, and stereotype, of white Creole literature in the Caribbean. Rhys's portrayal of Christophine in *Wide Sargasso Sea* is perhaps the most significant, but even here there are gaps in the record. In his characterisation of Josephine (Antoinetta in the 'Journal'), Scott reflects back on this tradition and attempts a shift in the relationship between the black nanny and the white Creole child.

Josephine is written early into the structure of the novel, and the 'Overture' introduces her as a key source and influence:

> Lavren tells these tales with the help of his beloved Marie Elena, his
> mother and muse, and with the help of black Josephine: cook,
> housekeeper, servant, nanny, nurse, doer of all tasks, comforter in
> the darkness and in the hot stillness of noon. (1993: 2)

Her voice interrupts to guide Lavren at various points in the tales and, as his remembering catches up in time and she emerges into history, her perspective on events becomes more important. When her own mother dies, for instance, she cuts across Marie Elena to tell the true story of her wake and the rituals of a local community. In this way, Josephine acts as a conduit for Lavren into the life of the gully that the Monagas have otherwise ignored. It is with Lavren's own birth, however, that Josephine herself comes fully into focus.

Like Christophine, the black housekeepers in *Witchbroom* have had to leave their own children in order to care for others. The pain of this situation is heightened for Josephine, who is pregnant at the same time as Marie Elena. The treatment of their parallel birthing is a poignant critique of social hierarchies and the gross inequality of their mistress/servant roles. Despite their partnership, their complicated relationship of co-dependency, as the novel later comments: 'there was no romantic eyewash about where Josephine could put her foot and where she couldn't' (1993: 249). Extra-busy in her chores for Marie Elena, Josephine pleads for the day off and slips quietly away to have her own child. Interestingly, the narrative forks at this point. While most of the attention is focused on Marie Elena and the imminent birth of Lavren, the narrative voice shifts to pick up Josephine as she walks home:

> Josephine cross over to the other side of the sugarcane-factory yard, beyond the secret garden with the pond, the poisonous lilies and the staircase leading nowhere, beyond the sugarcane fields and the gully where the barrack-rooms huddled; beyond this colonial compound and indentured skein of traces and rutted roads with their secret ditches of massacre and murder, the burial ground for untimely ripped babies. (1993: 194)

The use of dialect slows the pace and we draw closer to Josephine as she walks through the village and into her own home. The narrative voice is increasingly focalised through her, and we gain a vivid glimpse into her life and family, and the wider community of women who help in the birth of her child, 'with his green eyes, sandy hair, and skin the colour of cinnamon' (1993: 195). Although the narrative returns to events in the Monagas household, stories of Josephine's child shadow Lavren so that he becomes a parallel to Lavren's own life. As Josephine says directly:

> I have a boy like you, Master Lavren. He going read book. Madam say she going give me some old book all you throw out. He going go to school, but Madam say I can't bring him here. I can't bring him here to play with you. Must be she frighten you get black, or is something else. That is a story Master Lavren. (1993: 207)

It is to the older Lavren, the Creole boy she has loved like her own, that Josephine finally tells the story of her rape by his father — 'and she cried for the loss of herself in that far-distant afternoon when the sun was going down' (1993: 253).

In its attempts to include Josephine's story, *Witchbroom* also marks the decline of the Creole families and the collapse of their once-great houses. This is treated as a necessary purging, and the novel embraces the cultural traditions that emerge in their place. Crucially, it is the music of steelband that inspires Lavren in the womb, and Scott writes his own epiphanic moment as a direct tribute to the influence of Lovelace and *Dragon*:

> Up on Calvary Hill above the shimmering Belle d'Antilles, where Taffy was crucified and the Blessed Virgin Mary of Laventville looked down on the shanty towns, hallucinated in the blue air, tumbling down to the Gulf of Sadness, the first pingpong is picked out on a rusty dustbin cover. Lavren is stirred within the womb of his beloved muse and mother, Marie Elena. He is stirred by the first pingpong, pingpong, pingaling ping p'ding, and is tempted by the sound that was to transform the world's music, to be born early and become a douen escaped from limbo to jump up J'Ouvert morning. But Marie Elena held him beneath her heart and cradled him as he took that music down into his imagination, and began to learn that all which would last here in the new world would come from beyond the gutter, full up with dirty water; would come from the villages burning kerosene lamps, would come from beyond the bougainvillaea hedge, from the black galvanize barrack-rooms down in the gully where the grassy verge merely petered out. (1993: 189–90)

Carnival takes over as the organising metaphor in the novel, and in particular it is 'the reversal that happens in Carnival, the collapsing of opposites' that appeals to Scott (1993: 270). In J'Ouvert, the novel's encore, Scott stages his own version of the Carnival masquerade in which characters like Josephine and Marie Elena, Lavren and his mixed-race brother are finally able to cross historical divides and meet as equals, and where the white Creole can also come down from the Hill and find himself in a band.

★ ★ ★

In tracing these particular movements, these shifts in perspective, I hope it becomes clear that the titles to both novels are a call to arms rather than a negative statement. Both writers believe in the possibility of a fundamentally transformed society, and both outline models of personal and cultural renewal. By the end of the novels, various characters have managed to gather the parts of themselves and are ready to move forward. In *Dragon*, Aldrick, Pariag and Philo have all made deeper connections and are able to reflect on their quest for home and belonging. In *Witchbroom*, the multiple narrators and storytellers settle back into one voice to achieve a rootedness on the site of the old family house. In keeping with their use of Carnival forms, however, there is no sense of closure in these endings; history is already on the move and communities are once again on the brink of change. The Trinidad that emerges in both novels is very much an unfinished project, a liminal space where there is a necessary tension between nation and hybridity. The epiphanic moments in both, the celebration of cultural difference and diversity, do not suggest equilibrium in the future, but rather an awareness of perpetual movement.

It is through their particular use of language and form that Lovelace and Scott are able to achieve this balancing of a difficult hybridity. Although I have focused on character to illustrate some of their shared concerns, we must remember that both novels are primarily about community — their subject is Trinidad rather than the individual. There is a productive tension here in that sociological (Lovelace) and metafictional (Scott) perspectives are also sharply drawn, but the individual conflicts they explore are always part of the wider community. Writing in 1967 about the emergence of this kind of aesthetic, Brathwaite likened the West Indian novel to jazz music:

> The West Indian writer is just beginning to enter his own cultural New Orleans. He is expressing in his work of words that joy, that protest, that paradox of community and aloneness, that controlled mixture of chaos and order, hope and disillusionment, based on his New World experience which is at the heart of jazz. (1967: 279)

At the time, Brathwaite identified jazz 'moments' and hoped that the presence of a folk tradition would help create the jazz novel as an alternative to the European convention of social realism, which too often focused on the *ego* rather than the *gestalt* of community. *Dragon* contains many of the features of Brathwaite's jazz aesthetic — the style, the bravado, the emphasis on improvisation — to create a more collective form of expression. The passage from the Prologue quoted previously is a good example of the jazz 'riff' — the repetition of a 'theme' to mark the voice of the chorus — and this is continued through the novel with the repetition of key phrases — visibility, guts, people, self — and variations on the same theme. Although we identify with the individual's struggle for visibility, we also hear the chorus and the presence of a wider, communal identity. Through the oral, performative, improvised quality of the novel — in which characters move around each other like partners in a dance, sometimes together, sometimes at a slight angle — Lovelace adapts the social realist frame to produce a narrative that is still in flux. Even the closing chapters introduce new notes on the same theme: the insight into Philo's background provides a fine jazz moment with the 'duet' between Philo's parents. The description of Philo's mother is also the most vivid portrayal of religion and its music in the novel.

Dragon creates a version of the jazz novel through its immersion in the folk tradition of Carnival and calypso. Though Brathwaite was aware of the emergence of these indigenous forms, he was unsure of their capacity for articulating the tension, the pain (as well as the affirmation) of the individual in the community. 'Norman "Tex" at the Carnival Fête' is a perfect encapsulation of this kind of tension: the movement between the trio of musicians signifying exactly the 'controlled mixture of chaos and order' that Brathwaite saw at the heart of jazz. The band is mixing classic tunes with calypso — 'swinging them and mocking them and quarrelling with them and opening their bellies and bringing out the soul in them' (1986: 130) — and Norman 'Tex' in particular is 'blowing the saxophone like he wanted to blow into it not only the air from his body, but all the organs of his own life' (1986: 131).

Lovelace's characters want to be made visible; but they also want to lose themselves in a higher, communal identity and the tension and ambivalence of this struggle are powerfully evoked in the rhythms of this chapter:

> And all the time Norman 'Tex', writhing and straining and bending back from his waist, from his knees, from his ankles, his two hands stretched out pressing the sax to his lips, his face twisted up in this pain, this pain, this pain, and wanting to blow a note, the note, to blow it out, and already kinda half-knowing he would never get the note to blow, but, same time feeling, 'Now! Now I have it! I going to blow it now! (1986: 132)

In the final paragraph, in another riff on the main theme, Aldrick achieves a similar community with Inez while still managing the pain of his love for Sylvia.

The tension, and release, conveyed in this chapter are typical of the movement through the novel. Lovelace uses the rhythmic, thematic and structural features of Carnival to explore the dilemmas of community, but in a way that is always indicative of transformation. This becomes part of the Trinidadian frame that Scott is able to draw on for his own novel. *Witchbroom* expresses that same 'paradox of community and aloneness' and uses many of the same improvisatory effects — especially the repetition of images and phrases to signal the voice of a chorus. But *Witchbroom* does not sustain the same kind of rhythmic quality as *Dragon*, evident more of jazz moments, in Brathwaite's terms, than a jazz novel. The repetitions in *Witchbroom* are also intertextual riffs and Scott's mapping of the island of Kairi draws, perhaps, from Wilson Harris's epic vision of community.

Writing just before Brathwaite, and similarly concerned with the form of the West Indian novel, Harris drew metaphors from the land to articulate what he saw as a native tradition of depth:

> The native and phenomenal environment of the West Indies, as I see it, is broken into many stages in the way in which one surveys an existing river in its present bed while plotting at the same time ancient and abandoned, indeterminate courses the river once followed. When I speak of the West Indies I am thinking of overlapping contexts of Central and South America as well. (Harris 1967: 30)

Using the language of his native landscape (escarpment and watershed, tributaries and heartland) to trace the inherent cross-culturality of the region, Harris argues that only a novel of 'scale', a novel of associations, could begin 'to reconcile the broken parts of such an enormous heritage' (1967: 31). The very construction of Kairi suggests this kind of scale — both a representation of Trinidad *and* a tracing of the links that bind it to a wider region. The passage from the 'Overture' quoted previously is a good example of what Harris means by a series of associations working to create a scale or ladder into a wider drama of consciousness. Though Lavren remains precisely located, the narrative quickly expands to suggest links between multiple histories.

Witchbroom is particularly open to Harris's notion of scale through its intertextual borrowings. In its links with García Márquez' *One Hundred Years of Solitude*, for instance, the novel claims a tradition of magical realism for the Anglophone Caribbean and makes the form Trinidadian through its own Creolising structures. The early tales draw on García Márquez's use of myth, the grotesque, his exaggerated comic and ironic style, and excursions into the miraculous and supernatural to present cycles of colonial history as a series of absurd perversions. As in García Márquez, the desire for love and reconciliation is strong and Lavren resembles the trickster-like figure of Melquíades, mediating the generations across time and space. After the interlude of the 'Journal', and as we move into the twentieth century, the tales take on a more corporeal style. Lavren emerges as a figure playing mas, presenting history now as a series of Carnival processions. The lyrics of calypsos begin to thread the narrative to record historical events and Scott increasingly uses Trinidadian speech rhythms. The novel retains a faith in the marvellous and extraordinary, but it is Carnival that now encapsulates that spirit of transformation:

> If there was any magic left in the world it was to be found in the masquerade of history, a history whose calamitous waste had

produced the possibility of a new world. But this, only by the repeated creation and simultaneous destruction of beauty, the grasping at the ambivalence of nature in the masquerade of cruelty and horror, transforming it out of darkness into a sunlight of music and colour: Carnival! (1993: 226)

Just as the imagination of the poor 'had transformed the greed of capital, the new El Dorado, oil, into the music of liberation', so Trinidad also emerges out of multiple, and violent, histories to create the possibility of a new, hybrid community (1993: 190).

★ ★ ★

The process of hybridisation takes place at the level of form as well as content as both Lovelace and Scott are concerned to develop more appropriate ways of writing Trinidad. *Witchbroom* is a more experimental novel than *Dragon* — a more uneven novel (perhaps) as it tries to include so much. Even taken together, however, there is no sense of the layers of Trinidadian history and culture being exhausted. There are flaws, or gaps, in both novels and we may respond to these as part of an ongoing national project. For all their interest in gender, and their idealism with regard to love and intimacy, they remain largely male-driven novels. To adapt Brathwaite, we hear about Sylvia, but we do not *hear* Sylvia.[1] Scott approaches taboo subjects of homosexuality and homophobia but these stories are also underdeveloped. Though there are strong religious sources, especially Creolised Baptist (*Dragon*) and Catholic (*Witchbroom*) forms, these are never fully brought into dialogue.[2] Nevertheless, both are remarkable novels: powerfully written, deeply politicised, funnier and more compassionate on each rereading. They indicate a direction for the novel worthy of Brathwaite's jazz and Harris's native aesthetic; most importantly, they produce out of hybrid forms a narrative that is recognisably Trinidadian.

Notes

[1] Sylvia carries too great a burden as the object of desire in *Dragon*. We are constantly gazing at her (as in the passage quoted previously), rather than seeing the world through her eyes. Scott's story 'Sylvia's Room' (Scott 1994) can be read as a translation of Sylvia and her lack of agency in *Dragon*.

[2] Subsequent novels (Lovelace 1982, 1996; Scott 1998) engage with these aspects in interesting ways.

References

Braithwaite, E.K. (1967 [and 1968]) 'Jazz and the West Indian Novel' *Bim*, no. 44. [Continued in nos 45 and 46.]

Hall, Stuart (1993) 'Cultural Identity and Diaspora', in Patrick Williams and Laura Chrisman (eds), *Colonial Discourse and Post-Colonial Theory: A Reader* (London: Harvester Wheatsheaf).

Harris, Wilson (1967 [1964]) 'Tradition and the West Indian Novel', in W. Harris, *Tradition, the Writer and Society: Critical Essays* (London and Port of Spain: New Beacon Books).

Lovelace, Earl (1986 [1979]) *The Dragon Can't Dance* (Harlow: Longman).

—— (1982) *The Wine of Astonishment*. Oxford: Heinemann.

—— (1996) *Salt* (London: Faber and Faber).

Scott, Lawrence (1993 [1992]) *Witchbroom* (Oxford: Heinemann).

—— (1994) *Ballad for the New World and Other Stories*. Oxford. Heinemann.

—— (1998) *Aelred's Sin* (London: Allison and Busby).

7
PERFORMANCE AND TRADITION IN EARL LOVELACE'S *A BRIEF CONVERSION*: THE DRAMA OF THE EVERYDAY

Nicole King

'Do saints fight back?' asks a confused Travey, the 11-year-old protagonist of 'A Brief Conversion', the title story of Earl Lovelace's 1988 collection.[1] Travey's idea of saintliness is uncomplicated: it means he buttons up the top button of his shirt without protest, he submits himself to the 'Nazi-like' haircuts his mother forces on him, and he endures, again without protest, the teasing and bullying at school that a fresh haircut provokes every three weeks. But he can afford to be saintly, he feels, because he will eventually escape his small West Indian village: he, Travey, can see a future beckoning to him beyond the trials of adolescence in Cunaripo, Trinidad because he is sure he will be one of a very few village children who can use education as a springboard to a better life as he has already earned a place in the exalted exhibition class — a milestone in any British colonial education.[2]

His exhibition place has the power to save Travey from the fate awaiting his academically untalented elder brother and the bullies who will all leave school either to dig dirt or to 'be A-one coconut pickers', as his mother predicts (Lovelace 1988a: 19). An education will also relieve Travey from the pressure of living out his father's narrow dreams. But in the meantime, in the present, Travey's saintly posture — whilst convincing — crumbles rapidly as the bullying intensifies, prompting his question: 'Do saints fight back?' Eventually he, at any rate, does retaliate. And while standing up to bullies must be a universal right of passage, Travey's triumph, as Lovelace portrays it, is not so much increased credibility amongst his peers, but the shift effected at home in the interactions with his stern mother. The gruff script she habitually follows mellows as she realises that she is parent to a person making the transition into young adulthood. Travey's 'brief conversion' to saintly endurance is the spine of the story, while its controlling metaphor — a slow growth into independence and a dawning recognition of its sometimes treacherous landscape — is bone and sinew for each of the 12 linked stories, set in the early years of Trinidad's shift from colony to nation.

The title story serves here as the introduction to the project of this chapter: in paying particular attention to the everyday, I explore the performative framework of Lovelace's short stories and examine how they function as paradigms of a post-Independence literary form.[3] The performative is deployed by characters in these stories as a strategy for coping with the contradictory forces of political independence and the social norms of tradition in the nascent postcolonial period. I argue that, in Lovelace's short narratives of Caribbean lives, 'performance' is neither limited to the familiar dialogic relationship between performer and audience, nor does it afford the satisfaction of a definitive resolution. As such, these stories are usefully considered within paradigms of postcoloniality, where temporality gestures both forward and back, while demanding that the reader approach the text with a sense of history that encompasses European colonialism and modern Caribbean independence movements.

The many-sided aspects of performance — especially creative and experimental action and the interpretation of a role — fuel the audacity required, for instance, to stand up to bullies and to seek independence. As such, performance is also about possibility and hope, as a bravura performance can provide camouflage in the uncharted landscapes that comprise personal and collective identity after the end of official colonialism. Performance, masking and the assumption of different personas, like Travey's saintly posture, are all vehicles by which Lovelace's characters interact with each other and with the wider world. By tracing Lovelace's representations of performance — both ordinary and extraordinary — conducted by the people of Cunaripo, I ask how the construct of performativity operates as an analytic category in the reading of post-Independence literature. What does performativity tell us about the way subjectivity is conceived in the postcolonial condition? Lovelace's short stories are, I believe, particularly telling in this respect.

What follows is an analysis, with examples taken from three stories, of characters confronting and adjusting to aspects of lives led in a period when Independence is still new and strange, but when the traces of colonial rule nevertheless continue to linger. Lovelace's protagonists self-consciously stage their lives, in the face of disaster crafting modes of self-expression imbued with an optimistic sense of imagination and faith. Such faith in the *possibility* of change, in the-not-yet-real, lifts the postcolonial experience out of the hands of officially sanctioned recorders and makers of history, and relocates it in the everyday experiences of the putative citizens of the new nation. Familiar as much with disappointment and stasis as with triumph, the fortunes which befall Lovelace's characters reflect the false promises and false hopes bequeathed by the national project. Lovelace's overarching emphasis on the performative as everyday strategy signals a critical shift in how we apprehend post-Independence cultural practices.

While postcolonial critics have characteristically worked with categories at the level of the national or transnational, only relatively recently has attention been paid to what might be called the sub-national: the life that happens under the radar of what generally are these more abstract frames of analysis. Lovelace's work prompts this different analytic register, enabling us to grasp the workings of everyday life 'below' the stipulations offered by grand narratives of national identity. 'Lovelace's main preoccupation,' claims Birbalsingh, 'is with the quest for personhood ... and, his aim is to examine how wholeness and integrity may be achieved' (Birbalsingh 1991: 170). In the post-Independence era depicted in *A Brief Conversion*, this quest for personhood is continually hampered by everyday concerns: lack of employment, petty crime, poverty, limited opportunities for material or educational advancement and, often, the stifling norms arising from the prescriptions of gender. One of the key attributes of Lovelace as a 'post-Independence writer' is his determination to represent the grim reality and disappointments of this post-Independence era, even as he conveys and constructs avenues of hope for his characters who suffer continuing dispossession.

Performance and Postcolonialism

The idea of performance is central to Lovelace — an author perhaps best known for his representation of Carnival and the Trinidadian working class in the novel *The Dragon Can't Dance* (1981 [1979]). In all his fiction, whether or not the story is 'about' Carnival, the rhythms and performance traditions of Carnival are woven into his narratives. Funso Aiyejina (2005) goes so far as to say that nearly all of Lovelace's narrators can be described as 'chantwell figures', as calypsonians. His tales share calypso's grassroots loyalties and origins, as well as its subject-matter — although he is hardly alone in connecting the politics of Trinidad and Tobago's Independence to the genres of popular narrative. Indeed, during the 25 years of his political dominance, Eric Williams, the country's first prime minister, was both lovingly and derisively portrayed in multiple calypsos (Rohlehr 1988: 850). At one extreme — negatively — Williams was derided by some as a 'directing a nation of animated puppets' in 'a theater of the postcolonial Absurd' (Rohlehr 1988: 850). As I will show, Lovelace's portrayal of disillusionment with the political realities of Independence is more subtle than this, although the concept of the new nation as theatre is an image that recurs in *A Brief Conversion*.

Carnival and calypso are not the only instances of performativity that can be found in Lovelace's short stories. Other aspects connect him to a web of literary traditions stretching across and beyond the Caribbean. Derek Walcott, in particular, is an influential figure in any discussion of performance and postcoloniality, especially in Trinidad. As the founder of the Trinidad Theatre Workshop, Walcott intended to show:

> that the creation of great theatre by a great company was the true West Indian revolution, the true liberation from the burden and shame of history, in contrast to tyrannical post-colonial governments that falsely claimed to speak to the people. (Cited in King 1995: vii)

As the novels *Salt* (1997 [1996]) and *The Dragon Can't Dance* exemplify, Lovelace, like Walcott, understands the creative arts as a seedbed of ideas, voices and viewpoints in both the decolonising and in the neo/postcolonial eras. It is clear how the notion of performance, whether on a theatre stage, in a calypso tent, or nested in the metaphors and images of fiction and poetry, holds a dynamic, powerful place in the Trinidadian imagination.

In tandem with performance, Lovelace uses a multi-faceted notion of tradition as a structuring device for his characters and their actions. His characters never use the abstract vocabularies of 'tradition' or 'postcolonial' (though on occasion their creator does), but even so they are forced to negotiate the realities to which these concepts allude.[4] Taken as a whole, *A Brief Conversion* evokes the lived realities of Independence which exist outside the fanfare of political rhetoric. As such, Lovelace allies himself to the more plastic notion of 'postcolonial' outlined by Ania Loomba who maintains that 'it is more helpful to think of postcolonialism not just as coming literally after colonialism and signifying its demise, but more flexibly as the contestation of colonial domination and the legacies of colonialism' (Loomba 2005: 16). The short stories of *A Brief Conversion* are chiefly concerned with precisely these legacies as they are experienced by the working population of the new nation.

Debates abound in postcolonial studies about basic definitions and about the usefulness (or not) of designating an era, a region or a writer as 'postcolonial'. Loomba's efficient summary of the evolution of the term 'postcolonialism' is helpful for our understanding of the Trinidad which Lovelace portrays in *A Brief Conversion*. She states:

> A country may be both postcolonial (in the sense of being formally independent) and neo-colonial (in the sense of remaining

economically and/or culturally dependent) at the same time. We cannot dismiss either the importance of formal decolonisation or the fact that unequal relations of colonial rule are reinscribed in the contemporary imbalances between 'first' and 'third' world nations. The new global order does not depend on direct rule. (2005: 12)

In stories which variously depict the continuing influence of colonial moral codes together with the newer imperatives represented by the neocolonial order, Lovelace knows well enough the means by which indirect rule can replace the formal apparatuses of an earlier colonial system. His ambition is complex, for he endeavours to catch something of the doubleness of the postcolonial moment: on the one hand, the barely perceptible shifts in the practices of everyday life and, on the other, what he takes to be the profound psychic effects within the individual and social imagination. In terms of temporality, the stories occasionally do explicitly reference dates, as in 'The Coward', when a speaker proclaims: 'This, Brothers and Sisters is the year nineteen hundred and seventy. This, Brothers and Sisters is an independent country' (1988a: 48). More often, however, specific dates are not needed in order to signal to the reader that an ethos of historical change underlies the action of each story. The credulousness of the character Blues as he listens to the speaker (quoted above) intone Black Power rhetoric, or the disappointing emptiness of upward mobility in 'Those Heavy Cakes', are two examples of Lovelace's skilled evocation of the complexities of Independence which are not about chronology but rather about fundamental, if individual, shifts in perspective effected after 1962.[5]

As signalled earlier, Lovelace's post-Independence focus contributes to a wider Caribbean and postcolonial literary discussion. In addition to famous calypsonians such as Lord Kitchener, The Mighty Chalkdust and Black Stalin, and alongside poet/playwright Derek Walcott, Lovelace has obvious affinities with other post-Independence fiction writers (Rohlehr 1988: 888). *A Brief Conversion*'s publication can be read alongside a number of texts which all appeared within a few months of each other: *A Small Place* (1988) by Jamaica Kincaid, *No Telephone to Heaven* (1987) by Michelle Cliff, and *Angel* (1987) by Merle Collins.[6] These texts are closely related to *A Brief Conversion* through their shared disillusionment with Caribbean society after Independence. In their narratives, Cliff, Kincaid and Collins — like Lovelace — express feelings which range from disappointment to bewilderment to outrage. Unlike an earlier generation of writers who began publishing in the 1950s, such as George Lamming and Samuel Selvon, these authors are not concerned with explaining and introducing the Caribbean to a foreign readership. Their particular critical perspective looks inwards rather than outwards, and places the lives of Caribbean people — wherever they may be in the world — in relation to themselves, at centre stage. This distinctive shift is a critical aspect of a post-Independence sensibility.

It is worth highlighting as well that Lovelace is an accomplished dramatist with a keen sense of contemporary theatre, having worked with Walcott at the Trinidad Theatre Workshop, and having had a spell as a theatre critic (King 1995: 90, 249, 314–15). Lovelace's collection of plays, *Jestina's Calypso and Other Plays*, was published in 1984. I will not address Lovelace's work as a playwright or examine the performance-history of individual plays. Rather, I aim to capture and analyse how gestures and structures of performance have migrated to his short stories, where they provide a habitus for characters adjusting to Trinidadian life after Independence.

Character and Scene

For the characters in *A Brief Conversion*, Independence — by which I mean all the hopes and mythologies pinned to the achievement of nationhood and entrance on to the world stage — is frequently unrealised in historical terms. In their everyday lives, their quests for material prosperity, self-improvement, love and self-invention rarely come to fruition. Speaking of his Cunaripo community in a voice that echoes Thornton Wilder as much as it does Derek Walcott, Travey, the young martyr of the title story, discovers a heretofore unseen dimension to the ordinary people around him. With his own newfound maturity (and quite possibly voicing the author's opinion, if not his own experience), he sees his world with a profound clarity:

> These are our celebrities. Their escapades, their fights, their moments of madness, their sayings, these are the subjects of our conversations. And about each of them is a story: pride that has fallen; ambition that overleaped itself. Each story ends victoriously in defeat, penance, apology. This was our folklore. Until that Thursday evening I had not put them all together in that way. It was then that I felt the weight of their apology and defeat for the first time; and, for the first time, I looked at our town. (1988a: 25–6)

Travey's vision of the community's 'folklore' allows him, perversely, to recognise in their loneliness, alienation and outright failure something of great value. Their idiosyncrasies and sorrows can be understood universally, as they are in Wilder's celebrated play *Our Town* (1938), but I believe they are most powerfully understood when filtered through a historical lens of national independence and Trinidad and Tobago's entrance into the so-called postcolonial era. The community of Cunaripo symbolises what Wilson Harris would term the limbo state of the nation in the era of Independence, having neither fully emancipated themselves from colonialism, nor found their footing within the postcolonial world. Indeed, there is much of Walcott, Whitman and Homer echoed within the poetic form of Lovelace's narrative style. While he toys with epic formulations, such as the catalogue of Cunaripo's 'celebrities', the linked short story sequence is more episodic than epic. It frees Lovelace from the need continually to set the scene in each story, and allows him more space to investigate the peculiarities and particularities of his cast of characters. Thus, while the title story effects a panorama of Cunaripo, the subsequent stories telescope down and are character-led pieces. This is not to say that landscape and history disappear after 'A Brief Conversion', but rather — as the titles of the other stories indicate (10 of the 12 titles are names or nicknames of Cunaripo residents) — Lovelace is concerned with the speech, the emotions and the personalities of the individuals who inhabit that landscape and who are making that history. To illustrate these points, I will explore one of the more unusual stories and characters in the collection. 'Call Me "Miss Ross" for Now' is the only story with a female protagonist and it brings the calcified gender roles of colonialism into focus through the exalted position its protagonist holds in the community.

Miss Ross and the Postcolonial Epiphany

A Brief Conversion opens and closes with images of boys and men ritualistically involved in the business of getting and giving haircuts. In effect, they are involved in marking off and marking out their territory with and against one another. Lovelace's penchant for male protagonists is connected to the themes he addresses and the notion of personhood that, Louis James notes, runs through his fiction from *While Gods are Falling* (1965) to *Salt* (1996). The key theme for most of these male protagonists is 'the problem of heroism in a Trinidad where frustration turns energy to violence; the creative power of its popular culture, and the paradox of regeneration through the very loss of old traditions' (James 1999: 194). In what are mostly male-dominated homosocial environments, women characters are generally peripheral to the stories. Frequently, their narrative purpose is to shed light on the actions and personalities of their sons, husbands or boyfriends. By the final story, 'Victory and the Blight', which takes place in a barbershop, women characters are so extraneous to the subject and action that they do not appear at all.

In 'Call Me "Miss Ross" for Now', however, Lovelace makes an exception. He juxtaposes several themes which connect Miss Ross to women at the centre of early twentieth-century West Indian novels, such as *Jane's Career* (1914) and *Minty Alley* (1936). The most prominent of these themes are notions of respectability and class aspirations. But, unlike Maisie, Mrs Rouse or Jane in those earlier novels, Miss Ross is set uncomfortably apart from her village community. She is set on so high a pedestal she might well wish to ask, like Travey, if saints fight back.

Once the most eligible and refined young lady in the village, we meet Miss Ross as she is growing old waiting for a companionable suitor. She has said 'no' to many men who wish to marry her, but most significantly she refuses the only one who moved her deeply — a younger man called Fitzroy. She diligently convinces herself that he is too young and common to pair with herself, a woman of her maturity (she is 47) and stature in the community. She is still considered beautiful and remains widely respected by all, yet Lovelace suggests that these attributes are barriers to her happiness, imprisoning her while simultaneously keeping the crude world at bay. This point is driven home when Fitzroy takes up with a very young, 'jolly' woman (who is decidedly unrefined) when he realises he cannot win over Miss Ross. By keeping Miss Ross's first name a secret from the reader as well as from Fitzroy, Lovelace effectively conveys Fitzroy's frustration when confronted with the power of the fiercely, if illogically, held notions of respectability that attach to Miss Ross, and which she upholds with such diligence.

The narrative of Miss Ross alternates between her history and a present-day town council meeting called to elect new officials. With this parallel narrative, Lovelace introduces a parallel civic frustration: unlike the 'old days', the council now struggles to get enough people to come to the meetings and to be involved in the town governance, and this struggle is suggestive of a waning belief in the ability of politics to effect change.

The characterisations in 'Miss Ross' are an important counter-balance to what Shalini Puri calls the 'heroic masculine subject', which so often is located at the centre of chantwell/calypsonian narratives (Puri 2003: 31). In a significant shift, Lovelace renders Fitzroy powerless when faced with Miss Ross's fortress of respectability. The fortress is in fact a prison-house that has both confined and confounded Miss Ross since her girlhood. Miss Ross is caught up in a paradoxical existence in which she is both committed to a sense of who she is supposed to be according to a notion of middle-class respectability, even as she is stifled and tragically disappointed by it. The code of respectability to which she adheres is related to the notion of 'true womanhood' prevalent in the nineteenth-century United States: 'The attributes of True Womanhood ... [were] piety, purity, submissiveness and domesticity' (Welter, cited in Carby 1987: 23). As Hazel Carby notes, 'in terms of social and literary conventions, the qualities of piety and purity were displayed through action and behaviour' (1987: 25–6). Lovelace directly intervenes in the West Indian version of such conventions by creating a protagonist who exists on the cusp of emancipation from such social norms.

The odds against Miss Ross affecting her own emancipation are great. She has neither immediate guidance nor a model to follow, as her parents have died, and she stepped into her role as respectable woman so early in life (as a teenager) that she cannot remember a different mode of existence. Thus she is ill-equipped to negotiate the shifting (and class-based) gender norms in Cunaripo. Miss Ross enacts this dilemma in her own confusion and paralysis over how to be both her 'own' woman and a 'respectable' woman. She feels she cannot act as she desires, even though she is old enough, one might argue, to consider it her prerogative. An analogy can be drawn between the experience of Miss Ross and the group of Caribbean territories that received nationhood in the second part of the twentieth century. The newly independent Anglophone nations adopted political systems and government structures — such as prime ministers and bicameral legislatures — modelled upon that of the former colonial powers. As is commonly agreed (Knight and Palmer 1989; Cooper 1995; Edmondson 1999), issues of respectability and middle-class norms were as central to the political scene as they were to domestic ones. For instance, in the run-up to Independence, the nascent Trinidadian governments were led by the likes of middle-class Albert Gomes instead of the more flamboyant Uriah 'Buzz' Butler (Lewis 1968: 221, 207). Later, Eric Williams, in consolidating his power-base. eventually needed to contain the more radical elements of the People's National Movement and tone down its socialist agendas (Nielsen 1997: xxi, 124; Lewis 1968: 405).

While the figure of the alienated black woman (who is often in or aspiring to the middle class) is not unfamiliar in Caribbean literature (see Edmondson 1999, esp. Chapter 3), Lovelace's story manages to present a female protagonist, Miss Ross, who resists her own alienation. Rather than accept election to the village council — as all around her expected her to do — and its attendant psychic stasis, the resolution of the story sees Miss Ross literally dashing for the exit, for her freedom. Significantly, this flight is a solitary one, not connected to Fitzroy, to any other man or even to a specific destination, other than her best friend whom she can see disappearing down the road. But the fact that Miss Ross cannot reveal her name, cannot break down the wall of formality that has grown up around her, forms the tragic crux of the tale. Miss Ross repeats the phrase 'Call me "Miss Ross" for now' many times to a heartbroken Fitzroy. The tragedy is not so much Fitzroy's broken heart as her own expectation — evident in the repetition of the phrase 'for now' — that she will find a way to reveal her name and thus experience the intimacy of trust and love. In turn, the council meeting hall rings with her name as they pile more and more work at her feet. In the juxtaposition of silence (the unspoken name) and clamour (the repeated surname) Lovelace deftly conveys the vulnerability as well as the emotional rigidity which define his character. In the end, what cannot be done in speech is achieved through the physical action of flight.

It would be wrong not to acknowledge that Miss Ross's flight might have a great cost — what Puri and others (Cooper 1995; Edmondson 1999) would name as Miss Ross's 'respectability'. When she steps down from her pedestal, that act of self-determination carries a specific risk of acquiring a reputation as a loose woman. The freedom she seeks (and possibly never gains) is perhaps a freedom to be in the world on her own terms, unprotected and therefore unconfined by title, husband or social class position.[7] Miss Ross's transgression represents an attempt to reconcile her personal power with the expectations of her community; she was used to the latter, but ignorant of how to go about the former. The epiphany arrives when she recognises that her performance of ideal, respectable womanhood is one that she can refuse — hence her flight:

> [She] began to move towards the door and the disappearing Fedosia, feeling with each step a fear circling the pit of her stomach and spreading all over her insides, feeling as if she was stepping into an unknown wilderness, utterly alone. Out the door she didn't have any voice, even to call Fedosia. (1988a: 80)

The moment of epiphany, when Miss Ross withdraws her labour from the town council meeting and exits, is simultaneously the moment when she no longer sees her identity as mediated through the approval of *others*. In a Hegelian move, she frees herself by refusing to participate; she refuses to recognise the tradition of her participation on the council and the history of her standing in the community. And without the work of mutual recognition, the master/slave dialectic cannot cohere. The consequences of such a radical break are tangible: to lose that other self, that performed self, Miss Ross must strip bare and enter 'an unknown wilderness'. The reader is left hoping that she will find some truer, organic selfhood there.

Miss Ross's inability to speak her name is counter-balanced by her ability to move. The idea that (self-)expression can be manifested physically rather than verbally is an elementary aspect of drama, but perhaps marginally less familiar in prose and fiction. As a subject, the silencing of women and the idea of women then finding and using their voices as writers of their own narratives has been a key project of feminist literary criticism.[8] At the same time, the kineticism at the close of 'Call Me "Miss Ross" for Now' connects Miss Ross to Aldrick (in *Salt*) and Bango (in *The Wine of Astonishment*) and to other Lovelace characters. They are all descendants of what he calls the indigenous Trinidadians — those people brought from Africa and enslaved in the colony. Describing the simple but no less powerful ways that enslaved Africans found to resist their condition, Lovelace explains that:

> They claimed sovereignty over their voices, their bodies and their imagination. These were the only areas over which they had any control: what they could sing; how they could dance; what they could think. (1988b: 338)

To view Miss Ross's movement and thought as subversive is to relate her narrative to the larger history of Trinidad and of its people. Miss Ross is an important point of reference for other female characters in Lovelace's fiction because in Miss Ross he offers the reader a more complete account of her personal history than elsewhere in his writings, and a deeper understanding of the conflicts her character confronts. Thus, unlike Sylvia or Miss Cleothilda — 'princess' and 'queen' respectively in Lovelace's Carnival narrative of *Dragon* — Miss Ross achieves a welcome complexity.

In his discussion of enslaved Africans and of the freedom claimed through the movement of dance, Lovelace reasons:

> The body became an instrument over which they had control. And if you look at African dances you will see that they show the body in control of itself. The dancer is not seeking to traverse space, like in the waltz or other European dances, but concentrates on mastering his/her body within a limited space. The body becomes the universe. (1988b: 338)

The notion of the body as the individual's universe is a challenging way to think about Miss Ross: she takes her body out of the meeting hall as a way of changing her fate. She is not sure how she will achieve it and nor is the reader, but the fact of her agency is definite. So too is the theme of dance. Miss Ross escapes in an unambiguous manner: she claims sovereignty over her mind and body by running out of the council meeting. Although she simply runs to join Fedosia who is going to a fête in a nearby village, this action is momentous for Miss Ross. We learn at the opening of the story that going to this very dance is, by far, the activity Miss Ross would prefer over the council meeting, but she 'turns from that madness' and impropriety of two women going out unaccompanied and, until the moment of her flight, does the respectable thing by participating in the meeting (1988a: 59). This deceptively simple act of flight towards the dance, we suppose as readers, signals the turning point for Miss Ross. Indeed, earlier in the story we learn of how another village fête is the site of brief transgression for Miss Ross when she dares to slow-dance with Fitzroy. That dance was a place where she had proven to herself and to others that she need not be permanently imprisoned by her own, her parents' or the village's social aspirations for her. The tantalising conclusion of the story, with its lack of a definite resolution, is a powerful example of Lovelace staging a performance that exudes possibility and hope even as an alternative — the 'madness' of the community's disapproval and Miss Ross's loss of social standing — is equally possible.

Performativity and The Short Story

Although it is clear that aspects of performance are key elements within the themes and forms of Lovelace's short stories, the question of what is accomplished through them remains. Part of the answer is implicit in his keen awareness of the interplay between the short story form and calypsos as popular narrative forms in Trinidad.

A Brief Conversion implicitly comments on the short story form as it had previously been deployed during the period before Independence. Such commentary is partially evident in Lovelace's evocation of the style of Naipaul and Selvon. Louis James, for instance, charts a literary lineage that positions Lovelace as a principal inheritor of an episodic form of short fiction initially created by Naipaul and Selvon (2001: 107). James reminds us of the particularly rich history of the short story in Trinidadian literary history, beginning with the *New Beacon* writers in the 1930s. Historically, the short story was a way for writers to reach a working-class audience who had neither the money nor the leisure to spend on novels, whereas the frequent publication of short stories in newspapers made them more easily accessible (James 2001: 103–4). Given Lovelace's admiration for indigenous art forms, we can be sure of his awareness of the development of the short story in Trinidad, even if *A Brief Conversion* does not represent an explicit 'writing back' to his literary precursors. Lovelace, Naipaul and Selvon all use similar conventions to great effect, especially their shared determination to examine the particularities of everyday life set against the urban and rural Trinidadian landscapes. However, the orientation of Lovelace's stories is starkly different from these predecessors. The critical difference is one of the mediation, which affects *A Brief Conversion* both structurally and atmospherically. It is not the mediation of an omniscient narrator (Selvon and Naipaul do that too), but rather the mediation of performance and performativity. Protagonists such as Miss Ross negotiate the burden of expectation the community places upon them by altering the 'script' and breaking out of the role they are used to. Similarly, Travey confuses his mother when he takes on a *new* persona. In each case, Lovelace makes the performative aspects of a given scene transparent to the reader by signalling when characters make that shift between roles or personas. The plot of each story often revolves around the way a particular performance is received by the other residents of Cunaripo. And, in an analogous manner, *the reader* is always aware of the mediating function of performance because it overtly guides how the story is to be read.

The literary connections to Selvon and Naipaul are important. But these need to be read alongside his political connections to contemporaries who, in their fiction, explicitly engage with the consequences of the stalled progress of independence. In particular, I'm thinking of authors such as Jamaica Kincaid, Merle Collins, Nalo Hopkinson and Edwidge Danticat, all of whom structure dystopic visions of the Caribbean in their prose and prose fiction. Lovelace's characters, like ex-colonial nations themselves, cannot easily free themselves from patterns of behaviour perfected and policed in the colonial era; nor do they have access to promised prosperity and general good-living imagined when Independence lay just around the corner. They are instead caught 'recovering from the shock' of independence as best they can (Walcott 1980: 152).

For some, the strategy for 'recovery' is simple: one must leave. The story 'Joebell and America' illustrates both shock and strategy. Joebell, a petty gambler and an amateur calypsonian, is 'seeing too much hell in Trinidad so he make up his mind to go away' (1988a: 111). In the absence of a good life in Trinidad, he chooses the fabled riches and opportunities of America. The journey — and, one must assume, Joebell himself — are doomed from the outset. He is travelling to America from Trinidad via Puerto Rico, on a false passport which requires him to impersonate an American. His near-perfect performance is detected at the last moment by US immigration officers in Puerto Rico airport. Defeated but not destroyed, Joebell thinks to himself about 'how to go', which is as much about an actor trying to decide how to deliver his lines — what sort of heroism to portray — as it is about a young man savvy enough to know his one chance at a different sort of life has just been undone. This final scene abandons third-person for first-person narration, and in so doing the character takes on significance far larger than himself. Indeed, he can be seen to be speaking for a sovereign Trinidad of the imagination as he casts about for the proper idiom in which to express himself:

> They catch me. God! And now, how to go? I think about getting
> on like an American, but I never see an American lose. I think about
> making a performance like the British, steady, stiff upper lip like
> Alec Guinness in *The Bridge Over the River Kwai*, but with my hat
> and my boots and piece of cigar, that didn't match, so I say I might
> as well take my losses as a West Indian, like a Trinidadian. I decide
> to sing. It was the classiest thing that ever pass through Puerto Rico
> airport, me with these handcuffs on, walking between these two
> police and singing,
> Gonna take ma baby
> Away on a trip
> Gonna take ma baby
> Yip yip yip
> We gonna travel far
> To New Orleans
> Me and ma baby
> Be digging the scene. (1988a: 124)

For Joebell, to be 'Trinidadian' is positively defined as being a calypsonian. At the same time, Trinidadian-ness is also seen as identified with, in this international instance, being West Indian — which in turn suggests a reference to the short-lived Federation era at the end of the 1950s. To be Trinidadian (and West Indian) is also defined by Joebell in terms of what it is *not* — revealing the psychic paradigm shift following from the achievement political independence. To be Trinidadian is distinct and separate from being either British or American. In his characterisation of Joebell, Lovelace once again emphasises the promise and pride of the postcolonial/post-Independence era which coexists with the realities of social deprivation for the mass of the new nation's people. Joebell is related to Fitzroy, to Travey's father and to many of Lovelace's other characters in his search for meaningful work in the newly born nation. Joebell's turn towards the United States acknowledges its role as a neo-colonialist entity while the immigration agents function as the gatekeepers of the new social order.

Finally, as an 'indigenous' Trinidadian, Joebell does have power over his *voice*, though he is stripped of all other power and agency when he is handcuffed and marched through the airport. Yet it is sobering to consider that Joebell was first stripped of power by the social conditions he confronted in Trinidad, where his prospects were momentarily improved only as a result of his gambling: literally, by his random good fortune. He wins big at the game of 'wappie' and it is these 'earnings' that finance the purchase of the false passport and the airline ticket, and which also gain him the admiration of his friends. Without that win, Joebell faced a life no different from that of Travey's older brother: dirt-digging and coconut-picking. Travey's own place in the exhibition class, we might further reflect, is as much a lottery too: while he possesses the requisite intellectual ability, the prestige of gaining access to the exhibition class is based upon the limited number who get in and successfully climb to the top of the educational ladder — a point upon which Lovelace elaborates in Alford George's moment of 'conversion' in *Salt*. In the new Trinidad, Lovelace suggests, for the underclasses individual advancement can only be a matter of luck.

Stephano Harney claims that, at the end of *The Dragon Can't Dance*, Lovelace, in critiquing the vapid abstractions of the new nationalism, asserts the power of the individual or that of the nation. In so doing he effects, Harney argues, an 'estrangement with the past' (Harney 1996: 44). This 'estrangement', in combination with his attention to the everyday and to what I have called the subnational, are at the crux of Lovelace's powerful and creative representations. Invoking another Trinidadian theorist of politics and culture, Harney writes:

> C.L.R. James would see Lovelace as a product of a break in a nation's history, at the birth of postcolonial nationhood and all its disruptions of identity and ethics, but James would see in Lovelace the national and native writer as an artist who recognized the universal truth of the sovereignty of individual identity and creativity, challenging the very nation-state that produced him. (1996: 45)

This is what both Miss Ross and Joebell achieve, and perhaps what Travey will grow up to do: they challenge the very nation-state and colonial apparatus that produced them. Each either breaks out of, or deliberately manipulates, a performance dictated by the imperatives of colonial order.

As I have indicated, Lovelace shares a broadly political standpoint with many other Caribbean writers who question, critique and record the ongoing changes in the region since Independence. In Derek Walcott's play *Pantomime* (1976), a character — well aware of the travails of the post-Independence era — admonishes a British expatriate living in Tobago. I have already alluded to these lines: 'You mustn't rush things, people have to slide into independence. They give these islands independence so fast that people still ain't recover from the shock ...' (Walcott 1980: 152). These lines, with their deliberate comic element, capture the unevenness and unfamiliarity of the 'postcolonising' process. Walcott's play, like Lovelace's stories, signals the apparent impossibility of leaving colonialism behind, when its remnants and dregs, and sometimes more, continue to surface in everyday relationships. Travey, Miss Ross and Joebell each struggle and 'slide into independence'. Lovelace depicts them as sifting through the possibilities before them, occasioned by a nascent notion of self-determination in their own lives. While Joebell is turned back at the last hurdle of his quest for a better life, his faith in the possibility of change casts a curiously positive light on his journey. Like Travey's challenge to himself to endure his mother's orders and the heckling from the school bullies, Joebell, in his clash with the authorities in the Puerto Rico airport, acquires a sense of his own style. 'That is why I love America,' Joebell declares. 'They love a challenge. Something in my style is a challenge to them' (1988a: 123).

Like calypsos, self-conscious performances of identity provide a space in which to launch a critique of self, and of the community which may not otherwise be audible. The prerogative which Lovelace's characters assert for themselves — to play with their modes of self-expression — is a defining attribute of the post-Independence author. If, however, the realm of performativity is a symbolic zone that offers Trinidad's citizens in Lovelace's texts an arena in which to test the ways in which their own subjectivity might be conceived, Lovelace works hard to ensure that the reader does not lose sight of the ironies that are also in play. For the legacy of colonialism, in which performance can be reduced to pantomime alone, still holds. Nevertheless, it is a testament to Lovelace the chantwell that we believe in his characters. Indeed, Carolyn Cooper (2006) links the performative acts of these short stories to 'subversive masquerade aesthetics', in which the characters forge their own emancipation. Audacity links Travey, Miss Ross and Joebell. Yet, though spirit and style may be at the knife edge of a liberatory politics, and they cut sharp, the totems of post-Independence governments — the police, the social class system, the educational system — also loom large, and stand ready to knock back those would-be rebels whose audacity allows them to imagine their lives anew.

Notes

[1] I would like to thank Kandice Chuh and Bill Schwarz for their comments on earlier drafts of this chapter.

[2] 'Exhibition' in this sense, as per the *Oxford English Dictionary Online*, refers to the attainment of a place, via competitive examination, in a secondary school or college where the curriculum is focused on scholarly studies as opposed to vocational studies. The place often also comes with a full or partial bursary to offset the costs of this further education.

[3] In my juxtaposition of the performative and the quotidian, my essay shares a similar framework to Manalansan (2001).

4   Because this chapter is focused exclusively on Earl Lovelace's 1988 text and its representations of Trinidadian communities, I am using the terms 'postcolonial' and 'post-Independence' interchangeably. However, I do not wish to signal a rigid interpretation of either term. See, for instance, McClintock (1992); Appiah (1996); Shohat (1993); and Hulme (1995).
5   These also suggest why Lovelace should not, in my opinion, be categorised as a cultural nationalist.
6   This is a deliberately short list, but one which nevertheless highlights the varied timeline of independence for former British colonies in the Caribbean: Jamaica (the setting for most of *No Telephone to Heaven*), like Trinidad, became independent in 1962 while in Grenada (depicted in *Angel*) Independence occurred in 1974, and in Antigua (the subject of *A Small Place*) it took place in 1981.
7   Miss Ross faces similar approbation from her community as that experienced by Janie Crawford in Zora Neale Hurston's *Their Eyes Were Watching God* (1937). Janie disappointed her public by taking what they considered a common man as her lover and going off to do physical labour by his side.
8   In Caribbean literature see, for instance, Cudjoe (1990); Anim-Addo (1996); Chancy (1997); Edmondson (1999); and Davies (1994).

References

Aiyejina, Funso (2005) 'Unmasking the Chantwell Narrator in Lovelace's Fiction', *Anthurium: A Caribbean Studies Journal*, vol. 3, no. 2.

Anim-Addo, Joan (ed.) (1996) *Framing the Word: Gender and Genre in Caribbean Women's Writing* (London: Whiting and Birch).

Appiah, Kwame Anthony (1996) 'Is the Post in Postmodernism the Post in Postcolonialism?' in Padmini Mongia (ed.), *Contemporary Postcolonial Theory: A Reader* (London: Arnold).

Birbalsingh, Frank (1991) 'The West Indies', in Bruce King (ed.), *The Commonwealth Novel Since 1960* (Basingstoke: Macmillan).

Carby, Hazel V. (1987) *Reconstructing Womanhood: The Emergence of the Afro-American Woman Novelist* (New York: Oxford University Press).

Chancy, Myriam (1987) *Framing Silence: Revolutionary Novels by Haitian Women* (Piscataway, NJ: Rutgers University Press).

Cooper, Carolyn (1995) *Noises in the Blood: Orality, Gender, and the 'Vulgar' Body of Jamaican Popular Culture* (Durham, NC: Duke University Press).

—— (2006) 'The Politics of Style in Earl Lovelace's *A Brief Conversion and Other Stories*', *Anthurium: A Caribbean Studies Journal*, vol. 4, no. 2.

Cudjoe, Selwyn (ed.) (1990) *Caribbean Women Writers* (Wellesley, MA: Calaloux Publications).

Davies, Carole Boyce (1994) *Black Women, Writing and Identity: Migrations of the Subject* (London: Routledge).

Edmondson, Belinda (1999) *Making Men: Gender, Literary Authority, and Women's Writing in Caribbean Narrative* (Durham, NC: Duke University Press).

Hall, Stuart (1996) 'When was "the Post-colonial?" Thinking at the Limit', in Iain Chambers and Lidia Curti (eds), *The Post-colonial Question: Common Skies, Divided Horizons* (London: Routledge).

Harney, Stephano (1996) *Nationalism and Identity: Culture and the Imagination in a Caribbean Diaspora* (New York: Zed Books).

Hulme, Peter (1995) 'Including America', *Ariel*, vol. 26, no. 1.

James, C.L.R. (1971 [1936]) *Minty Alley* (London and Port of Spain: New Beacon Books).

James, Louis (1999) *Caribbean Literature in English* (London: Longman).

—— (2001) 'Writing the Ballad: The Short Fiction of Samuel Selvon and Earl Lovelace', in Jacqueline Bardolph (ed.), *Telling Stories: Postcolonial Short Fiction in English* (Amsterdam: Rodopi).

King, Bruce (1995) *Derek Walcott and West Indian Drama* (Oxford: Clarendon).

Knight, Franklin W. and Palmer, Colin A. (eds) (1989) *The Modern Caribbean* (Chapel Hill: University of North Carolina Press).

Lewis, Gordon K. (1968) *The Growth of the Modern West Indies* (New York: Monthly Review Press).

Loomba, Ania (2005) *Colonialism/Postcolonialism* (New York: Routledge).

Lovelace, Earl (1988a) *A Brief Conversion* (Oxford: Heinemann).

—— (1988b) 'The Ongoing Value of Our Indigenous Traditions', in Selwyn Ryan (ed.), *The Independence Experience 1962–1987* (St Augustine: Institute of Social and Economic Research, University of the West Indies).

—— (1981 [1979]) *The Dragon Can't Dance* (Harlow: Longman).

—— (1997 [1996]) *Salt* (New York: Persea).

Manalansan, Martin IV (2001) '*Biyuti* in Everyday Life: Performance, Citizenship, and Survival Among Filipinos in the United States', in Kandice Chuh and Karen Shimakawa (eds), *Orientations: Mapping Studies in the Asian Diaspora* (Durham, NC: Duke University Press).

McClintock, Ann (1992) 'The Angel of Progress: Pitfalls of the Term "Postcolonialism"', *Social Text*, nos. 31/32.

Nielsen, Aldon Lynn (1997) *C.L.R. James: A Critical Introduction* (Jackson: University Press of Mississippi).

Puri, Shalini (2003) 'Beyond Resistance: Notes Towards a New Caribbean Cultural Studies', *Small Axe*, no. 14.

Rohlehr, Gordon (1988) 'The Culture of Williams: Context, Performance, Legacy', *Callaloo*, vol. 20, no. 4.

Shohat, Ella (1992) 'Notes on the "Post-colonial"', *Social Text*, nos 31/32.

Walcott, Derek (1980) *Remembrance and Pantomime* (New York: Farrar Straus Giroux).

Welter, Barbara (1976) *Dimity Convictions: The American Woman in the Nineteenth Century* (Columbus, OH: University of Ohio Press).

8
A 'LIMITED SITUATION': BREVITY AND LOVELACE'S *A BRIEF CONVERSION*

James Procter

Sandwiched between various drafts of 'Shoemaker Arnold' in the Earl Lovelace Archive at St Augustine Library, Trinidad, is a slip of paper headed 'The Short Story'.[1] The sheet contains typed notes listing definitions and aims of short story writing: 'one aspect of character'; 'limited situation'; 'single effect'; 'Thus the short story does not aim at creating a world as much as explicating a world'; 'At showing views of the world'; 'The significance of incidents in a world'. Circled in pen, the only other word on the page is 'Selvon'. There is no indication of when or where these notes were made, or where they come from. What they suggest, however, is Lovelace's self-consciousness about the short story as a distinctive genre, his awareness of a Trinidadian tradition of short fiction (Selvon) and, above all, his appreciation of the formal qualities of the modern short story: its impressionism ('one aspect of character'), its economy and enclosure ('limited situation'), and its unity ('single effect'). What follows is an exploration of Lovelace's use of the short story form in *A Brief Conversion* (Lovelace 1988).

Relatively little attention has been paid to Lovelace's short writings, with critical discussion focusing predominantly on the novels.[2] Perhaps this is unsurprising given the many striking thematic parallels between the stories and the novels, which make it easy to overlook the generic and formal differences between them. Yet Lovelace's temporary break with the novel form in *A Brief Conversion* invites a consideration of how such differences mark our reading of what are otherwise well-established preoccupations and concerns in Lovelace: stickfighting and crises in masculinity; village rituals and alienating urban modernity; masks and masquerading. Where earlier Trinidadian writers like C.L.R. James, Alfred Mendes and Samuel Selvon first published their short stories in a variety of magazines, journals and newspapers, and they were subsequently edited for anthologies and collections, all but two of the 12 stories in *A Brief Conversion* appear to have been written specifically for the collection. This suggests that the architecture of *A Brief Conversion* was more premeditated and self-conscious, less haphazard, than was traditionally the case with the Trinidadian short story.³

For Lovelace, the short story was no 'apprenticeship form', a genre imposed from above by a publishing industry unwilling to gamble with an unknown writer; his self-conscious turn to the short story after the publication of three successful novels was less a pragmatic than a creative act that must affect our appreciation of the stories (James 2001: 104). Like the slip of paper sandwiched between drafts of 'Shoemaker Arnold' (the penultimate tale in *A Brief Conversion*), what the drafts themselves expose is just how carefully crafted Lovelace's stories are. The Earl Lovelace Archive reveals that the short stories of *A Brief Conversion* typically went through between five and 10 typed drafts, each heavily annotated for further revision with Lovelace's pen.

It is important to stress these points about the constructedness of Lovelace's prose partly because the author has arguably been too straightforwardly aligned with an unreconstructed and spontaneous folk culture. Lovelace has associated himself, and in turn tends to by associated by others, with the bacchanalia of the village rather than the cosmopolitanism of the city, the spiritual over the material world, tradition as opposed to modernity, nationalism rather than migration. His early journalism appeared in the tabloid *Express* because it was 'the first locally owned press in the nation' rather than the broadsheet *Trinidad Guardian*, with its prestigious literary connections: Seepersad Naipual and Samuel Selvon (Lovelace 2003: vi). He has stressed the need for an indigenous Caribbean aesthetic that can avoid the error of 'guiding ourselves by the "inherited" institutions, the "inherited" ceremonies, accepting the bewigged judges, irrelevant communications media, irrelevant school books, irrelevant cinema shows' (2003: xii). He has been involved in folk theatre at a grassroots level and, unlike most other contemporary writers from the region who have migrated to the United States and Europe, Lovelace remains in Trinidad.

It is valuable to note within this critical and biographical context that, in using the short story form for *A Brief Conversion*, Lovelace seemingly adopts a paradoxical genre, closely bound up with the experience of modernity and migration in the Caribbean in the first half of the twentieth century. Where we might expect Lovelace to pursue the affinities of short fiction with oral storytelling, or the yarn's emphasis on denouement, anecdote and revelation, he employs modernist devices such as epiphany, curtailment and ellipsis. The short stories of *A Brief Conversion* are narrated less by griots and calypsonians than by journalists and reporters. Even when a folk tale tradition is evoked in a story like 'Shoemaker Arnold' (where 'the good cobbler' of Grimm's story is replaced by the cantankerous and antisocial Arnold), it is only inverted. Lovelace's note on 'single effect' borrows directly from the father of the modern short story, and from Edgar Allan Poe's remarks on 'singularity of effect'.

A Brief Conversion's complex attachments to modernity are most apparent in the three stories that together form a brief cycle within the collection: 'The Fire Eater's Journey', 'The Coward' and 'The Fire Eater's Return'. The narrator of these consecutive pieces is the enigmatic Santo, a man whose intelligence and self-consciousness mark him out (and to a certain extent distance him) from his peers in Cunaripo. He commands an authority and respect among the other boys, but Santo remains aloof from the village, and eventually moves to Port of Spain to become a newspaper reporter with *The Standard*. His destiny in this respect is tied to Blues (the fire eater), an outsider for very different reasons (his lack of formal education, and of authority), who moves to the capital with an acrobatic troupe in search of recognition. In contrast to the sceptical Santo, Blues entertains innocent fantasies about travelling to England as a performer.

Before their move to the city, Santo regards Blues with a mixture of suspicion and muted admiration: they are 'sorta friends' (1988: 37). However, their encounters in Port of Spain are stilted and uncomfortable, their relationship becoming increasingly fragile and unpredictable. For Santo, Blues is hiding behind a series of masks, a grotesque 'repertoire of gestures' (1988: 39). He is variously a victim of masquerade, 'holding himself as if on display' (1988: 38) like the white mannequins in a shop window (1988: 39), or knowingly exploiting the city as 'lie, a sham, a con ... appearance' (1988: 42) in his fraudulent performance as the 'Iron Man' (in which Blues 'breaks' an already broken bar on his chest). Yet, in a contradictory gesture typical of the collection as a whole, Santo also implies that his is a misreading of Blues: 'I had the feeling that the city, after all, without a knowledge of Blues, might take his exuberance in the wrong spirit and might not be giving him the welcome his sincerity and delight merited' (1988: 39). Santo's narrative generates uncertainty around Blues (is he superficial or sincere, substantial or sham?), inviting us to question the narrator's authority and perspective.

Of crucial significance here is the increasingly prominent relationship between reporter (Santo) and reported (Blues) in the three stories. In 'The Coward', the second story in the cycle, Blues gets drawn into a Black Power demonstration as it marches on Woodford Square. Blues appears to be in a dream-like state as he is pulled hypnotically into the crowd, 'the drums were beating in his head' (1988: 46). At the same time, the event constitutes an *awakening*, a coming into (black) consciousness for Blues, as he catches himself in a shop front:

> Blues followed them down the street, past show windows with mannequins with blond hair modeling tweed jackets and Parisian blouses. In the mirror of a display window, he caught a glimpse of himself and realized with a shock that suddenly he didn't look so tall,

that he wasn't cool at all, that his tie was a rope around his neck and where was the crown in his hair? (1988: 46)

Blues, who is dressed for work as a security guard, is exposed to the black skin behind his white mask: he experiences an epiphany, one of a series of brief conversions that dominate the text, a moment of being that is quickly deflated and undermined in what follows.[4] As Blues is exposed to the social and economic inequalities of the city, what he experiences is not growing conviction, but a nervous condition, a sense of rising uncertainty: 'Blues found himself trembling. He felt his head buzzing. The drums were filling his belly. He looked at his watch. It was nearly three. He had to get back to the bank to do his security' (1988: 48). Blues turns to leave, only to come face to face with Santo, who accuses him of cowardice:

> 'And you frighten?' I said coldly, 'Frighten to die?'
> 'Yes, Santo,' he said. 'Yes.' Suddenly his face was very sad. 'But I ain't frighten to dead. I frighten I kill somebody. Let it go. Let them go with what they thief. Let them keep it.'
> 'And we will go to sleep. Leave things just so and go back to sleep?'
> I thought he was going to strike me, so fierce were his eyes. Instead he said softly, 'Yes. But I don't know how sound a sleep it will be.' (1988: 49)

In these closing lines, we return to the opposition between sleep and consciousness that has already been undermined through Blues' (sleep) walk towards black consciousness. There is no external, authorial comment or reflection on this verbal exchange within speech marks, and in his suspension of commentary, Lovelace exploits the brevity of the short story in a way that generates uncertainty. Because if Santo's accusation of cowardice concurs with, and affirms, the title of the short story ('The Coward'), then the emotional sincerity of Blues's reply might be said to reveal a bravery and honesty of which Santo is incapable. Blues's retreat is not out of fear for his own life, but for the lives of those around him. Moreover, if he seems willing to return to a state of unconsciousness, it is one still marked by a social conscience — a conscience that will not allow him to sleep soundly.

Santo's somewhat self-righteous attack on Blues is further undermined by the context in which it appears. Unlike Blues, who has risked his job in order to attend the march, Santo is present not out of personal curiosity, but professional duty. As he explains to Blues: '"I come to see what's happening," I said, waving my notebook. "I covering the demonstrations for *The Standard*"' (1988: 48). If

Blues does not see the irony in his reply — 'Keep your distance and write your story, but don't get involved. I going. Just write your story and keep out of this.' (1988: 48) — it is harder for the reader to ignore that, for all the worthiness of his diatribe, Santo is essentially a detached, passive, even parasitic presence at the demonstration.[5]

In the last of the three stories, 'The Fire Eater's Return', the problematic relationship between newspaper reporter and the events he reports is tragically foregrounded. Blues has lost his former innocence and optimism, and seems broken mentally. Now dressed in African clothes, the positions at the close of the 'The Coward' appear reversed as Blues accuses Santo:

> 'The Black race is under threat. They are stealing our dreams, our rhythms. Santo,' he said seriously, 'you have to stop sleeping. What you doing with yourself? You have to get out of the rat race. People have to care, Santo. People have to care about people.' (1988: 55)

Blues now associates his performances as iron man and fire eater with a political cause, a quasi-religious conversion: 'People want something more spectacular than words, something more grand. Faith needs spectacle' (1988: 57). Nevertheless, Blues relies on the words of the newspaper to generate this spectacle, persuading Santo to cover his performance in *The Standard*. Santo's story is rejected by the editor, and he has to miss Blues's next performance to cover events in parliament. It is during this performance that Blues's struggle for the spectacular goes tragically wrong, and he is consumed by the flames he blows. Belatedly, and ironically, Blues becomes a spectacle, grabbing the next day's headlines as Santo's story is resurrected for *The Standard*:

> Next day they had my story in the paper with pictures of Blues with flames pouring out of his mouth and they had a big headline: THE RETURN OF THE FIRE EATER and below that, The Fire Eater Eats His Last. (1988: 58)

The inadequacy of these words in capturing the character we have glimpsed through the three stories is striking. The brutal economy of journalistic discourse and the absences it carries as a close to this short story cycle recalls the kind of symbolic violence associated with the District Commissioner's clipped narrative of Okwonkwo at the end of Achebe's *Things Fall Apart*. However, as a literary device, it perhaps shares more in common with V.S. Naipaul's *Miguel Street*, where the short story cycle presents a recurring disjunction between the stories of the boy narrator and newspaper accounts of the same event.

Such narratives do not simply reinforce a disjunction between journalism and short story, they also remind us of the proximity of the two genres in relation to the emergence of the modern short story in Trinidad in the early twentieth century. The advent of the commercial press and newspapers, notably the *Trinidad Guardian* established in 1917, was contemporary with the rapid rise of the magazine and journal in the Caribbean in the 1920s, 1930s and 1940s. These new print spaces played a considerable, constitutive role in shaping the architecture of Trinidadian fiction in the early twentieth century. I am thinking here of the enclosed nature of the short story, its primary existence as an interstitial document, sandwiched between adverts, essays and artwork in little magazines, or 'locked' into the narrow, carefully measured columns of the newspaper. In Trinidad in 1929, C.L.R. James and Alfred Mendes established *Trinidad*, which after two issues became *The Beacon*. Also in 1929 (the same year Seepersad Naipaul began writing for the paper), the *Trinidad Guardian* was overhauled and modernised, having previously been a failing colonial paper. It was the Guardian Commercial Printery that produced the first print run of Seepersad's short story collection *Guredeva and Other Indian Tales* in 1943. If he was horrified to discover one of his short stories had been printed in the format of the newspaper column, his letters to his son Vidia reveal his use of the term 'story' interchangeably to refer to both short fiction and journalism. It is perhaps no coincidence in this context that many of Trinidad's most famous short story writers have also been journalists, from James and Mendes to Sam Selvon and, of course, Earl Lovelace.

This journalistic context is important for understanding the modernity that Lovelace inherits through the short story form. Along with other media which are recurring referents in the collection and which include magazines, radio, television and cinema (which have also had a marked influence of the modern short story form in Trinidad), the newspaper is associated variously with sensationalism, a fleeting culture of speeded-up technologies, the inauthentic, neo-colonialism, commodification and the cosmopolitan city.[6] However, this fact should not eclipse the material 'embeddedness' of Lovelace's narratives within a modern print and media culture that inevitably helps give form and meaning to his fiction. The shortness, singularity and impressionism of the short story serve to encapsulate an increasingly fleeting, superficial world with which Lovelace is troubled at the level of content. In stories like 'The Fire Eater's Journey', 'The Coward' and 'The Fire Eater's Return', the journalist Santo might be said to foreground the limitations of narrative brevity, and the incapacity of the artist to provide a more sustained, holistic vision of character and community.

Thus many of the short stories of *A Brief Conversion* dramatise a tension between form and content that Evelyn O'Callaghan has already noted in Lovelace's novels. Questioning the idea that Lovelace merely presents a nostalgic and Edenic pastoral vision of the Caribbean as an alternative to the decay and corruption of the purgatorial city, O'Callaghan notes that in *While Gods are Falling* and *The Dragon Can't Dance*: 'There's almost a contradiction between the pile-up of violent or squalid images and the vitality of the prose' (O'Callaghan 1989: 50). Similarly, in the short stories, there is an apparent contradiction between the prevailing distaste for modernity in Trinidadian society to be found within the stories, and Lovelace's formal embrace of the short story as a thoroughly modern vehicle for the expression of this distaste. In order to understand such contradictions, it is necessary to appreciate what O'Callaghan describes as Lovelace's attempt 'to engage the wider world of contingencies' (1989: 50) in which the modern city is at once a negative site of dehumanisation, an inferno or spiritual wasteland, *and* a potential space of reinvention, change and transformation. Lovelace himself makes a similar point in relation to the question of modernity:

> It is possible to look at a folk culture as a way of life falling away before the impact of modernization. And perhaps to expect those of the affected culture to be engaged in the nostalgic mourning for what has been lost ... It is ... with a consciousness of loss, but with a greater emphasis on gain, that I find it most profitable to look at the question of Caribbean folk culture *within* the process of modernisation. (Lovelace 2003: 25, emphasis added)

In the short story 'Fleurs', the elderly stickfighter comments on the younger generation: 'A set of impressionists, that is what they is: just giving a impression. They don't really want to fight. They want to make style. They want to look pretty' (1988: 100). In 'The Fire Eater's Return', Blues says to the narrator: 'Santo, the world today is gimmick' (1988: 57). Meanwhile, in 'Victory and the Blight', Victory insists that 'Everything in the world losing taste, everything quick, quick, quick ...' (1988: 136). At such points, the characters seem mouthpieces for Lovelace's mournful modernity. Yet impressionism and brevity are also formal qualities of the short story that I wish to argue Lovelace embraces in *A Brief Conversion and Other Stories*, with its lack of incremental vision, and its elliptical plot structures.[7]

A Brief Conversion exploits the formal qualities of the short story collection in a way that illuminates the contingency of modernity. Gathering together 12 related, but nevertheless self-contained, discrete narratives allows Lovelace to adopt different, often discrepant positions, or — to adopt one of the dominant metaphors of the collection — to don different masks. Many of the stories are told by unidentified third-person narrators whose voices frequently merge with the central characters through the use of free indirect discourse. These voices range from the calypsonian Creole of Joebell (in 'Joebell and America') to the prim and proper Miss Ross (in 'Call me "Miss Ross" for Now'). Meanwhile, as we have already seen, the brief cycle of stories that includes 'The Fire Eater's Journey', 'The Coward' and 'The Fire Eater's Return' are narrated by the educated, dispassionate Santo, a reporter in Port of Spain.

This is not simply to suggest that *A Brief Conversion* is a polyphonic collection (see Kohn 1997). During the course of individual stories, the perspective and very spirit of the narratives seem to shift in disconcerting ways. In 'Shoemaker Arnold' and 'Victory and the Blight', the traditional folk figures of the barber and the shoemaker are deliberately undercut through the anti-social behaviour of Arnold and Victory. The setting of 'Shoemaker Arnold' in the pre-war past further undermines the aura surrounding tradition in some of the earlier tales. Meanwhile, the barber's nostalgia for the recent Trinidadian past in 'Victory and the Blight', his rants against the evils of the modern world, are — as we shall see — dramatically disturbed in the final epiphanic moment of that text. In this way, what appears to be the very premise of many of the stories folds as the narrative progresses.

As the final story of the collection, 'Victory and the Blight' might be said to carry a particular burden of representation, and on one level this story of a barber brings the book full circle, recalling the opening narrative of Mr Fitzie, the itinerant barber, in 'A Brief Conversion'. At the same time, the story appears to unbalance, or at least unsettle, the prevailing positions of the stories that precede it. Victory senses a blight come over him when he sees Brown and a stranger playing draughts in his just-opened shop. Victory's 'stiff aloofness' (1988: 133) towards these men, his suspicion of the outsider, and his cantankerous comments seem inexplicable given the warmth and affection that Brown and the man he introduces as Ross show towards him. As Victory cuts the hair of another customer (Pascal), the protagonist's attitude gradually becomes clearer. Pascal wants his head shaved, which Victory takes as an affront to his barbering skills, his status as a traditional craftsman:

> Look, I have one of those machines here that you could just plug in ... they call it a clipper. I could just plug in the clipper and put it on your head and bzzz! Just like that, and all your hair gone. But, I don't call that barbering. Barbering is playing music. Everything have to flow. Things have to fit. (1988: 136)

To Victory, the clippers represent a speeded up, technological world in which traditional folk values, and the daily rituals that once bound the village together, are threatened. They connote dissonance ('Barbering is playing music'), the breakdown and fragmentation of 'flow' and 'fit'. This fragmentation embodied in the clippers is ultimately linked to diaspora, and the emigration of West Indians from the village. The clippers are a gift from a former cricketing teammate who has migrated to the United States. His departure, which for Victory represents a kind of betrayal, is itself symptomatic of a wider culture of movement and migration in the vicinity threatening the centrality of both the cricket team (called, ironically, the Wanderers) and the barbershop. As Brown wistfully pitches in:

> Those was the days when Wanderers was Wanderers ... This barbershop was the centre. On a Saturday morning you couldn't get in. All the young teachers and civil servants lined up to talk cricket and boxing and waiting to trim. Those days real drafts used to play, with Castillo and Cecil and Mr Arthur leaving Libertville to clash with Paul. Now Paul, too, gone away. (1988: 136)

Victory's hostility towards modernity stems from the increasing pace of everyday life, an experience of acceleration that he finds both superficial and lacking in substance. As he sums it up in his diatribe against the American clippers: 'You always feel it have an easy way in everything. Some things aint have no short cut' (1988: 136). Victory's defensiveness regarding the cricket team is grounded in anxieties concerning the new transience of an ever more mobile community: 'You build a club to last, to stand up. They say nothing can't last in Cunaripo. They say we can't build nothing. And you build a club and next thing you know, bam! fellars you building it with gone away' (1988: 138).

For Victory, the newcomer in his shop seems a further signal of flux and the modern blight that has set in: the erosion of a familiar, knowable community. As the conversation continues, a difference of opinion emerges when Pascal, Brown and Ross express an empathy with the emigrants that Victory cannot countenance. Where Victory reads emigration as a betrayal of the traditional loyalties of the village community, Brown argues: 'You have to be able to afford to care' (1988: 138). When newcomer Ross adds that it is not the going away that matters, but what the men did while they were here, Victory loses his patience: 'You come in this barbershop a stranger and making more noise than anybody and now you telling me "is not the going away"?' (1988: 139).

If, on the one hand, it is difficult to dismiss Brown's pragmatism or Ross's optimism, we cannot deny the validity of Victory's argument that a price cannot be put on care, either. The verbal economy of the short story allows Lovelace to exploit this undecidability in a manner that seems to exploit the qualities of modernity mourned at the level of content. In short, the dissonant, fragmentary quality of the short story collection appears, like the clippers themselves, symptomatic of the fleeting culture that is 'blight' to Victory. Victory's suspicion of Ross is founded on an understandable anxiety concerning modernity and contemporary change, but the fact that these suspicions are proved spectacularly incorrect at the story's close also exposes the limits of an insular and unchanging folk culture intolerant of newness. At the end of the story, the bench on which Brown and Ross play draughts suddenly collapses. The agility that Ross displays in recovering from this fall makes Victory see, for the first time, the newcomer's ability as an opening batsman. This epiphany appears to bring about a change Victory's perspective:

> 'And, you know,' Victory said as he drew the ends of the cloth
> securely around Ross' neck, 'When you step through that door this
> morning, I sure you was a blight.' (1988: 141)

But whether this change is passing or permanent remains uncertain, as it coincides with the close of the story. The short story's brevity, its potential to curtail narrative, is exploited by Lovelace to refuse any definitive alignment with folk culture, *or* modernity, at the collection's conclusion.

At a very basic level, the problem of how to read Victory in 'Victory and the Blight' — is he the heroic defender of folk traditions, or a symptom of the very blight he diagnoses in others? — is produced by the omission of character exposition. All we know of Victory comes from a single, fleeting episode, a conversation (lasting the duration of one haircut) in his shop. Parts of Victory's past are glimpsed metonymically (we learn of his sporting prowess through the photographs on the wall), but we do not know enough about him to 'take sides' in the argument. Moreover, by locating the epiphany at the end of the story, it is not possible to say how or even whether the revelation about Ross will change Victory.

Epiphany, or 'brief conversion', is a recurrent device within Lovelace's collection. Often retaining Biblical connotations, these epiphanies provide one of the clearest thematic and structural links between the stories. Suzanne Ferguson has argued in her classic essay on impressionism and form in the short story that the 'notion of single "moments" of experience as determiners of the quality of a whole life' results in 'the deemphasis of the orderly unfolding of an action through time':

> In the short story, we frequently see only one such privileged
> moment, which takes the place of the traditional 'turning point,' the
> climax of the plot. Not much actual dramatized time passes,

although in the memory and fantasy of the characters large reaches of 'time' may be covered. (Ferguson 1982: 20)

In the title story 'A Brief Conversion', we have several such epiphanic moments, which themselves seem to challenge the tradition notion of turning point or climax in the text. First, we have the conversion of Travey's father from warrior, stickfighter and *parang* reveller into 'family man' (1988: 12) as he finally settles down and marries the mother of his children. Second, we have Travey's own conversion as his warrior spirit is tamed at the hands of his father:

> 'Button up your shirt, Travey.' And as I looked at him, 'Yes. Don't frighten, button it up,' nodding encouragement as if, yes, it was all right. It was the thing to be done.
> I felt a strange, relief and a flow of sadness. It was as if we had come to an end, the two of us. The hoping was done. It was as if he had come finally to acknowledge that he could no longer ask me to wait upon his dreams, that my freedom was to be severed from his own, that I was to go it alone. (1988: 16)

There is a misogynistic logic to this revelation, in which it is implied that the rigid will of domesticated femininity, working hand in hand with colonial ideology, civilises, stifles and represses a potentially liberating black masculinity that still remains latent in Travey's father. Nevertheless, Travey succumbs, seeing in his conversion 'a redemptive penance that shall lead me to glory, that shall remove the strange burden from my father and make my mother proud of me' (1988: 16). Following his conversion, Travey is bullied mercilessly by the other boys at school until he instinctively hits back. Now Travey faces a dilemma: should he give the boy he struck his marbles as a 'peace offering' (1988: 23) or should he stand his ground and fight?

On the evening before he must resolve this dilemma, Travey wanders alone through his home village of Cunaripo. There he sees Miss Priscilla flaunting her dirty, decaying body shamelessly before a crowd of men. The once-beautiful woman, a model whose pictures had appeared in the papers, has gone to seed. Continuing his journey, Travey encounters, in a condensed, elliptical moment that seems to emerge internally from his own stream of consciousness, rather than externally in the street itself, the various characters of the community:

> Now Science Man prowls the street with a grimace on his face and now and again butts his head forcefully against the wood of the telephone post. Britain, in her unchanged dress of red, white and

blue; Graham, with his hernia, Pretty Foot, our transvestite; Fowl, who still crows like the cock he stole from Mother Alice; the Shango priestess. These are our celebrities. Their escapades, their fights, their moments of madness, their sayings, these are the subjects of our conversations. (1988: 25)

Through these figures, Travey evokes both a vibrant folk alternative to Hollywood and the media celebrities that corrupt the village elsewhere in the collection, and a paralysing parable (like Miss Priscilla before them) of 'pride that has fallen; ambition that overleaped itself': 'Each story ends victoriously in defeat, penance, apology' (1988: 25). It is through this elliptical ensemble of stories that Travey experiences a further epiphany:

Until that Thursday evening, I had not put them altogether in that way. It was then that I felt the weight of their apology and defeat for the first time; and for the first time, I looked at our town.

The architects of Cunaripo have placed the police station on a hill commanding the main street. On another hill, the steeple of the Roman Catholic church raises against the sky like a shaft of white light; seeing it, men make the sign of the Cross, women genuflect. Men, coming out of Kee's rum shop, stumble upon the serene and anchored power of the police station, with its thick masonry and its Union Jack and its walk of whitewashed flagstones, about it a distant and secret air, like that of a monastery; and they make a bow, not a bow of bending the back but of bending the knees, recognizing before them a power that can render them as sober as the surrounding estate's cocoa trees ... Overpowered by the sense of penance and apology, I head for home. (1988: 26)

Epiphany here does not lead to change or transformation, but to a new or heightened awareness in Travey of his lack of agency in a towering landscape that commands ultimate symbolic authority. The striking stylistic economy that Lovelace uses to represent Travey's seeing of the village for the first time is achieved through an impressionism that substitutes condensed and partial vision for holistic verisimilitude. The sense of abundant, absolute power is achieved, paradoxically, through minimalism, curtailment and restraint. The distilled, painterly image of the village seems suspended in time and appears contrary to conventional plotting and exposition through action and event.

At this moment, Travey decides to hand over the marbles. But no sooner has he made the decision than he experiences another epiphany that undercuts the previous one. It occurs as he encounters his uncle Bango. For the second time in the text, Travey feels 'saved' (1988: 26): 'Out of this landscape, I had plucked a hero' (1988: 26). Bango is a lovable rogue, a stickfighter and streetfighter, womaniser and gambler. His body appears relaxed and unrestrained, and his undone shirt and upturned collar present an alternative to the neatly dressed, buttoned-up Travey. As his Uncle Bango hails him by his father's nickname (Bull), Travey comes to realise a new sense of comradery, of being 'part of the struggle' (1988: 27). Travey goes on to confront his bullies, and wins his fight with the boy. However, if the revelatory encounter with Uncle Bango seems straightforward in this sense, what is a moment of enlightenment to Travey (as he embraces his inner masculinity) appears as a moment of confusion and uncertainty for the reader (as that masculinity is troubled). Indeed, Travey's own account of his Uncle Bango articulates a number of uncertainties of which he appears unconscious.

Travey begins by expressing a desire to see his Uncle Bango in terms of the classic, romanticised male hero of cinema, television and the media:

> I would like to embellish Uncle Bango with power and purpose and a war, give him two pistols and a rifle and a double bandolier; and, with a *sombrero* tied around his neck and falling on his shoulders, put him on a white horse and make him a bandit chieftain at the head of forty, fifty, a hundred lean desperadoes who appear out of nowhere to battle for the poor. I would like to tell of his being pursued by the cavalry, riding through a hail of bullets to meet the woman that is waiting for him, and his name will be Pancho or Fidel or Che. (1988: 27)

Yet Travey tells us he is not blinded by this fantasy of his uncle, in reality a local hero, far from clean cut and unknown beyond the village of Cunaripo. What appeals to Travey, however, is Uncle Bango's essential *style*:

> It was not style as adornment, but style as substance. His style was not something that he had acquired to enhance an ability; rather, it existed prior to any ability or accomplishment — it was affirmation and self looking for a skill to wed it to, to save it and maintain it, to express it; it was self searching for substance, for meaning. (1988: 27)

There is a slippage in Travey's account here as we move from style *as* substance to style *searching for* substance. Is style here a core, authentic expression of an inner, substantial masculinity, or is it as insubstantial and superficial as the cinematic images of masculinity presented elsewhere in the text? This is an uncertainty that only becomes more pronounced as Travey goes on to relate an anecdote or rumour of the knife-wielding Cut Cake who once confronted Bango at a fête: 'And before he butt Cut Cake, he said, "Don't do that stuff, kid." No doubt it was something he had heard in a movie; but, the spirit, the desire for meaning, the style, that was Uncle Bango's' (1988: 27). There is a troubling of the origins of masculinity here as Bango speaks both in the style of the Hollywood actor, and in a style that is identifiably his.

Throughout the collection, epiphanies serve to undermine authoritative revelation, to signal the provisional and contingent. Elsewhere in this chapter, we have seen how Lovelace uses a variety of devices associated with the short story — brevity, impressionism, condensation — in ways that unsettle an unequivocal alignment of his writing with a spontaneous, or anti-modernist, folk culture. If, in the fire eater trilogy, Lovelace attends to the limitations of narrative brevity through the analogy with journalism, more generally he exploits the limited situation of short prose. Arguably, the short story form frees him from a didacticism and instrumentalism that can sometimes be detected in his longer works. The firm historical groundings of many of the novels become condensed metaphorical moments.[8] While brevity is a symptom of corrosive modernity for characters like Victory, for Lovelace it provides a way of articulating what it means 'to live in the midst of contradiction', not in the form of detached undecidability but as 'an everyday struggle':

> People have always faced the tough choice between individual advancement and group concerns: there's always this area of tension. Some Calypsonians today still maintain their role as the people's voice, while others see themselves as entertainers. But I don't want to make it a straight line between those who sell out and those who don't. I'm sympathetic to the kind of pressures that people face, why very often they don't fully understand themselves. One of my intentions is to show what these problems are and how people respond to them: they are trying their best, even as they fail. And, more important than making judgments about what they finally do, is to understand their situation and the questions they have to answer, as well as the reasons for their failure to lift themselves above their circumstances. (Jaggi 1990: 26)

Notes

1. I am grateful to the British Academy for providing me with a small research grant to visit this archive.
2. Of the 32 articles, book chapters and interviews on Earl Lovelace listed in the MLA International Bibliography (searched in August 2006), only one focuses on the short stories. Unfortunately I was unable to consult Kohn (1997) before the publication of this essay. The most frequently discussed novel is *The Dragon Can't Dance*. More neglected than the short fiction, even, are Lovelace's plays and theatre work. A valuable bibliographic resource in terms of Lovelace is Johnson (2004).
3. The ordering of the stories was being experimented with at least three years before final publication. An undated draft version, which appears to have been produced in 1985, contains 13 stories in the following order: 'A Brief Conversion', 'Shoemaker Arnold', 'Joe Bell and America', 'Midnight Robber', 'Fleurs', 'Victory', 'Bicycle Pump', 'Heavy Cakes', 'Plain Talk', 'Fire Eater's Journey'; 'The Coward'; 'The Fire Eater Eats His Last'; 'Call Me "Miss Ross" for Now'. Earl Lovelace Archive, St Augustine, Box 2A.
4. Significantly, this revelation — a Lacanian moment of (mis)identification in the mirror — signals a separation from the spaces of commodified urban modernity that are associated with depthlessness, mimicry and white masks in this collection. It is a revelation that reverses the moment in the first fire eater story when Blues stops 'to look in on a display window at the banlon jerseys and tweed jackets displayed on the mannequins with pink faces' and his eyes 'light up with the delighted amazement as he saw reflected there the man in long sleeves with folded newspaper, carrying so effortlessly that magnificent chest' (1988: 39).
5. In the third of the 'fire eater' stories, Santo speaks of his own 'cowardice' (1988: 52), when he hides from Blues during Carnival, only to check the coverage of the event in the press the next day.
6. Cinema is particularly significant here. In 'Joebell and America', Lovelace offers us an (exaggerated) equivalent of Bogart in *Miguel Street*. Joebell is a mimic man completely immersed in a North American culture of film and television. Meanwhile, in 'A Brief Conversion', the violent, vain and sadistic masculinity that Ronnie embraces derives from his time in the De Luxe cinema, Port of Spain.
7. Where impressionism at the level of content is associated with popular cultural forms — television, cinema, high street fashions — at the level of form it is more frequently employed as avant-garde impressionism.

[8] This is perhaps best illustrated in 'The Coward', a story which — like *The Dragon Can't Dance* — contains allusions to the Black Power rebellion in Trinidad in 1970. In 'The Coward', Lovelace reserves his most poetic descriptions for the portrayal of the harshest realities: 'he [Blues] flowed with them into Woodford Square where the grass lay down panting in the huge shadow of a samaan tree at the table of whose roots vagrants with serene indifference to the noises around them were preparing a meal with the salt of their tears' (1988: 46). See also the description of Shanty Town where Blues sees 'black emperors stepping out of their palaces of cardboard into the ooze of the suffocating vapours of decay to contest the squalling *corbeaux* and mangy stray dogs the rights to the treasures in the unmined mountains of refuse dumped upon their doorsteps' (1988: 47).

References

Ferguson, Suzanne C. (1982) 'Defining the Short Story: Impressionism and Form', *Modern Fiction Studies*, vol. 28, no. 1.

Jaggi, Maya (1990) 'Interview: Earl Lovelace', *Wasafiri*, no. 12.

James, Louis (2001) 'Writing the Ballad', in Jacqueline Bardolph (ed.), *Telling Stories: Postcolonial Short Fiction in English* (Amsterdam: Rodopi).

Johnson, Nadia Indra (2004) 'Earl Lovelace: Selected Bibliography', *Anthurium: A Caribbean Studies Journal*, vol. 4, no. 2.

Kohn, James (1997) 'Polyphony in the Short Stories of Earl Lovelace', *Language and Literature*, vol. 22.

Lovelace, Earl (1988) *A Brief Conversion and Other Stories* (Oxford: Heinemann).

—— (2003) *Growing in the Dark: Selected Essays*, ed. Funso Aiyejina (San Juan, Trinidad: Lexicon).

O'Callaghan, Evelyn (1989) 'The Modernization of the Trinidadian Landscape in the Novels of Earl Lovelace' *ARIEL*, vol. 20, no. 1.

9
'ALL O' WE IS ONE': CARNIVAL FORMS AND CREOLISATION IN *THE DRAGON CAN'T DANCE* AND *SALT*

John Thieme

The Dragon Can't Dance (1979) opens with a familiar Trinidadian story: an account of a man who, supposedly believing he is Christ, stages his own crucifixion and asks onlookers to stone him, but rapidly relinquishes his Messianic fantasy when the stones thrown at him turn out to be larger than expected (see Dance 1992: 152–3).[1] Lovelace's single-paragraph version of this urban myth is an apt curtain-raiser to a novel which, among other things, will deal with the ambivalences of carnivalesque role-playing. It is also, I would suggest, an invitation to consider his relationship to other Trinidadian writers who have told the same story and of whose versions, one assumes, he would have been aware when he came to write the novel, specifically Naipaul's 'Man-man' in *Miguel Street* (1959) and the account of Brackley's crucifixion which Moses relates to Galahad in the closing pages of *The Lonely Londoners* (1956).[2] The intertextual relationship points towards a superficial similarity in the three writers' subject-matter more generally, so I should like to begin by comparing the ways in which Lovelace, Naipaul and Selvon retell this piece of modern folklore. Arguably, it can be seen as a metonym for their different approaches to late colonial (and in Lovelace's case, early post-Independence) Trinidadian society and its storytelling traditions. So, using the crucifixion story as a departure point, this chapter offers a few comments on the three texts' fictional practice more generally, particularly comparing *The Dragon Can't Dance* with *Miguel Street*, and then goes on to identify some of the more distinctive aspects of the *Dragon*'s treatment of the Carnival society and its consideration of the extent to which the annual festival can be seen as providing a site for national unity. Subsequently, I provide a briefer discussion of aspects of *Salt* (1996) in an attempt to see whether Lovelace's representation of Creolisation and the possibility of arriving at a consensual discourse of national or communal 'oneness' has undergone a change in the later novel.

First, though, let's look at Selvon's version of the crucifixion story. It forms part of a nostalgic conversation between Moses, the central figure in *The Lonely Londoners*, and his friend Galahad. Placed in Moses's mouth, but narrated in one of Selvon's own distinctive Creole registers, its form is typical of the anecdotal style of the novel and, although it is a self-contained narrative episteme, the storytelling moment foregrounds the distance between the characters' present London situation and 'those characters back home' (Selvon 1972: 112). Its mood is bitter-sweet: after hearing it, Galahad laughs until tears come to his eyes, while Moses suddenly sobers up, reflecting on the divergence between the pleasure of such 'oldtalking' and the harsher realities of the Windrush generation's life in Britain. There is no real evaluation of the tale, simply the sharing of the pleasure, and the nostalgic sadness, that comes from remembrance of Trinidadian things past, as personified by Brackley, the individualistic eccentric who has staged his own crucifixion.

Naipaul's version, which provides the climax to his story of the trickster Man-man, is the fullest of the three. Initially it seems richly comic, but the comedy relies on the discrepancy between Man-man's very proper English and the realities of the Creole society. When he objects to the size of the stones being thrown at him, his mimicry of Biblical English speech gives way to no-nonsense Caribbean cussing. Unlike the other two versions, a coda is added. The story ends with the words: 'The authorities kept him for observation and then for good' (Naipaul, 1971: 44). It has begun with its ingenuous boy-narrator querying whether Man-man is, as is commonly assumed, mad. The ending provides a kind of closure by making it clear that, as far as the 'authorities' are concerned, he is. And it is typical of the kind of comic deflation around which the majority of the stories in *Miguel Street* are structured. Characters aspire to fulfilment through the enactment of some kind of role, very often a role centred on manliness, which becomes the central theme of the volume, but despite the use of calypso themes and comedy, Naipaul's irony works to negate all possible avenues to self-fulfilment, with the single exception of emigration.

So how does Lovelace's version compare, and how, more generally, does the *Dragon* respond to the problems of writing about male identity in late colonial and early post-Independence Trinidad? The crucifixion story is concisely related in the first paragraph of the first section of the Prologue, which is mainly devoted to evoking the cultural geography of Calvary Hill. 'This is the hill,' Lovelace tells his readers rhetorically, where 'Laughter is not laughter; it is a groan coming from the bosom of these houses — no not houses, shacks that leap out of the red dirt and stone' (Lovelace 1979: 10). Calvary Hill is a site of urban Creole dispossession, and the would-be Christ — a man named Taffy — seems to represent the possibility of transcendence through suffering, but his suffering is of course only role-playing. In some ways his failure echoes that of Man-man since, although the account here is very brief, he too subsides into Creole when his attempt to stage the ultimate Western fantasy collapses. However, unlike Naipaul, Lovelace does not offer a coda by way of commentary. Moreover, he introduces the tale as a beginning, a point of departure for his account of the predicament of Trinidad's urban proletariat and the social codes through which they have contested the dehumanising aspects of their situation. After the first section of the Prologue has sketched in the world of the Hill, it moves on to sections on Carnival and calypso, suggesting the potential for release that the Carnival-centred popular culture (the trinity of Carnival, calypso and steelband) offers to the Hill's residents. Lovelace's use of Carnival forms engages with the perennial debate about whether the pre-Lenten festival is simply a forum for licensed escapism, as in the Carnivals sanctioned by the Catholic church (which is one side of the provenance of Trinidad's Carnival) or whether it contains genuine revolutionary — or at least transformational — possibilities, as suggested by the other side of its origins: the nineteenth-century Afro-Caribbean association of Carnival with Emancipation (see Hill 1972: 16–22). Tied in with this debate is a consideration of the extent to which Carnival can enable the society's men — and to a lesser extent its women — to fulfil a Creolised, but African-based, ideal of manhood — or, as Lovelace sometimes renders it, 'personhood'.

Miguel Street is centrally about diminished manhood. Characters affect macho roles, but most of the stories employ a common formula: their protagonists pursue a particular ideal or code of behaviour, but by the end their aspirations are deflated and they are left stripped of dignity. Lovelace addresses similar issues, albeit while locating his story on the east side of Port of Spain — on the Hill (Laventille) — as opposed to the lower middle-class world of Miguel Street's location — in the Woodbrook district on the west side of the city — where social deprivation is less marked. However, Lovelace's tone is altogether different. The ideal of manhood — or 'personhood' — survives amid the bricolage of the Hill and particularly asserts itself through Carnival performance arts and role-playing, which often define characters' year-round identities, not simply the personae they adopt during the two-month Carnival season. Like both Naipaul and Selvon, Lovelace assembles a broad cast of characters and the 'mulatto' Miss Cleothilda's early assertion, 'All o' we is one' — a phrase that is subsequently repeated in two different contexts and with different implications — raises the issue of whether the miscellaneous inhabitants of the Hill really constitute a community or whether they remain divided by their affirmations of individuality and the inequalities prevalent in their society.

Miss Cleothilda's articulation of the 'All o' we is one' cliché seems to be self-serving. A self-styled Queen of the Band, she holds herself aloof from the Hill's other residents for most of the year, only emerging from her supposed superiority to assert a commonality of concerns with them during the Carnival season, when the discourse of unity is uppermost, during a period when, in words that Bakhtin uses to describe Carnival, 'all hierarchical rank, privileges, norms and prohibitions are suspended' (Bakhtin 1965: 10). Miss Cleothilda's version of a long-established Carnival role is followed by three chapters which also define the characters on which they focus in terms of stereotypical roles: Sylvia is a Princess, Aldrick the eponymous dragon and Fisheye a badjohn. These early chapters, then, follow a pattern in which the characters' staged personae are those of so many Carnival masqueraders. With the novel initially structured around the movement towards the actual occurrence of Carnival, which does not in fact provide a climax, one of the questions it asks is whether the highly individualistic role-players can form a successful ensemble cast or whether they will remain a collection of self-preoccupied individualists. The characters in *Miguel Street*, despite some mutual support systems, never really come together and, although the text's form — a collection of linked short stories — allows for the protagonists of some of the stories to reappear in others, many remain solipsistically isolated in their own stories. *The Lonely Londoners* maintains a delicate balance and, although its episodic structure presents its readers with a series of 'ballads' centred on accounts of particular individuals' lives, the characters' loneliness in London as first-generation migrants also promotes a degree of collectivity: every Sunday morning they congregate in Moses's room in what he jokingly refers to as a 'coming to church' (Selvon 1972: 24).

Lovelace is a good deal more complex in his representation of the issue of community cohesiveness. Shaped by a discourse of 'rebellion and warriorhood' (1979: 59), male identity on the Hill has traditionally had to assert itself through battles with the members of rival steelbands (which in the pre-Independence period operated as gangs) and Fisheye, the badjohn, particularly seeks fulfilment through forms of combat, which are the antithesis of 'unity'. When his girlfriend Yvonne suggests an alternative version of 'All o' we is one', joining up to 'Fight the people who keeping down black people. Fight the government' (1979: 59), Fisheye — lacking political awareness at this point — demurs, feeling that such action would lead to the loss of his reputation as a dangerous man and with this his self-esteem. Changes in the society quickly initiate him into politics, though. He attends Woodford Square meetings and is introduced to another version of the 'All o' we is one' slogan: the People's National Movement (PNM)'s employment of it in the service of a discourse of *national* unity. The dividing line between Yvonne's use of the phrase to suggest that the dispossessed of the Hill should unite to improve their lot and the nationalist political rhetoric that Fisheye encounters in the Woodford Square meetings is a thin one, and Lovelace suggests both the overlap and the divergence between these two uses of the term. This, of course, mirrors the way a calypsonian such as the Mighty Sparrow, who provides at least part of the inspiration for the character of Philo in the *Dragon*, managed to elide potential differences between the more dispossessed sectors of the Afro-Caribbean urban population and the nationalist politicians. In Gordon Rohlehr's words, in the period from 1956 to 1966: 'Sparrow sang mainly to celebrate the faith of the predominantly African urban masses in the new political movement' (Rohlehr 1971: 7).

This convergence of the new nationalist politics and the cultural forms associated with Carnival soon became difficult to maintain, and Lovelace's chapter on Fisheye reflects the transformations that Carnival was undergoing in the years before and immediately after Trinidadian Independence. Older notions of steelband warrior identity break down with the arrival of sponsorship, and Fisheye is disturbed to find Carnival becoming respectable, as it is appropriated by the middle classes: Desperadoes become Gay Desperadoes and he hopes no one will suggest his band should become Gay Calvary Hill; Carnival, which Fisheye regards as 'slum, street corner territory', is taken over by 'light-skinned boys from prosperous families and well-off schools' (1979: 65). Disgusted by this pre-emption of Carnival by the middle classes and unable to understand what the nationalist politicians have 'won', Fisheye reverts to type as a badjohn, but his former status as a culture hero is now an anachronism (1979: 66).

The novel offers two other close studies of manhood in the characters of Philo, the calypsonian, and Aldrick, the dragon. Philo is central in the final chapter, which outlines his rise to fame and commercial success. The placing of this chapter at the end is arguably appropriate as a reflection of the cultural changes attested to by the popularity of Sparrow and their association with the political mood of the nationalist era. Philo's 'Axe Man' calypso evokes Sparrow's 'Village Ram', and more generally he is representative of the changes in aesthetic taste that were occurring around this time.[3] The success he achieves with the 'Axe Man', described as 'a simple metaphor of male sexual conquest' (1979: 112), comes from abandoning his earlier commitment to criticising social deprivation and corruption, and his physical relocation, away from the Hill in the suburb of Diego Martin, also suggests a betrayal of his former ideals, as well as the extent to which the codes of warriorhood and brotherhood, associated with steelband culture, are being eroded in the nationalist era.

In the chapter titled 'The Dragon Dance', battle is joined when Yvonne's advocacy of uniting together to fight the government is embodied in the 'Calvary Hill Nine's' abortive and unplanned attempt at revolution, a fictionalised version of Trinidad's failed 1970 'Black Power' revolution. However, lacking both ideology and organisation, the putative revolutionaries find themselves isolated. This section posits the possibility of transferring the revolutionary potential of Carnival into political action — Aldrick thinks of it as a masquerade and feels he is 'in a dragon costume on Carnival Tuesday' (1979: 177), but any suggestion that Carnival aesthetics can solve social problems is exposed as futile when the authorities decline to intervene, because they have 'trusted these men to fail' (1979: 183).

Of the trio of main characters, Fisheye becomes an anachronism and Philo sells out to commercialism. Aldrick alone seems to maintain a lifestyle that perpetuates the African-based codes of manhood, which appear to offer the possibility of dignity and fulfilment within the Creole society. But, although people turn to him, when the values by which they live are challenged — for example by the Indian Pariag's purchase of a bicycle, an act which is seen as a first step on the road to entrepreneurial consumerism — Aldrick too runs the risk of being seen as a repository of outdated codes of behaviour when he emerges from prison after serving five years for his part in the uprising.

All of the characters discussed so far personify possible responses to the situation of urban deprivation and the attempt to attain dignity through the creativity of music and the culture of warriorhood associated with it. Naipaul also makes extensive use of music in *Miguel Street*, quoting or referring to a dozen calypsos, but doing so in a very different manner from Lovelace.[4] Far from seeing kaiso as a liberating force, Naipaul simply introduces it as a vehicle for choric commentary, sometimes ironic, sometimes more neutrally contrapuntal, and frequently suggesting that Miguel Street is a microcosm of Trinidad. There is no serious engagement with the possibility that the music may offer release or fulfilment to Trinidad's urban populace, and ethnicity is often occluded in the text. Characters such as Hat and Bogart initially seem to be Afro-Caribbean, but comments by Naipaul in his later 'Prologue to An Autobiography' reveal that he based both characters on Indo-Caribbean models, Creolised Indians who had retained few traces of their Hindu origins (Naipaul 1984: 19–20). And curiously, despite the negative nature of Naipaul's vision, from one point of view this elision of ethnicity makes for a less divisive view of Trinidadian society than one finds in Lovelace, albeit by ignoring what most people would see as crucial markers of identity. This said, the *Dragon* does a much better job of squaring up to the realities that lie behind discourses of national unity and Lovelace particularly addresses the issue in the chapter entitled 'The Outsider', in which he focuses on an Indo-Caribbean character. This character's name, Pariag, suggests 'pariah' and this is the role he is forced to occupy. He comes to Port of Spain keen to be absorbed into Creole society, but the extent to which he is constructed as an outsider comes across in the various nicknames attached to him: he is variously called 'Boya', 'Bottles', 'Colts', 'Channa Boy' and 'Crazy Indian'.

Whereas the Creole characters exercise a degree of self-determination through the personae they occupy (badjohn, dragon, and so on), even though their chosen roles are products of Carnival and more general Trinidadian tradition, Pariag's various identities are conferred on him by others and so he emerges as the constructed other of a colonial populace which, despite *its* internal divisions, closes ranks against someone from another community.

So *The Dragon Can't Dance* depicts urban Creole society as practising exclusions, but to what extent is its own practice inclusive? Its careful and discriminating treatment of Pariag and his wife Dolly expands the frame of reference, and so in textual terms they are given a presence that the society of the Hill refuses them in the social world, but the novel is distinctively pessimistic about the possibility of their being incorporated into any meaningful form of 'All o' we is one' discourse. The various people who mouth the phrase use the 'we' pronoun to suggest different notions of community: Miss Cleothilda tries to incorporate herself into a 'we' that comprises herself and her neighbours; Yvonne advocates the bandsmen joining together to fight the common enemy of the government; the nationalist government uses the slogan in a supposedly inclusivist way, glossing over the ethnic, class and economic divisions in the 'we' of the society at large. Of the three versions, Yvonne's communal usage is the only one that the novel takes seriously, but the botched charade of the revolution suggests that this kind of rebellion is futile, little more than a form of temporary Carnival role-play.

So one is left with Carnival itself, the great leveller, as a chronotope in which egalitarianism may possibly be achieved, but Carnival has been appropriated by the middle classes. For all the lyrical prose of its accounts of Carnival and related forms, *The Dragon Can't Dance* remains pessimistic about the possibility of society cohering in any kind of unified way. The culture that Fisheye represents is superseded by the commercialised Carnival values of the nationalist era; Philo sells out to achieve success. Only Aldrick is left as a personification of the ancestral codes of manhood, embodied in his dragon persona. The novel is ambivalent about whether he can sustain this role year-round: he thinks of Ash Wednesday, the day after Carnival, as 'the wickedest day of the year on the Hill' (1979: 129) but, despite the sense of deflation he feels when his two days of being a dragon (1979: 123) are over and his elegiac sense that he is 'the last one, the last symbol of rebellion and threat to confront Port of Spain' (1979: 121) as Carnival becomes increasingly sanitised and respectable, in the first half of the novel Aldrick *does* play the role of dragon year-round. Carnival has him coming into his own, as masqueraders become ancestral masks, forging links back across the Middle Passage with the sacred traditions of West African society, but out of season, as he works on his costume in preparation for Carnival, he engages in a creative activity that preserves and renews the older traditions of Afro-Creole society.

Lovelace's conclusion seems to be that the spirit of rebellion inherent in the version of Trinidad Carnival that had its origins in the freed slaves' struggle against continuing injustice has largely been crushed by the commercialisation of Carnival in the nationalist era, with local politicians having succeeded where the colonial authorities failed. But in one sense the dragon continues to dance: Aldrick's resistance to co-optation suggests that Carnival can still be more than licensed escapism and the novel itself articulates a view which associates Carnival with a view of manhood predicated on African retentions that have been metamorphosed in the Creole present. The novel ends with a report that Sylvia, the Hill's Princess, who is the natural heir to Miss Cleothilda's crown, has gone looking for Aldrick and if one reads the man–woman relationship as a trope for social relations more generally, this suggests a coming together of Aldrick's dragon persona and the promise of the Trinidadian future.

There is, though, little sense of unity in the community. The commercialisation of Carnival and the social codes associated with it seem to have eroded any real sense of the need for the collective. Lovelace's novel gestures towards this need, but the positive aspects of the ending are tempered by a sense that the 'All o' we is one' refrain is a sham. Passing by the shop that Pariag now owns, Aldrick has been tempted to go in and talk to him, but decides against this on the grounds that 'Each man — Pariag included — had the responsibility for his own living, had the responsibility for the world he lived in, and to claim himself and to grow and grow and grow' (1979: 204). Ultimately it seems that the communal ideal is impossible; growth can only come from individual effort.

That, at least, is *The Dragon Can't Dance*'s apparent verdict on the Condition of Trinidad at the time of the nationalist moment. In an interview conducted two years after the publication of the novel, Lovelace commented: 'We do not authorize our own existence ... We respond more than we create, we react more than act. I think our historical situation has made us act "self" for "other"'.[5] Needless to say, such a statement takes issue with the social situation it describes, and Lovelace's approach in the *Dragon* is similar in that it portrays a situation in which most of the residents of Calvary Hill 'act "self" for "other"', while his own aesthetic project, as embodied in the form and structure of the text, outlines an alternative praxis. The novel's panoramic account of the relationships between the individuals who make up its extensive *dramatis personae* moves towards a notion of community that is effectively realised in the constitution and structure of the book, while being represented as unattainable in the immediate present of the *social* world of the Hill, a microcosm for Creole Trinidad. In *Salt*, a novel that goes much further in adumbrating the consequences of the 'historical situation' of Trinidad and their perpetuation in post-Independence public policy-making, Lovelace appears more sanguine about the possibility of achieving a cohesive community, but still views it as an aspirational ideal rather than an attainable reality.

In the intervening years he had published *The Wine of Astonishment* (1982), where much of the emphasis falls on ordinary people's need for leadership in the struggle towards achieving an egalitarian, plural society. Mediated through the consciousness of the novel's narrator Eva, who functions as the voice of her village community, the novel offers two compelling studies of putative leaders, both of whom become alienated from the village. Bolo, a champion stickfighter from pre-war days, becomes embittered when, like Fisheye in the *Dragon*, he sees the cultural norms that have made him a heroic figure vanishing in the face of the new fast-and-loose values encouraged by the 'Yankee dollar'. And, again like Fisheye, he becomes a badjohn, loses the community's respect and eventually destroys himself. Ivan Morton, the most educated boy in the village, is elected to Trinidad's Legislative Council, but instead of fighting for the villagers' rights, he becomes increasingly concerned with feathering his own nest, only remembering his constituents at election time. The novel ends with an election looming and the villagers left to choose between Ivan Morton and two candidates who look even less likely to represent their interests. As in Naipaul's first two novels, *The Mystic Masseur* (1957) and *The Suffrage of Elvira* (1958), universal suffrage has been achieved during the period covered by the novel's action, but the failure of leadership among the emerging generation of politicians leaves people as disenfranchised as ever. However, *unlike* Naipaul's two early novels, the *Wine* does not reject all possibilities for meaningful individual and communal fulfilment. Throughout, the vernacular voice of Eva functions as a *discursive* alternative to the *social* impasse in which the villagers appear to be locked, and the novel ends with the lifting of a ban on Baptist worship, which has been the main rallying-point for the villagers' own, and owned, culture, reopening one important conduit for forging a new Creolised identity, grounded in African values, in the New World.

Salt covers a much broader social and historical canvas and has a more extensive repertory of characters, but follows *The Wine of Astonishment* in placing two contrasted male protagonists, Alford George and Bango, who initially seem to have affinities with Ivan Morton and Bolo respectively, at the centre of its design. Like Ivan Morton, Alford George is a product of the colonial education system and he remains within its fold when he becomes a teacher himself. He can also be seen as an extension of a type that Lovelace had earlier treated in the figure of Mr Warrick, the eponymous hero of his second novel, *The Schoolmaster* (1968). Warrick is a personification of late colonial modernity who succeeds in disrupting the over-idealised calm of the village, Kumaca, to which he brings education. In Kenneth Ramchand's words:

> What Lovelace is really saying in *The Schoolmaster* is that the kind of
> education and progress coming to these islands (for the novel is
> parabolical, Kumaca stands for the island), and the selfhood of those
> whose responsibility and privilege it is to be the means of that
> coming are closely related matters; if we fail to take this into
> account, there can be no moral authority, only pappyshow, betrayal
> and dreadful autumn for the patriarch. (Ramchand 1979: 11)

The Gabriel García Márquez allusion here may read awkwardly, but the emphasis on education failing to provide 'moral authority' seems to echo Lovelace's interview comment that 'we do not authorize our own existence' and Warrick anticipates those of aspects of Alford George which, in Alison Donnell's view, make him a Naipaulian mimic man, although this assessment *finally* seems harsh in relation to the later character.[6]

As the novel progresses, Alford George emerges as an altogether more complex study of late colonial modernity grappling with the forces of change that are occurring around the time of the nationalist moment. The problems surrounding the colonially educated protagonist's capacity to serve as a people's leader who can help to bring about genuine community cohesiveness remain to the fore, but Alford is presented more sympathetically than Warrick and Ivan Morton. Comparing him to Ivan Morton, M. Keith Booker and Dubravka Juraga relate him to Gramsci's comments on 'the crucial importance of intellectuals in leading the fight for justice' (Booker and Juraga 2001: 181). The reference to a political theorist whose work was influential in the founding of the Subaltern Studies movement is interesting, given Lovelace's attempt to give voice to extra-colonial discourses (see Guha 1982: vii). But Booker and Juraga follow Gramsci in emphasising the particular problems faced by intellectuals from the 'peasant' classes: 'even intellectuals who originate in the peasantry tend, by virtue of the process that makes them intellectuals, to lose their sense of organic connection to their former class' (2001: 181). They support this by quoting a passage from Gramsci, which suggests that intellectuals who 'originate in the peasantry' are co-opted by other social groups: 'the mass of the peasantry ... does not elaborate its own "organic" intellectuals ... although it is from the peasantry that other social groups draw many of their intellectuals' (cited in Booker and Juraga 2001, from Gramsci 1971: 6). Applying this to *The Wine of Astonishment* and *Salt*, it seems to offer a reasonable summary of what happens to Ivan Morton, but Lovelace's account of Alford George's career, which seems to be following a similar trajectory until the later stages of the novel, is a more nuanced and intricate study of the potential of the village-born, colonially educated intellectual, and it is complemented by the figure of the unintellectual Bango, who is a more obvious repository of subaltern values.

As a boy, Alford feels 'alien' and 'inferior' in his society, and 'dreams of the other world', an imagined site of fulfilment, constructed from a 'legion of heroes' that ranges from those of Greek myth to those in American comic books (Lovelace 1996: 28, 27). When he subsequently apprentices himself to a career as a schoolmaster, feeling that this is the first step towards the outside 'world', his resolve is only shaken once; this happens when he encounters the rhetoric of the National Party and its Leader (fairly obvious fictional surrogates for Trinidad's PNM and Dr Eric Williams), who hold out the promise of creating the 'world' at home. Lovelace stops short of offering a direct critique of the Nationalist Party's agenda, allowing its promise of achieving unity and self-fulfilment within the society, as seen through the mediating consciousness of Alford George, to stand as a viable alternative to a greater extent than is the case in *The Dragon Can't Dance*. Once again, though, he suggests that the ruling post-Independence faction's rhetoric fails to incorporate Trinidadian subalterns into its version of national unity. As with Miss Cleothilda in the earlier novel, one has the sense of a self-serving use of the language of communal cohesion. Lovelace's inventory of the elements that have gone into the Party's 'mantras' — a mélange ranging from classical thinkers, iconic 'third-world' figures and, incongruously, random if exotic place-names ('Socrates, Tacitus, Timbuktu, Tagore, Delhi, Nkrumah, Nehru, Gandhi, Senghor, Toussaint, Césaire') (1996: 35) — suggests that it too is importing cultural baggage from overseas, although the Leader deftly synthesises Western ideology with elements from the local Carnival culture in a discourse of national unity, based on a personality cult.

However, the novel both exposes and reinstates the possibility of the politics of leadership bringing about a more inclusivist and unified society, since it offers Alford George as an alternative to the prime minister, very obviously so in a chapter in which he sits 'in the PM's Chair' (1996: 166–88) but more generally in its account of his being persuaded to become a National Party candidate and, as Minister of Social and Environmental rehabilitation, developing an inter-racial vision, in which Carnival arts assume a central importance:

> See these islands with new eyes, he encouraged. See past the slums, see past the racial divisions, see past the present ownership of resources, see a people who have been thrown together and are working to make this a new world place ... He wanted to make the steel band the central symbol of the nation, an icon encapsulating our struggle for freedom to express ourselves in our own idiom. He wanted the Laventille slums transformed into a shrine to the steel band with art galleries and restaurants and a theatre. He wanted the Carnival arts placed at the centre of the educational system. There is no profit in imitation, he said. What we have to do is see ourselves

with new eyes, see a land where it is possible to create a new people and a culture of prosperity and dignity and freedom. (1996: 128)

Just as in the *Dragon*, the dividing line between the nationalist political rhetoric of the Woodford Square meetings and Yvonne's use of the 'All o' we is one' cliché is a thin one, so here Alford George's vision overlaps with that of the prime minister, but crucially — unlike his — it makes no appeal to imported cultural and intellectual traditions. And significantly, it expresses a view that seems close to Lovelace's own aesthetic practice in the novel. The syntax and rhythms of *Salt* articulate 'our struggle for freedom to express ourselves in our own idiom' in various ways: in sentences, such as the one that opens Chapter 4, which snake down the page, threatening to end but meandering onwards in a manner that resists 'standard' notions of grammatical closure; in a style that wanders from character to character, interweaving multiple stories; and sometimes, again as in Chapter 4, where the title 'Eye' foregrounds perception without indicating which Eye/I is the narrator at this moment, leaving it unclear which of the text's many voices is speaking. Lovelace has likened his use of multiple voices to those that 'appear in a Shango ceremony' (cited in Hewson 2004: 2), and the net effect of his polyphonic Babel of voices is to give the sense of a community trying to talk itself into existence.[7] The focus of interest changes repeatedly, and biographies of minor characters are introduced late on in the novel, seemingly to direct readers to expand their view of what constitutes the Creole community by recognising both its diversity and the distinctive individuality of its various members. Chapters 11 and 12, respectively centred on the French Creole Carabon and the Indo-Caribbean Lochan, serve both to expand the repertory of the novel's characters and enlarge *its* inclusivist nationalist project.

As a potential people's leader, Alford George is committed to Carnival arts, inter-racial dialogue and the need for expression 'in our idiom', but Lovelace eventually creates a distance between Alford and what he, as author, represents as the National Party's espousal of similar ideals. Nevertheless, he remains a Gramscian 'peasant' intellectual, in danger of being alienated from his 'sense of organic connection to [his] former class' and dialogue with his complementary opposite, Bango, is needed to give full expression to the people's 'idiom'. Through the interaction of the characters of Bango and Alford George, Lovelace suggests what is needed to take the society forward. Bango is a carnivalesque storyteller, with a developed sense of subaltern history, a commitment to Trinidadian popular culture (including steelband, cricket and stickfighting) and a stubborn resistance to succumbing to what he sees as the continuing condition of 'unfreedom'. In the opening chapter, he is introduced as the teller of an ancestral subaltern legend, the story of his ancestor Guinea John who escaped slavery by flying back to Africa, 'taking with him the mysteries of levitation and flight'

(1996: 3). This, though, is just part of Bango's story, which includes accounts of Columbus's arrival in the New World and Emancipation Day, when his great-grandfather JoJo was arrested for cursing the governor for 'granting him a halfway freedom instead of giving him the liberation that was his due' (1996: 45), and relates these historical events to the present social situation, in which the problem is no longer 'how to keep people in captivity. It was how to set people at liberty' (1996: 7). Bango emerges as a Trinidadian griot, a contemporary incarnation of JoJo, equally unwilling to accept anything less than full freedom, which he feels should take the form of reparation through the openly acknowledged granting of land that he feels is rightfully his. In the novel's central encounter, he lectures Alford George 'in the PM's Chair' about the need to accept an alternative oral historiography: 'They write their history down and you don't ask them nothing. You swallow it down even when it don't make sense. But as soon as Blackpeople start to talk, you want date and name in the story' (1996: 185). The conversation persuades Alford George both of the justice of Bango's case and of the historically determined inequalities that have been perpetuated in the post-Independence nationalist politics, in which he has become implicated.

The novel moves to a conclusion amid Independence Day celebrations, with Alford, who had been dumb as a boy, realising that 'Bango had kept the self that he, Alford, had lost' and in an epiphanic moment feeling 'shame, at himself and his community that had left it to Bango alone to be outraged at the indignity its people continued to live under' (1996: 257). So now, aligning himself with Bango — who, as on an earlier occasion, has assembled an inter-racial troop to represent the different races of the island as *his* personal statement of Independence and communal unity — Alford George attacks the 'conditions of unfreedom' (1996: 257) under which ordinary Trinidadians are still consigned to live. The novel ends with the 'I' narrator of this section marching with Alford George and Bango and his troop, and hoping that Carabon and Lochan will join in this inter-racial action. Significantly, whether they will or not is left as an open question and there is no suggestion that there can be an easy reconciliation of the ethnic divisions that have plagued the society.

Nevertheless, the ending of *Salt* remains more affirmative than that of *The Dragon Can't Dance*, since the journey towards a genuinely egalitarian vision of national unity, rooted in the Creole community's popular culture and led by a subaltern figure who has refused to surrender to colonial appropriations, is underway. Significantly, it is represented by the trope of the march which, like the wandering, exploratory quality of Lovelace's prose style, puts the emphasis on movement and progress, rather than consolidated achievement, in the quest to arrive at a point where 'All o' we is one'.

Notes

1. I am grateful to Aaron Love for directing me back to this interview.
2. Other retellings occur in The Mighty Wonder's calypso 'Follow Me Children' (see White 1975: 50), and in Wynter (1962) and Khan (1987).
3. Similarly, the trope of African cannibalism in 'I Am the Ape Man Not Tarzan' (1979: 230) evokes Sparrow's 'Congo Man' and his 'Hooligans' is reminiscent of Sparrow's tongue-in-cheek assertion of his respectability in calypsos such as 'Carnival'. Sparrow calypsos are more explicitly alluded to in *Salt*, which includes references to 'Get to Hell Outa Here' (1996: 115, 117) and 'Jean and Dinah' (1996: 134).
4. For further discussions, see Thieme (1981) and — reprinted with alterations — Thieme (1987: 14–33).
5. Earl Lovelace, 'The Baptists Preserved the African Roots of Our Music' *People* (March 1981), quoted in O'Callaghan (n.d.: 9).
6. '... although Alford is Naipaul's mimic man in a way that Forster [in Selvon's *An Island is a World*] never is, Alford does not migrate and Lovelace's novel is not an account of the damage and trauma that has been enacted on the colonial subject by the epistemic violence of the colonial motherland' (Donnell 2006: 123).
7. See too the reference to 'chanting voices in the Shango palais' in the first paragraph of Chapter 4 of *Salt* (Lovelace 1996: 44).

References

Bakhtin, Mikhail (1965) *Rabelais and His World*, trans. Helene Iswolsky (Cambridge, MA: MIT Press).

Booker, M. Keith, and Juraga, Dubravka (2001) *The Caribbean Novel in English: An Introduction* (Oxford: James Currey).

Dance, Daryl Cumber (1992) *New World Adams: Conversations with Contemporary West Indian Writers* (Leeds: Peepal Tree).

Donnell, Alison (2006) *Twentieth-Century Caribbean Literature: Critical Moments in Anglophone Literary History* (Abingdon: Routledge).

Gramsci, Antonio (1971) *Selections from the Prison Notebooks*, ed. and trans. Quintin Hoare and Geoffrey Nowell Smith (New York: International Publishers).

Guha, Ranajit (1982) 'Preface' to *Subaltern Studies* 1 (Delhi: Oxford University Press).

Hewson, Kelly (2004) 'An Interview with Earl Lovelace', *Postcolonial Text*, http://journals.sfu.ca/pocol/index.php/pct/article/view/344/122.
Hill, Errol (1972) *The Trinidad Carnival: Mandate for a National Theatre* (Austin: University of Texas Press).
Khan, Ismith (1987) *The Crucifixion* (Leeds: Peepal Tree).
Lovelace, Earl (1979 [1968]) *The Schoolmaster* (London: Heinemann).
—— (1979) *The Dragon Can't Dance* (London: André Deutsch).
—— (1982) *The Wine of Astonishment* (London: André Deutsch).
—— (1996) *Salt* (London: Faber and Faber).
Naipaul, V.S. (1984) *Finding the Centre: Two Narratives* (London: André Deutsch).
—— (1971 [1959]) *Miguel Street* (Harmondsworth: Penguin).
—— (1957) *The Mystic Masseur* (London: André Deutsch).
—— (1958) *The Suffrage of Elvira* (London: André Deutsch).
O'Callaghan, Evelyn (n.d. [1987?]) *The Lovelace 'Prologue': Ideology in a Nutshell* (Coventry: University of Warwick Occasional Papers in Caribbean Studies).
Ramchand, Kenneth (1979) 'Introduction' to Earl Lovelace, *The Schoolmaster* (London. Heinemann).
Rohlehr, Gordon (1971) 'Calypso and Politics', *Moko*, no. 73, 29 October.
Selvon, Sam (1972 [1956]) *The Lonely Londoners* (London: Longman).
Thieme, John (1981) 'Calypso Allusions in Naipaul's *Miguel Street*', *Kunapipi*, vol. 3, no. 2.
—— (1987) *The Web of Tradition: Uses of Allusion in V.S. Naipaul's Fiction* (Aarhus: Dangaroo/London: Hansib).
White, Landeg (1975) *V.S. Naipaul: A Critical Introduction* (London: Macmillan).
Wynter, Sylvia (1962) *The Hills of Hebron* (London: Jonathan Cape).

10
ENGAGING THE WORLD: LOVELACE'S *SALT* AS A CARIBBEAN EPIC

Louis James

With *Salt*, which won the Commonwealth Writers' Prize for its area in 1996, Lovelace engaged with a new kind of fiction. Each of his previous novels had been centred on specific areas of contemporary Trinidad society, and on a particular aspect of the island's culture. But *Salt* moved across many aspects of island life and some 400 years of Trinidad history, from the first slave plantations to post-Independence politics. *Salt* touched on many lives, and was ultimately concerned not with individuals so much as with the community as a whole. Where Lovelace's early work had focused on life histories, *Salt* attempted a national epic.

I define 'epic' in its Caribbean form as a work of the imagination conceived on a heroic scale, in which individual narratives become representative of the cultures within which they have evolved. However, in contrast to the European and Asian models, which feature great men and gods, the Caribbean epic is given life by the peasantry of the region, by the heroism of the common people and by their place in the natural environment. Caribbean epics, by the time of *Salt*, also resound with the echoes of other national epics. Derek Walcott, when he received the Nobel Prize for his masterpiece *Omeros* (1990), reflected on the 'fragments of epic memory' which composed the culture of the region. He recalled watching a folk festival in Felicity, a small village in rural Trinidad, at which the villagers re-enacted the Indian saga of the *Ramayana*. As they recreated the story in voice and action, they entered the cultural world of an Indian people of another time and place. Unself-consciously, without any pretension to create high dramatic art, the villagers returned the third century BC saga to its origins in the life of the common people. Distanced by time and place, these 'epic memories' gained a new poignancy in fragmentation:

> Break a vase, and the love that resembles the fragments is stronger
> than that love which took its symmetry for granted when it was

whole ... Antillean art is this restoration to of our shattered histories, our shards of vocabulary, our archipelago become a synonym for pieces broken off from the original continent. (Walcott 1998: 69)

Walcott traced the epic form back to the beginnings of modern Caribbean literature in the work of St-John Perse, who had been born in Guadeloupe in 1887. The imagined world of his long poem *Anabase* (1924), with its barren wastes of 'poisonous lakes, horsemen burnoosed in sandstorms', was very different from the 'cool Caribbean mornings' he remembered from childhood. But in his instinctive creation of a new world literature out of the fragments of the old, St-John Perse anticipated the villagers of Felicity whom Walcott watched recreating one of the most ancient Indian sagas under the blue skies of present-day Trinidad. Referring to perhaps the most powerful of the island's traditions, Carnival, Walcott comments:

From the *Ramayana* to *Anabasis*, from Guadeloupe to Trinidad, all that archaeology of fragments lying around, from the broken African kingdoms, from the crevasses of Canton, from Syria and Lebanon, [remain] vibrating not under the earth but in our raucous, demotic streets. (Walcott 1998: 79)

While the conventions of the colonial period led generations to believe that the Caribbean had been incapable of generating anything resembling a culture, or a civilisation, the new Caribbean epic asserted the creative potential of its peoples.[1] Aimé Césaire's *Cahier d'un retour au pays natal* (1939) opens in a poverty-stricken hovel in Martinique, but envisions dawn breaking on to a world cataclysmically recreated by the spirit of the resurgent black peoples, by the forces of *négritude*. Césaire was to have a seminal impact on the emergent Caribbean Francophone and Hispanic literatures. He shifted the focus of the region's writers from a preoccupation with material reality into an exploration of their *consciousness* of that material world, and in so doing disrupting the given logics of Western history, probing the psyche, the subconscious and the phenomenology of Caribbean time and place, and everywhere discovering the human potential for survival and growth. Offering a radical alternative to a European obsession with order and control, Césaire's epic imagination privileged energy and emotion. Politically subversive, it focused not on individuality but community.

In Haiti, Césaire influenced Jacques Rouman's peasant novel *Gouverneurs de la rosée* (1944, translated as *Masters of the Dew* in 1947); and in his native Martinique he left his mark on Edouard Glissant's *Le Lezard* (1958; *The Ripening*, 1985).

From Glissant's radical theories, a novelistic tradition evolved in the Francophone Caribbean that persists to this day in the work of writers such as Maryse Condé from Guadeloupe, whose *La Vie Scelerate* (1987; *Tree of Life*, 1994) represented an important moment in the feminisation of the Caribbean epic tradition. In Cuba, Alejo Carpentier's *Los Pasos Perdidos* (1953; *The Lost Steps*, 1956) invoked the hidden life of the South American interior to interrogate the values of the Old World civilisation. From the Caribbean coast of Colombia — an integral part of an 'expansive' Caribbean — Gabriel García Márquez's *Cien Años de Solidad* (1967; *One Hundred Years of Solitude*, 1970) explored communal history in terms of the 'marvellous real' which was to have a profound, electrifying effect on the literatures of the region (see Zamora and Fari, 1995; Bénitez-Rojo 1996).

Writers in the more pragmatic Anglophone tradition were slow to respond to this visionary perspective. An independent and largely unacknowledged pioneer was the Guyanese writer Edgar Mittelholzer, whose epic series beginning with *Children of Kaywana* (1952) combined massive historical research with exploration of psychic violence and the disorienting presence of the jungle world to venture beyond the conventions of any realist models of writing. This was followed up in Wilson Harris's seminal *Guyana Quartet* (1960–3), which explored the mythic constitution of the New World, and investigated the human possibilities generated within extremes of social fragmentation. 'What in my view of the West Indian in depth is this sense of subtle links, a series of subtle and nebulous links which are latent within him, the latent ground of old and new personalities' (Harris 1967: 31). The Caribbean peoples, he argued, possessed instinctive bonds with the natural world. 'The smallest area one envisages, island or village, prominent ridge or buried valley, flatland or heartland, is charged immediately with the openness of the imagination ...' (1967: 28). In *Palace of the Peacock* (1960), as he progresses into the interior the demonic lust of Donne, the colonial oppressor is transformed by self-knowledge, and by deepening understanding of the different racial personalities of Guyana, reflected within the crew of his boat. Climbing the giant waterfall at the journey's end, transcendental love transforms a history of oppression into an alternative vision of spiritual quest, and the colonialist's 'heart of darkness' fades into El Dorado, the City of Gold, Celestial City.

Harris's style has proved inimitable. But his work has had a liberating impact on younger Caribbean writers, including Lawrence Scott in *Witchbroom* (1992) and Pauline Melville in *The Ventriloquist's Tale* (1997). Yet quite other epic perspectives have also emerged in the region. Wilson Harris, like Derek Walcott in *Omeros*, moved through Caribbean specificity to find — beyond it — a universal human psyche and a shared collective unconscious. But Lamming's *Season of*

Adventure (1970) and *Natives of My Person* (1972), for example, like Kamau Brathwaite's great poetic trilogy *The Arrivants* (1973), were rooted in a discernibly Caribbean time, encompassing Africa and the Middle Passage as constituent elements of modern West Indian life. Much earlier, and conforming to a more conventional historical epic envisioning an independent national identity, V.S. Reid's *New Day* (1949) celebrated Jamaican nationhood emerging out of the horrors of the colonial past and, more specifically, out of the trauma of the Morant Bay rebellion of 1865.

Strands from many of these conflicting epic forms, as we will see, are to be found in Earl Lovelace's *Salt*. But the novel also strikes out on to new ground. The great wave of literary creativity that followed the granting of national independence to Caribbean territories reflected the exuberance of the discovery that, with the passing of the colonial era, a great fund of creative energy lay latent in the common people. Movements spearheaded by, among others, Louise Bennett, Samuel Selvon and Kamau Brathwaite liberated writers so that they could build on the resources of popular culture and of the 'nation language' which previously had been despised and denigrated by the colonial authorities. But in 1996, when *Salt* was published, the Old World still remained obstinately implicated in the New. Over four decades of self-government, the new nations of the Caribbean had struggled to relieve the social tensions and poverty left by colonial rule. They had faced the break-up of the Caribbean Federation, and suffered from the persistent neocolonialism of Europe and the United States, and the pressures of IMF economics. After the celebrations, there came a period of sober reflection. It is this Caribbean that Lovelace addresses in *Salt*: the collapse of the nationalist dream.

When many fellow writers emigrated to Europe or North America in search of fame and creative opportunity, Lovelace remained immersed in the life of his island. In 1980 he described himself as 'largely a self-educated person', in childhood voraciously reading whatever books he could find (Dance 1986: 276). Where the British educational system directed most writers towards English writers, Lovelace preferred American writers for their vitality, drawn initially to Faulkner and Hemingway. His literary apprenticeship came as a proofreader for a local publishing firm, and then, like Wilson Harris, he worked in the island interior as a government forestry ranger, gaining knowledge of life in its remote villages he later was to put to creative use in his fiction. He was never self-consciously a 'literary' author. He drew on his experience of drama and journalism as much as of prose fiction, and the vivid speech of the common people, the island idioms of calypso and Carnival, flowed instinctively into his orally based prose (see Rohlehr 1970, 1992). While many West Indian authors felt that the role of an artist isolated them from their roots, Lovelace began and ended within the experience of his community.[2] He felt the Caribbean writer had a particular responsibility to support traditional — local — social values threatened by the dehumanising effects of the modern era. As he wrote in 1984:

> I think we must see that life is much more complex, much more textured than the straight line of technological advance called progress. We must see that while technological advance brings life, it also brings death, and most importantly that while it provides services, it does not provide meaning ... Two things strike me in a very personal and disturbing way today: the breakdown of the group, and the loss of revolutionary fervour in much of the world. I suppose this goes hand in hand. (Lovelace 1984: 3–4)

While countering the effects of modern advance required political action, Lovelace was aware that politics by itself was not enough. Politicians, he maintained, created predictive programmes that simplified the human condition, were vulnerable to their own personal ambitions, and were out of touch with the constantly shifting realities of everyday life. The crucial role of the creative writer was then to envisage and explore human possibilities and to discover a public voice in which the latent aspirations of the people could be articulated. Lovelace has declared that starting 'from where we are, with the experiences that we have, what we share is language, imagination' (Lovelace 1984: 4). His successive novels, to adapt George Eliot's phrase, have been 'a set of experiments in life'. The name Walter Castle, that of the main character in *While Gods are Falling* (1965), echoed the title of George Lamming's *In the Castle of My Skin* (1953). Both Lamming's G. and Lovelace's Walter painfully seek selfhood in a society fragmented by a legacy of slave culture and colonialism. But where G. moves into exile abroad, Walter — at first despairing of life in a Port of Spain slum — finds a new sense of purpose when he takes personal responsibility for helping a teenager unjustly charged with murder. Lovelace rooted his hopes for social change in the communal life of the people. In this he was in sympathy with radical shifts in Trinidad in the 1970s and 1980s. But where the government of Eric Williams's People's National Movement (the PNM) pushed for a wholesale return to the popular culture of calypso and Carnival, Lovelace was sceptical. Cultures change within developing societies, and so do the consequent political imperatives. In his novel *The Wine of Astonishment* (1982), the power of the Spiritual Baptists' ecstatic worship, suppressed as a threat to public order in 1917, fails to return when the ban is lifted in 1951. But, he insists, the old inspiration appears elsewhere, in unexpected, different, displaced locations in the contemporary nation society: in this instance, Lovelace suggests, in the new sound of the steelbands. The narrator realises it is 'that same Spirit that we miss in our church ... and listening to them, my heart swell and it is like resurrection morning' (Lovelace 1983: 146). In *The Dragon Can't Dance* (1979), the spirit of popular resistance embodied in the Carnival dragon loses its meaning as the event changes, and Aldrick — who has carried its mask as Carnival's most zealous upholder — has to abandon the past in order to search for a new selfhood.

The need for society constantly to renew its quest for justice and humanity is central to *Salt*. The title has several meanings. It recalls is the bitter sweat of the slaves and of the indentured labourers imported to work the plantations. Implicit also is the New Testament parable of salt as the human spirit, useless if it has lost its vital identity: 'Ye are the salt of the earth; but if salt has lost its taste, how shall its saltness be restored?' (Matthew 5:13). But the most explicit reference is the salt of the circumambient, undrinkable sea, the ocean that physically binds together the island peoples, both imprisoning and liberating them into their unique community.[3] The book is in two sections. The first covers the evolution of the island society up to its Independence in 1962 under Eric Williams, and the second explores the deepening search for national identity as his leadership, and that of his party, falter. The subject required a new form. Lovelace sought to go beyond a conventional novelistic focus on the individual, and turned towards the historical vision that Faulkner brought to the Deep South. He also largely abandoned the materialist focus of the conventional European novel that privileged physical appearance. Apart from broad categories of race, there are few physical descriptions of individuals, their dress or their manners, and accounts of locales are limited to the natural environment.

Nor is Lovelace concerned with the classic 'well-structured novel'. Roberta F. Knowles wrote that Lovelace's plot 'is, at times, downright puzzling ... For one thing, it takes a few chapters just to figure out who is telling the story and what the timeline is' (Knowles, 1999: 268). However, Lovelace is not writing a conventional novel, but rather a form of folk drama in prose in which different voices speak for the community rather than for the individual. The first-person narrator, who irregularly alternates with the omniscient author, appears to be the son of a black father, Bertie (who is barely introduced), and his wife Pearl. But this narrator is given no name, and all we know that he eventually becomes a barber (1996: 76). Undefined, he becomes everyman and everywoman. Lovelace, like Brecht with his *Verwremdungseffekt* (dramatic distancing), here denies us the satisfaction of a first-person story in order to direct us to his underlying concern, which is with the community as a whole, composed as it is of the entirety of its disparate, antagonistic elements.

Like the narrative voice, which shifts to give a sense of the island's multiple perspectives, the style itself is fluid. At one point it invokes a precise moment:

'"Where am I?" Myrtle asked herself. "Where is myself?"' (1996: 157). At another point, sentences snake down long paragraphs, only punctuated by intermittent commas, invoking a timeless consciousness:

> He had walked in the heights of the forest where the monkeys howled and snakes waited at the end of the traces near fruit trees, where cut vines sprung water, high up where parrots feasted on balata trees, into this far space where bands of wild hogs root among wild yams and up to the early paths of streams, high above the waterfall in among the guatacaire and mora trees, among the angelin and the perfumed laurier into a freedom precarious like the fern rooted on stone, all about it rooted itself anywhere it could hold, all about him, everywhere, breaking forth in the songs of birds, in the brilliance of flowers, ants crawling, with helicoptering honeybees, until after three days wandering, one morning with dawn breaking he saw at the side of a mora tree the huge eyes of a half-naked boy with his brother's face looking at him. (1996: 178)

Parts of the novel are made up of conventional historical narrative. But it opens in the temporal dimension of eighteenth-century folk memory, where Guinea John is described putting 'two corn cobs under his armpits and flew away to Africa, taking with him the mysteries of levitation and flight' (1996: 3, 169). Later, when knowledge of government corruption disturbs popular confidence, a woman sees the dragon weathervane on the government Red House in Port of Spain come to life in order to seize a pigeon, and a reported cataclysm of disasters terrifies the islanders (1996: 238–40). The emergent history of Trinidad is represented by a wall covered with portraits of eminent figures in public life, and by a huge mural celebrating the country's diversity and achievement (1996: 125–7). In contrast, political speeches by the members of the 'National Party' (a reference to Eric Williams's vision of Caribbean history) show the Caribbean as 'a new world puking blood, murky with corruption' (1996: 153). Costumed Carnival bands and annual independence marches bridge past and future and, as they re-enact different roles, further shift and exchange social identities. Everything has to be examined, revalued.

The natural environment itself plays a decisive part in the narrative, and the revolutionary Bango feels that even 'the sky, the sea and every green leaf and tangle of vines sing freedom' (1996: 5). It is valuable here to compare *Salt* with another great Caribbean novel, V.S. Naipaul's *A House for Mr Biswas* (1961). Throughout the story, Biswas struggles to bring meaning to a life constantly disintegrating amid the bourgeois clutter of colonised Trinidad, and his final triumph is to create a physical structure within which he and his family's lives 'would be ordered, their memories coherent' (Naipaul 1969: 581). But in *Salt*, personal meaning can only be found by those who submit themselves to change. Where Biswas ends up in his jerry-built house, Bango and Myrtle establish a chaotic home in the forest which is constantly coming into shape, where 'the back door was an open space, the front door swung on a single hinge and to open or shut it you had to lie it into place' (1996: 140).

Through the book's language and imaginative reconstructions, we gain a sharpened awareness of the great diversity of the Trinidad communities:

> In his speeches, pursuing his central theme of people looking at themselves and their islands afresh [Alford] called for people exchanges, between rich and poor; Indian and African and Chinese and French Creole and Syrian; between Caroni and Laventille, Morant and Goodwood Park, Elleslie Park and John John; Morvant and Carpichaima, Trou Macaque and Rio Claro; Roxborough and Cascadu; Canaan and Matura. (1996: 123)

Lovelace represents the three main ethnic elements in Trinidad society through specific family histories. The white landowners, the inheritors of the slave plantations, appear in the Carabons. Lovelace shows that the plantation owners, facing financial hardship and physical danger at the time of slave emancipation, had a very different view of the situation from those, however high-minded, in remote London. Nor, he insists, has Independence solved the problems of land-ownership. If land was to be restored to the rightful owners, were not these the massacred Caribs and Arawaks? How could the land be now redistributed without introducing new inequalities and injustices? Chapter 11 is given over to the birthday party for the old landowner, Adolph Carabon. This is attended by his lawyer son, Michael, and by his youngest son, also named Adolph, although nicknamed Myrrh. Michael wants to solve the land issue in legal terms, but the more perceptive Myrrh finds himself in an ambivalent position. His inherited status as a white is compromised in a predominantly black society, and he is aware that he is addressed 'with an undertone of condescension, setting him up as a mamaguy Captain Marvel, a pappyshow Tarzan, his talents making him the inferior, his earnestness making him a arse; and that was how it was' (1996: 200). However, he realises too that: 'We have to live here' (1996: 216). In a double gesture, he embraces Michael as a commitment to the legal process, while at the same time preparing to find a new social identity as he joins the Independence Day march alongside the Indians and Africans.

The Indians brought into Trinidad to supply plantation labour after emancipation are introduced by Moon and his descendants. Moon's name is not obviously Indian, and suggests an island confusion between Indians and Chinese: he has become deracinated from his ethnic roots. But his Hindu sensibility is revealed in his love of ritual and drama, and he turns the sidewalk in front of his shop into 'the stage for the carnival pantomimes of Police and thief, Babydoll and Jabmassie' (1996: 221). Like Naipaul's Biswas, he has a mystical delight in natural objects — 'he loved the look of bamboo, he feel of it ... He loved the smell of bread' (1996: 221). Constantly active, he 'loved the idea of craftsmanship, of work, of all the various wonderful stupid things that people made with their hands' (1996: 221). But, unlike Biswas, he is able to become a successful entrepreneur. He turns even disaster to his advantage, and when a drunken truck driver demolishes his shop and puts him on crutches, he extracts from the government compensation that allows him to move into a bigger shop in which to employ his wife, sisters and children. Becoming financially successful, he remains politically naïve. When he tries to buy votes by handing out wholesale free credit, he is cheated of his loans and is defeated in the election. However, he is not embittered, and in his final years he begins to recover his ancestral roots. He is found dead sitting, a smile on his face, 'bare backed like Mahatma Gandhi, his head wrapped in a white cloth, with his favourite tall boots on his feet and a pair of binoculars in his hand' (1996: 226).

Two generations later, his great-grandson Sonan has to reconcile his Asian selfhood with his multicultural location in an independent Trinidad. Cricket reveals his political difficulties as he finds his skills as a batsman dissolving when called on to play for his school or town. Before he can represent others, he has to be sure of himself. A political crisis projects him towards power. Moon's beneficent intentions are belatedly recognised, bringing support for an Indian candidate. As the corruption of the National Party comes to be confronted publicly, Sonan is propelled forward as a Democratic Party candidate. Placed on a rally rostrum, he feels 'he was the one to make the difference' (1996: 242). But, like Moon before him, he too is politically naïve. He begins to speak from his deepest convictions. The party officials are horrified by his departure from the party line, but then realise that the matter was of no concern as no one could hear him. 'What he was saying was drowned out by the chutney tassa calypso music, coming from the enthusiasm of a people who would not be denied the victory they were scenting for the first time' (1996: 243).

Lovelace's most extended treatment is given to those of African origin. The ex-slaves are traced from Guinea John, a rebel slave and Shango priest in the seventeenth century, through his great-grandson Jo-Jo who lives through the 1834 slave emancipation, to emerge, three generations on, into the present with three brothers, descendants of Guinea John: Bango, who marries Myrtle; Dixon who marries May; and the barely mentioned Bertie, the husband of Pearl. Each is an inheritor of the unresolved crises created by the plantation past. Dixon works his life away in the futile hope of making enough money as a labourer to buy the land he cultivates. The spirit of African resistance lives on in Bango, who is too proud to receive a handout of land that would ignore the past injustices of slavery. His anger channels itself into organising annual semi-military marches each year on Independence Day. For much of the story, these appear to have no specific object, and achieve nothing. They run like a theme through the book, underlining both the need for change and the absence of a vision that would give a meaning to change, until at the end they become the triumphant focus for a unifying nation.

None of the three main ethnic components of post-Independence Trinidad peoples can in themselves shape the islands' future. The character of Alford George, in this context, assumes a strategic significance. Alford is racially African, but life in modern Trinidad has left him without a clear identity. He is an anti-hero, clumsy, unsure of himself. Yet his dogged determination turns his weaknesses into a kind of triumph. A physical failure at playing cricket, he is relegated to scoring and umpiring, but makes such a success of this that, although he never plays a single game, he becomes an indispensable figure in the local cricket scene. Lacking a social niche, he throws himself into self-improvement with the indiscriminate earnestness of Naipaul's Mr Biswas:

> He bought a book called *Improve your Word Power* ... He read the sonnets of Shakespeare. He read the novels of Marie Corelli, *The Decline and Fall of the Roman Empire, Of Human Bondage,* the essays of William Hazlitt. He bought an umbrella ... Free to prepare for the world, he began to lift weights, to pull strands under the correspondence tutelage of Charles Atlas, the universal strongman. He acquired the habit of drinking raw eggs in with Guinness stout and condensed milk. (1996: 33–6)

Yet his enthusiasm for knowledge enables him to progress through this mix of cultures and to become an effective and obedient, if over-eager, schoolteacher. But training his charges to become *like him* induces in him a crisis. He impulsively leaves his post to protest that the attention given to prospective Exhibition winners discriminates against the education of the other pupils, dressing in white and conducting a month-long fast outside out parliament house. His Quixotic action verges on the absurd. But his actions finally win the day from an embarrassed government, and he himself sets out on the path to political power in the independent government of the National Party.

Alford's career represents Lovelace's critique of Eric Williams's place in Trinidad's history. Williams's intellectual brilliance, crystallised into his famous slogan, 'Massa Day Done' — a phrase that is repeatedly invoked in Lovelace's novel — enabled him to lead Trinidad from the formation of the People's National Movement in 1955, to his becoming the first prime minister of the independent nation in 1962, a post he held until his death in 1967. From July 1955 he reached out to the people in his famous public lectures and demonstrations, given in the heart of Port of Spain, at the so-called University of Woodford Square. Yet he remained too much the academic to have the common touch, and his growing isolation from the people was exacerbated by his increasing autocracy, as seen in his famous response to his critics when he refused, in 1965, to sack a minister for his high-handed behaviour: 'If you all don't like it,' snapped Williams, 'get the hell out of here.' The incident is enshrined in two of the Mighty Sparrow's calypsos, and is repeated in *Salt*.[4]

The careers of the historical Williams and the fictional Alford are sharply contrasted. When he rises to ministerial office, Alford becomes conscious that authority turns him into a 'pappyshow' (1996: 129), an empty figurehead of power. He declares that:

> I have forgotten my mission. I have become part of the tapestry of the pretence of power. I who ought to have been the one to disturb this numbing peace have now become keeper of that peace, I have joined the gang of overseers that help to keep this place a plantation. (1996: 130)

He comes to understand the danger of all abstract political slogans and ideologies.

> He had to think and work things out. He had to find meaning in his captivity, his enslavement, his enduring, to re-examine his relationship with women, his role as a man, he had to think of power, or what it was, of what must be its function ... He had to re-examine all the old questions, to look again at the old songs, the old sayings, the stories — the meaning. And he had to be careful about looking back to what things might have been. He had to look towards the future. He had to find the elation, the zeal for this new life. For, what he had woken up into was a new world. (1996: 172)

There are no easy answers in the politics of Independence. Lovelace believes passionately in the dignity of being fully human. But he also recognises that to be human is to be fallible, stupid and capable of wrongdoing. He argues that individuals can only fulfil themselves by being part of their community. But reliance on other people to set about achieving emancipation compromises human independence, comprises true selfhood. These dilemmas are central to the maturing liaison between Alford and his partner Florence, a creative love that reflects the importance Lovelace places on sexual relationships in the quest for social realisation. When Florence understands that Alford is becoming reliant on her, and that he needs his independence to find his role as a leader, she prepares to leave him. But, paradoxically, her readiness to sacrifice herself for a greater cause transcends her personal desires, and instead of forcing them apart, their unselfish love releases them to discover in each other the redemptive power of a wider community. Here Lovelace reworks the memory of his own childhood experience of being taken by his mother to a service in the Spiritual Baptist church, which made a deep impression on him. In *The Wine of Astonishment*, he had described the Baptists' religious practices, which the colonial rulers tried to stamp out, calling them elsewhere a 'culture that gave meaning to their actions ... their efforts were for visibility and affirmation of self' (Lovelace, 2003: 5). In *Salt*, at the time of the Independence march, Alford's thoughts go back to the ritual ceremony at which, when he was seven, the traditional priestess Mother Ethel had exorcised his inability to speak:

> As the praying went on, [Alford] felt himself taken back past that past, beyond the mysteries of the ceremony to the edge of a chasm he could no cross. Africa was out there. Out there was part of his self that all at once he longed to recover, to claim and reclaim a wholeness for himself. He strained to reach back to that child, to that past he felt belonged to him And he could feel it, sense it, right behind the wall, behind Mother Ethel and the Orishas, behind Ogun and Damballa and Yemanja and Shango. It was out there, with Africa, out of reach. (1996: 256)

His yearning reaches across the chasm of dispossession, searching for fulfilment in a new identity. Liberation from the colonial past, if it leads only to the corrupting values of modern Western culture, is to create — Lovelace suggests — a new imprisonment. As Alford ruminates at the end of the novel: 'How can you free people? he asked. When every move you make is to get them accept conditions of unfreedom, when you use power to twist and corrupt what it is to be human ...?' (1996: 257). He realises that he can no longer remain a spectator: 'He had to find his way back to the people from whom he had stood apart from he beginning ...' (1996: 257–8).

The book's conclusion is uncompromising. It combines Fanon's political cry for revolution to liberate the consciousness of the colonised 'damned' with

Kamau Brathwaite's spiritual call to return to ancestral gods. The village community sets out on a great Independence Day march, led by Bango. Along the route, the marchers encounter a rally of the ruling National Party. Their speaker declares Alford George is carrying on 'his campaign of political revenge', denying 'the Tolerance [sic]' that has been the watchword of the island's development and that has 'enabled us to live with such goodwill despite our different histories' (1996: 258–9). Alford is condemned by the National Party for attempting 'to invoke the spectre of racial division by claiming reparation for Africans' (1996: 259). But in marching beside those of every ethnic element in Trinidad, including Michael Carabon of the old planter class, the narrator knows that Alford's search is not one which is racial, but rather one for each Trinidadian to recover a true sense of selfhood. The end is not hatred of other cultures, but the possibility of spiritual rebirth into one's own, a transformation that has to begin with acceptance of the deprivation in the past. 'The tragedy of our time is to have lost the ability to feel loss, the inability of power to rise to its responsibility of human dignity' (1996: 259). The narrator cannot know the future, but concedes that 'I suppose what I have learned is not to despair because of our errors or to be afraid to try again ... I was thinking that if what distinguishes us as humans is our stupidity, what might redeem us was our grace' (1996: 259).

> Once more I worked my way through the crowd up to the front where Miss Myrtle was now at the side of Bango, who was marching with a sad stateliness and sense of distance as if he was keeping his strength in reserve, making me feel that this march of his was for all of our own lives and had to be carried on, even if it took us to the very end of time. I got in beside them. (1996: 259–60)

Lovelace has created a distinctive Caribbean epic that is at once communal and personal, a national saga that focuses on the responsibility of the individual. Its refusal to see any simple way forward makes it all the more challenging. At the 1996 ceremony at the Commonwealth Society at which Lovelace was awarded the Commonwealth Writers' Prize for *Salt*, I asked him to autograph my copy. 'In Brotherhood,' he wrote, 'keep up the work.' He saw the award not primarily as a literary distinction, but as an endorsement of fiction written to change the world.

Notes

1. A view notoriously echoed by V.S. Naipaul: 'History was built around achievement and creation; and nothing was created in the West Indies' (Naipaul 1964: 29).
2. See, for example, Lamming's famous lament: 'This may be the dilemma of the West Indian writer abroad: that he hungers for nourishment from a soil which he (as an ordinary citizen) could not at present endure' (Lamming 1960: 50).
3. See, for example: 'You hear any [Rastafarians] talking about Africa? You don't see any of them going back? Eh? Too much salt'; and Moon 'felt that his journey across the big stretch of salt water ... ought really to have elevated him' (Lovelace 1996: 213, 218).
4. He 'was ready for their backside — who don't like it could get the hell out of here' (1996: 115).

References

Bénitez-Rojo, Antonio (1992) *The Repeating Island. The Caribbean and the Postmodern Perspective* (Durham: Duke University Press).
Dance, Daryl Cumber (ed.) (1986) 'Earl Lovelace', in *Fifty Caribbean Writers* (New York: Greenwood Press).
Harris, Wilson (1967 [1974]) 'Tradition and the West Indian Novel', in W. Harris, *The Writer and Society* (London: New Beacon).
Knowles, Roberta Q. (1999) 'Salt', *The Caribbean Writer on Line*, no. 13, http://rps.uvi.edu/CaribbeanWriter/toc/tocvolume13.html.
Lamming, George (1960) *The Pleasures of Exile* (London: Michael Joseph).
Lovelace, Earl (1983) *The Wine of Astonishment* (Oxford: Heinemann).
—— (1984) 'Engaging the World', *Wasafiri*, no. 1.
—— (1996) *Salt* (London: Faber and Faber).
—— (2003) *Growing in the Dark: Selected Essays*, ed., Funso Aiyejina (San Juan, Trinidad: Lexicon).
Naipaul, V.S. (1969 [1961]) *A House for Mr Biswas* (Harmondsworth: Penguin).
—— (1964 [1962]) *The Middle Passage* (Harmondsworth: Penguin).
Rohlehr, Gordon (1970) 'Sparrow and the Language of Calypso', *Savacou*, no. 2.
—— (1992) 'Literature and the Folk', in G. Rohlehr, *My Strangled City and Other Essays* (Port of Spain: privately printed).
Walcott, Derek (1998) *What the Twilight Says: Essays* (London: Faber and Faber).
Zamora, Lois Parkinson and Faris, Wendy B. (eds) (1995) *Magical Realism: Theory, History, Community* (Durham: Duke University Press).

11
'BEAUTY AND PROMISE': SONIC NARRATIVES AND THE POLITICS OF FREEDOM IN THE LITERARY IMAGINATION OF LOVELACE

Tina K. Ramnarine

In the opening passages of *Salt*, Lovelace takes his readers into a world of island performance, plunging us into themes of music, freedom and captivity. One of the main characters, Bango, tells the story of flying Africans:

> Jo-Jo's great-grandfather, Guinea John, with his black jacket on and a price of two hundred pounds sterling on his head, made his way to the East Coast, mounted the cliff at Manzanilla, put two corn cobs under his armpits and flew to Africa, taking with him the mysteries of levitation and flight, leaving the rest of his family still in captivity mourning his selfishness. (Lovelace 1996: 3)

This is a myth that is narrated through the Caribbean region in performance traditions like the Big Drum ritual of Carriacou. The myth of the 'Flying Africans' recited by the Carricouan performer Gentle Andrews provides a framework for an interpretation of the title of the novel: 'The Africans who were brought here did not like it. They just walked to the sea. They all began to sing as they spread their arms. A few rose to the sky. Only those who did not eat salt left the ground. The Africans flew home.' (Andrews, cited in McDaniel 1998: 2). Musical parameters can be linked to the myth of flight, a reading contained in the story itself — the Africans sing as they spread their arms in preparation for flight. For McDaniel, the myth deals with a 'flight from enslavement' on one level and, on another, with 'compositional flight'. In ethnographic interpretation, musical creativity is an aspect of the politics of freedom, just as it is in Lovelace's *Salt*.

Bango's storytelling is an example of virtuosic display in the verbal arts that characterises many Caribbean oral traditions. It heralds the novel's engagement with island verbal arts interplaying with a performative mode of writing in the spirit of W.E.B. Du Bois's *The Souls of Black Folk* (1999), a text in which each chapter opens with musical notation of spirituals in evocation of African-American performance environments. Lovelace's sonic narrative, therefore, is an attempt to write island sounds into the novel (made explicit through drawing on the verbal arts) as well as to describe and evoke that soundworld. The story told by Bango is also presented as an oral historical narrative; later on, we learn that Jo-Jo was Bango's grandfather. As oral history, the narrative points to colonial inscriptions on social life in Trinidad (the family left behind in captivity) and to an unrecoverable cultural knowledge (the mysteries of flight are taken back to Africa). Ethnographic studies similarly emphasise the ways in which the past is evoked and knowledge is recuperated in performance. Practitioners of the Big Drum ritual claim that one's ancestral identity can be uncovered through becoming aware of the particular rhythms in the performance to which one is drawn. Carriacou drummers identify nine rhythmic patterns, 'nation rhythms' that signify ancestral heritages: Cromanti, Igbo, Manding, Arada, Moko, Kongo, Temne, Banda and Chamba (McDaniel 1998: 86–7). Singers like Ella Andall see the roots of calypso in Orisha ritual performance (Henry 2003). Chutney, the popular music represented as an 'Indian-Caribbean' genre, is habitually described as having emerged from the traditional ritual spaces of Hindu wedding ceremonies and celebrations at the birth of a child (Ramnarine 2001).

In considering *Salt* in relation to Caribbean performance traditions, I'll offer an ethnographic reading of the text that emphasises the intersections between creative expression and political visions concerned with the possibility of shaping a new, postcolonial society. The focus will be on three of the novel's central characters: Bango, Alford George and Sonan, in order to explore how musical performance is treated as a medium through which ideas about unity and liberty in a postcolonial Trinidad can be expressed. Lovelace also points to the different kinds of histories that shape contemporary Trinidadian sensibilities, such that one can ask how musical performance reifies the ethnic politics that continue to mark the island's political landscape and how the novelist approaches the distinctions drawn between the island's populations. I discuss Lovelace's sonic narratives in relation to the revival of Orisha performance (dancing 'bongo on the graves of the colonialism whose death they had come to celebrate') (1996: 35), the musical traditions associated with the island's Indian population (chutney, tassa drumming), and the formation of Carnival bands that foster national inclusiveness.

The Redefinition of Ownership and an Island Welcome

Bango is a practitioner of performance arts — a storyteller, musician, instrument-maker. Later in the novel we find out that he leads cricket teams and Carnival bands, but at the beginning he is described making toy steeldrums from 'bits of wire and condensed milk tins' and selling these in the market. He is the character who introduces the idea of acoustic ecologies within which island history unfolds. In his stories, he weaves together strands of history, performance and landscape to present a vision for liberty. 'Watch the landscape of this island,' he says, 'and you know that they coulda never hold people here surrendered to unfreedom. The sky, the sea, every green leaf and tangle of vines sing freedom. Birds frisk and flitter and whistle and sing. Just so a yard cock will draw up his chest and crow. Things here have their own mind' (1996: 5). Within the acoustic environment of the landscape, Lovelace explores the concerns of the island's people. Human sonic production is understood as dealing with both musical memories that dwell on cultural legacies and a politics of liberty that looks to the future. This temporal, cultural and political linkage is expressed in Bango's story. The imperial authorities are described as having

> to put up with the noise from Blackpeople. Whole night Blackpeople have their drums going as they dance in the bush. All those dances. All those lascivious bodies leaping and bending down. They couldn't see them in the dark among the shadows and trees; but they could hear. They had to listen to them dance the Bamboula Bamboula, the Quelbay, the Manding, the Juba, the Ibo, the Pique, the Halicord, the Coromanti, the Congo, the Chiffon, the Banda, the Pencow, the Cherrup, the Kalinda, the Bongo. (1996: 5)

In Lovelace's listing, we witness the narration of 'nation naming' that characterises performances like the Big Drum ritual of Carriacou. Bango's opening story, however — like ritual performance — is not only a reclamation of the past but also an affirmation of a present and a future that would have to be forged on the Caribbean island. Guinea John appears to his children in a dream telling them that: 'His wisdom was theirs to have; but they had eaten salt and made themselves too heavy to fly' (1996: 3).

Through the character of Bango, Lovelace introduces the reader to the theme of political possibilities for freedom. From descriptions of the natural environment (the 'tangle of vines sing freedom') to performance practice (the 'noise of Blackpeople'), the reader is alerted to political life as being bound up with the acoustic ecologies and human sonic environments of the island. At the centre of the island's political and sonic environments lie questions about land ownership, and it is Bango who both listens to the landscape and struggles ('waits') for the resolution of land issues in the postcolonial era.

While the sonic landscape is evoked to defy a state of unfreedom, Lovelace also uses musical metaphors to express the confines of island environments — a contrast that serves to highlight the political struggles towards freedom. Of note are the metaphors that are mapped on to the female body and citation of song texts to discuss both the violence of colonial power and the resistance of enslaved people: 'To get a man to follow your instructions you had to pen him and beat him and cut off his ears or his foot when he run away. You had was to take away his woman from him and his child. And still that fellow stand up and oppose you.' The rebelliousness of those men is demonstrated through the citation of song texts: 'Mooma, Mooma, your son in the grave already, your son in the grave already, take a towel and band your belly' (1996: 6).

While this chapter focuses on three male characters, the women in the novel are pivotal in drawing attention to the gendered dimensions of colonial and post-colonial politics, an interesting aspect of the novel that can be noted here. Violence against female bodies is expressed through notions of the body and colonial desires in musical terms: the women are banned from talking and walking, from 'shaking their melodious backsides' (1996: 7). In these descriptions, we glimpse the biopolitics of colonial attitudes to the unseen (and therefore imagined) 'lascivious dancing bodies' and the violence of enslavement that allows the continual practice of the dancing body to be fully understood as a political body. If the problem eventually becomes not how to keep people in captivity but 'how to set people at liberty', a lack of post-emancipation liberty is highlighted in the continuing pain of the female body (1996: 7).

The first descriptions of Alford George's mother, Miss May, relate to her death pains: 'the metronome of her mind keeping time to the rhythm of her distress, trying to find within the music of her pain a space in which to breathe' (1996: 8). Later in the novel, Miss Myrtle (Bango's wife) is described as detesting the sounds of Mighty Sparrow's 'Jean and Dinah', a calypso that dealt with female prostitution and American economic interests in Trinidad and Tobago (1996: 134). Perhaps one of the most dramatic examples of the island's confines expressed in musical terms appears in the episode when Alford George, working as a teacher, says goodbye to Gloria Ollivera, who sails for London alone because Alford feels he should stay on the island to 'save' the children despite his long held wish to escape. Thinking of Gloria had made Alford sing at home ('oh my love, my darling ...'), at which his pet bird would also sing, pouring its soul out as Alford felt his heart folding (1996: 66) — a duet that locates the human voice within its wider acoustic ecological space and refers back to Bango's notion of a landscape that holds clues to the courses of human action.

Despite the reference, this episode shows Bango's and Alford's different perceptions of the landscape. In contrast to Bango's understanding of a landscape that sings freedom to the extent that it cannot be held as 'property', Alford is conscious of an oppressive landscape, a sense that will ultimately lead him to seek reparation in the form of land ownership. When Gloria has left, Alford tells the bird that he knows where nowhere is, but receives no response and finds that the bird has starved to death in its cage. The aspirations and confines of both the cage and the island are marked by moments of song and silence.

As the reader follows the unfolding of Bango's life story, three key moments marking the narration of island postcolonial and diasporic politics in relation to performance are revealed. The first moment is a development of Bango's opening statements on landscape and the refusal to surrender to unfreedom. Myrtle attends the National Party meetings where she hears about 'Democracy, Brotherhood, Liberty' and about 'Discipline, Productivity and Tolerance' (1996: 154). The political speeches give Myrtle a 'sense of release' that comes from seeing land that was once owned by a few now shared between everybody. But Bango struggles with the dilemmas of postcolonial sensibilities in a radically different way. Myrtle, whose view of land is shaped by colonial concepts of ownership, tells Bango that they could have bought land only to realise that 'he had never thought of the plantation as property, as something you buy or sell, that to him it was more of a monster to struggle against, to outwit and outlast and defeat. His struggle she understood then had been not to buy the land but to make the land witness his undefeat' (1996: 155). Bango's undefeat is all the more forceful in that it subverts colonial assumptions about property and landownership that might also raise questions about the ownership of people. In his struggle, we see the potential for a postcolonial sensibility to reach beyond the heritage of colonialism, to think in very different ways about one's relation to the island space. But Bango himself doesn't know what he is fighting for (1996: 155), even though he is a performer whose practice reveals his political aspirations and through whom the rehabilitative and inclusive qualities of Carnival are explored.

The second key moment, then, is in the formation of a Carnival band. Bango's Carnival band idea is the first expression of the possibility of unity through creativity in the novel. Carnival is presented as a unifying force, as a way of welcoming people in the island — welcome becoming a trope for allowing all people to find a place in the island. Bango tells Myrtle about his plans to put a band together:

> This time he proposed to add to his presentation four boys, each to represent one of the major races in the island. He was going to deck them out in dhoti and turban; the European in Scottish kilt; the

Chinese to have on a big Cantonese hat and two false plaits of long hair; and the African a grass skirt on, beads around his neck and a spear in his hand. (1996: 46)

Myrtle does not understand why he troubles himself with this band when participants are not forthcoming and her sister, Florence, has to explain the 'beauty' of Bango's plans, 'the wonderful welcome he is making to each and every race of people in this island' (1996: 47).

Bango spends a lifetime marching for his cause, to the extent that Myrtle asks Alford George not to invite him to be a figurehead at an Independence parade. While all the major themes of the novel are introduced in Bango's opening story, the questions at the heart of postcolonial projects are posed in Bango's meeting with Alford, another key moment and one to which I shall return. At the end of the novel, an ongoing struggle for 'human decency' is described in Bango's march, this time with Myrtle and his nephew (the narrator) at his side. Bango is the most 'African' of the novel's characters (he adheres to traditional performance and ritual practices, and remembers the long durations of the past), but he is also the one who values all the island's people and seeks a postcolonial society that does not rest on the foundations of colonial legacy. In this respect, he represents the endurance of a sense of African self, worth and heritage and is a medium for articulating the ideas of twentieth-century black political speakers who sought to redress the image-making of colonialism that imprisoned people within their own skins as well as on plantations; who argued that the problems of Africans in the New World were problems for all humanity which should be addressed as such; and who marched for a better world (Garvey, Fanon, Malcolm X, Martin Luther King). The novel ends with Bango continuing his march, but the philosophical and ideological complexities of civil rights, passive resistance and movements towards freedom from 'mental slavery' that also embraced repatriation (Garvey) and separatism (Malcolm X) are depicted in Alford George's political journey. While Malcolm X changed his early views on separatism to embracing a global brotherhood, Lovelace's reversal of that stance in the development of Alford's political thinking engages with the realities of ongoing ethnic politics at work in the Caribbean. The novel's central question about how people might live in an independent society reflects a dismantling of the colonial project that extends into the postcolonial era.

From National Unity to Ethnic Reification

Alford George's first election campaign is constructed around the theme of 'Seeing ourselves afresh' — a postcolonial re-envisioning of island society that includes valuing steelbands, steelband yards, calypso tents and masquerade camps as island accomplishments (1996: 122–3). He also calls for 'people exchanges' that challenge the ethnic stratifications of island society. The campaign accords with Eric Williams's arguments regarding the place of folk arts, calypso, steelband and Carnival as 'a flowering of native forms of culture' (1964: 248) in the Independence movement, as well as of his critique of lingering colonial policies to 'separate racial groups'. Williams famously wrote: 'Together the various groups in Trinidad and Tobago have suffered, together they have aspired, together they have achieved. Only together can they succeed. And only together can they build a society, can they build a nation, can they build a homeland' (1964: 288). The extent to which cultural forms have formed the basis for postcolonial political, social and economic development is illustrated aptly by the pre-Lenten Carnival of Trinidad and Tobago, which has become one of the region's major musical spectacles, providing one of the most well-known representations of island performance traditions in the international forum and contributing to the tourist economy.

In contrast to Bango, whose commitment to the principles of unity and responsibility remains constant, Alford George has, by the end of the novel, begun his campaign of 'political revenge' (1996: 258), moving from an idealistic stance of people exchanges to racial division and the claim for reparation for Africans. The optimism of political possibility for freedom and a new social order at the beginning of the novel gives way to a pessimistic view of ethnic politics at work that is only somewhat appeased by Bango's continued marches and by Sonan's attempts — albeit silenced — to speak of unity. In the course of Alford's career, we see the pitfalls of party politics and the contradictions between island narratives of common postcolonial destiny versus ethnic mobilisation in pursuit of new hegemonic structures to control the nation's resources.

In his early idealistic phase, Alford George decides that the College Exhibition class should be abolished so that the teaching programme could be revised to provide an appropriate education for every schoolchild. He embarks on a public fast in front of the Ministry of Education. It is a 'performance', and Alford dresses appropriately in church robes, Hindu clothes and Orisha turbans, attracting the attention of those, like Kennos, who volunteer their services to encourage him to set up a new political party. A successful fast leads to the reinstatement of his teaching position and in returning to the classroom he transforms the curriculum of post primary education to include Anancy stories, calypsos and talks by various religious and healing practitioners. His students go on field trips to Shango, Hosay and Divali ceremonies (1996: 85–9). His programme to give each group a space in the curriculum is broad. Eventually he decides to organise a Carnival band to 'depict the beauty and the promise of the people of the island' (1996: 90).

The band would 'portray the Amerindians, the coming of Columbus, the importation of Africans, the arrival of Indians, of Chinese, of Portuguese, Europeans, Syrians. In order for people to understand one another, he wanted them to take on the role of the other: Africans were to be the Conquistadores, the Buccaneers, the Pirates; Europeans were to be African warriors; Indians were to be Amerindians; and Chinese and Syrians were to be enslaved on sugar plantations' (1996: 90). He publishes his vision of Carnival as 'the future religion of the island, because it was the single celebration in which disparate races and classes of people could come with whatever was their contribution to celebrate freedom and fellowship' in response to a pastor from the Tabernacle of Righteousness and Light who calls Carnival 'devil worship' (1996: 91). Controversy reigns.[1] The Maha Sahab call for traditional festivals, the Muslims for self-respect, the Adventists for the Toco Carnival retreat. The political scholar and visionary, Kennos, supports Alford's position:

> Carnival belonged to all the people of the islands. Living as we were so close to one another, any creation or practice by any group in the island achieved its character because of the presence of others in their midst, that in a way we all share in the creations and practices done by everyone in this island. (1996: 92)

It is Kennos, too, who observes that everybody feels like a victim, and that what is needed is 'someone to make the others welcome' (1996: 93). Yet, in the idealism of the Carnival band, one can note the roots of Alford's later politics of division that return to rest on the familiar colonial legacies of classification of people and land policies. Alford's Carnival band presents rather rigid reification of 'races' that does not allow any permeability between ethnic boundaries. The irony is that the alternative possibility of moving beyond 'race' is also present in Alford George's Carnival vision.

While Bango's Carnival band idea is to depict different people in their traditional dress as a way of recognising origins, Alford George wants people to reach an accommodation through understanding each other and seeing island history from the perspectives of one another. The differences in their approaches accord with Carnival as a long-standing forum for highlighting island struggles, from the efforts of colonial authorities to control Carnival performance to contemporary debates about its origins. If Bango's and Alford's Carnival visions present variations on how to perform national unity which resonate with Eric Williams's notions of developing national culture (1964), a return to the ethnic politics of cultural life has emerged in those groups seeking to claim the origins of Carnival. Recent contributions to Carnival scholarship struggle to reconcile diasporic sensibilities with national aspirations. In short, the African origin of Carnival thesis has turned to ancient Egypt (Nehusi 2000). This, in turn, has been challenged by those who propound an alternative connection to ancient Egyptian festivals, emphasising the Saivism (Hindu) origin thesis (Persad 2001).[2] Contributors to these debates seem to be concerned with the different ways in which memory flows through performances, cultural heritages and origins. They demonstrate the island contestations that arise when ethnicity is mapped on to performance practice or when cultural production is implicated in diasporic politics. Yet they also pay attention to contemporary politics in Trinidad and Tobago, dealing with economic development and the potential to expand Carnival as a tourist industry (Ramnarine, forthcoming) rather than familiar concerns with developing Carnival as a national expression.

In Chapter 9, 'Alford in the PM's Chair Listens to Bango', two people who have been promoting island performance and struggling for liberty meet. Bango explains his views to Alford (who 'happens' to be sitting in the prime minister's chair), acknowledging the latter's offer of land by way of compensation for the brutalities of the past, but insisting that what is needed is an assumption of responsibility that might enable the restoration of a sense of humanness. Bango and Myrtle suggest to Alford that the land must be given openly. In the discussion, Bango articulates questions that lie at the heart of the postcolonial project: 'How do you face in liberty a people who you organize a whole island to keep in prison?' 'How you going to live in liberty with a people whose bondage you make the basis of your land settlement policy?' 'How you going to free a people who you root up from their homeland and force against their will to give their labour for three hundred years to you?' (996: 168) The episode is central to the narrative, bringing to the fore the issues generated through colonial policy that plague the postcolonial moment and introducing the complexities of post-slavery colonial policies in which accounts for African labour were not settled (1996: 184) but new systems of indentured labour were established. Bango tells Alford about his grandfather, Jo-Jo, a singer and drummer who, 'for all the noise that he made in ordinary life ... wanted to shout and mash up the silence he had lived in' when he heard emancipation was coming (1996: 169). Music marks all the moments of political struggle. Jo-Jo learns the power of parody, of double entendre, songs, dances and beating drums (1996: 171); he sings stick-fight chants ('the song of a warrior with a battle before him') (1996: 175); and when others desert plantation life, he turns up for work demanding compensation for the 'mashing up' of lives (1996: 182).

The issues over colonial land policies and labour systems reach a climax in Bango's story as he tells Alford about his grandfather's first encounter with an indentured labourer from India. Jo-Jo hears a stranger working with a cutlass nearby and asks the man: 'You don't see people living here? How you could come in here just so and don't tell nobody nothing?' (1996: 185). Jo-Jo is surprised to discover that the man (Feroze) has land because of his contract. Feroze is puzzled that Jo-Jo does not have a contract and speculates that this might be because he has made a long journey across the sea, while Jo-Jo is local. The telling moments in this encounter are when Feroze learns that Jo-Jo's origins are also from across the sea and when Jo-Jo realises that his anger at Feroze may have made an enemy of him. Through this encounter, Lovelace contrasts the experiences of Jo-Jo and Feroze, delving into frictions created by colonial policies that have led to enduring ethnic reifications and then proceeding with depictions of the island's soundscapes that lead to a more optimistic view of the possibilities for dissolving such ethnic polarities. It is instructive to read the dialogue between Jo-Jo and Feroze within the frameworks of historical research that highlights the continuum of colonial policies on labour from enslavement to indentureship (Williams 1964; Dabydeen and Samaroo 1987). While Jo-Jo insists on settling of accounts, wages for indentured labour could be withheld illegally. No legislation provided for the recovery of wages but labourers remained legally compelled to fulfil their contractual obligations under penalties of fines or imprisonment (Mangru 1987: 165). In Williams's succinct observation, indentureship was 'slavery plus a constable' (1964: 105).

Such similarities in the experiences of Jo-Jo and Feroze become apparent as the novel turns to a closer exploration of the Indian presence. Lovelace's sonic narrative moves to increasingly heterophonic sonic textures that make audible the connections between the island's people and which parallel the attempts of Sonan to develop a party politics that reaches across ethnic divides. Before turning to Sonan's life story, Lovelace attends to the Carabons, the plantation owners whose struggle to find their place in a society moving towards Independence is narrated with reference to the national anthem ('Here every creed and race find an equal place'). The reference is poignant. In the nexus of musical performance, party politics and land ownership, we see all of the novel's characters (as well as Lovelace the novelist) adhering to an idea of 'race' that served colonial justifications with regard to differences between humans. 'Race' inscribed into the nation's anthem reveals the extent to which such colonial ideologies persist even as its categories crumble — as islanders recognise each other as fellow islanders. The paradox for the Carabons is that once the hierarchy of a society based on superiority and inferiority disappears, they are lost because they do not know where their equal place might be in an independent island nation state. A postcolonial project that remains committed to colonial representations, viewing and locating its population groups in discrete places, carries the burdens of the past. In the final chapters of *Salt*, Lovelace hints at the possibilities of a route towards the 'beauty and promise' of island people in everyday life rather than in party politics, a route that is made audible in the island's musical environments.

Sonic Connections

Moon, the grandfather of Sonan, was in 1946 the first in his family to run for election. He is an entrepreneur, building up various businesses and gaining a government settlement for an 'accident' with which he buys a store opposite the wealthy Gopisingh Hardware. In a quiet street he enters into a competition with Gopisingh in which they both shape the sonic environment of Cunaripo:

> Seeing how successful ... Moon was getting, Gopisingh bought a loud hailer as well and to get the edge, began to play music from the soundtrack of Indian films. Moon hit back with chutney singing from Trinidad Indians ... and when Gopisingh turned up the volume of his own hi-fi, Moon added calypso music to his arsenal of musical bombshells. Every Friday the street was a bedlam of chutney, calypso and songs from Indian films. Cunaripo started to be a real town.
> (1996: 220–1)

From an ethnographic reading of this novel, mention of chutney in the 1940s raises issues of representation and the reinvention of the past. If Lovelace promotes contemporary understandings of this genre as the distinctive musical contribution of the Indian population in Trinidad, efforts to introduce chutney into a public arena were made as recently as the 1970s, especially through the performances of Sundar Popo. By the 1990s, however, chutney had been established as the main musical medium through which ideas about Indianness in the Caribbean could be expressed, and the performance of this genre had become an integral aspect of Carnival. The reifications of island ethnicities are disputed, nevertheless, through the sonic connections of Cunaripo's musical soundscape — as, indeed, they are in island musical collaborations. Moon is also a patron of the island's diverse musical genres, encouraging stickfighting, drumming, chantwels and Carnival pantomimes in front of his store. These are diverse genres, which speak to the ways in which the island soundscape does not emerge from a simple mapping of musical genre on to ethnicity. Whereas chutney has been interpreted as the Indian version of (or alternative to) calypso in local discourses, musicians have laid claims to both genres without distinguishing so clearly between them. The extremes of diasporic imaginations displayed through visions of musical genres or performance spaces as 'African' or 'Indian' have the hallmarks of a politics of difference configured and transposed in terms of ethnicity around them.[3] While diaspora as history is vital to an understanding of the past and its effects on the present, why should anyone be confined by the 'ethnic' any longer? Is not the island home an appropriate place to begin challenging these boundaries?

This is the challenge that faces Sonan, who starts his career as a cricketer, but does not know how to cope with the pressure of batting as an 'Indian' with the hopes of the entire Hindu School resting on him. In his political speeches, he uses the cricket stories to promote a vision of unity. He goes to see Alford George as he fasts in protest in front of the Ministry of Education and joins forces with him. He is disappointed by Alford's subsequent move to the National Party, which he sees as a return to the 'African' fold, and follows by moving to the 'Indian' party. Alford George invites Sonan to appear with him at an Independence Day celebration. There are cars blasting chutney, calypso and Indian songs, and men beating tassa drums. Sonan feels a speech forming in response:

> The music was carrying him. It was taking him over. He was going deep down inside it. Out of its depths, to his surprise, he heard the sound of his mother's singing, a bhajan, a sacred song ... And he heard himself telling the story of Moon ... and the part he had always let out — out of sensitivity — of coming to this place, of finding those creole people, of their misunderstandings, of the need to welcome each other. (1996: 242-3)

Sonan's speech resonates with Bango's welcome to all the island's people as well as with Alford George's 'seeing ourselves afresh' and people exchanges. But in the audience, Mr Bissoon is horrified, believing that Sonan's determination to be politically inclusive will lose them the election again. As Sonan continues speaking, however, Bissoon's mood visibly changes: it is only afterwards Sonan realises that 'what he was saying was drowned out by the chutney tassa calypso music, coming from the enthusiasm of a people who would not be denied the victory they were scenting for the first time' (1996: 243).

This is the most explicit moment in the novel where music is used to silence a political vision of unity. In this episode, we see the conflict between creativity in unity (Sonan's speech) and creativity as a divisive force (music drowning political expression of island unity in favour of ethnic nationalisms). The passage is also a commentary on the recent party politics of Trinidad and Tobago, in which the rise of chutney music in the popular imagination paralleled the rise of the United National Congress (UNC), widely perceived as being an 'Indian' party.

We may recollect Bango's grandfather, Jo-Jo, who lived in silence though he was a drummer and singer (1996: 169) and Alford George's early silence, which had gone unnoticed amidst the noise of everyday life. Sound and silence are held in creative tension as another example of the various polarities that are woven through the novel: colonial/postcolonial; African/Indian; landowners/landless; ethnic particularity/unity; diasporic/national imagination. Silence is thus an important part of Lovelace's sonic palette. Silence marks crucial political and ritual moments. While Bango's stories draw attention to a sonic landscape, the entrance of Alford George is marked by non-speech.

When May realises that her son Alford has not spoken in six years, she seeks help from the Shango woman, Mother Ethel. She is advised to hold a thanksgiving feast and offer a young ram in sacrifice. The sacrifice brings an important sense of connection to the past for May.

> It would bring her to a past that she had neglected, to place herself within the shelter of a new and ancient force that would take her into a new space and meaning. She felt herself crying; but it wasn't sadness she felt as Mother Ethel held her to her bosom, it was a feeling of homecoming, of being found, being rescued. (1996: 22)

The reclamation and recovery of the past is a feature of many postcolonial movements. Lovelace indicates the redemptive and reconciliatory capacities of music that might make the island 'home' for its diasporic populations by locating the expressions of national unity in ritual contexts. Sonan's speech therefore stems from Hindu songs, Alford's from Orisha rituals. The vigour with which these beliefs are reclaimed represents a counterpart to the energies that had once gone into their denigration. While May feels a sense of homecoming, her husband, Dixon, responds in a very different manner. Ridiculing these 'superstitions', Dixon finally reveals his childhood stories, breaking his silence on his earliest experiences, informing May of his grandfather who had been an Orisha priest and bush doctor, who had been arrested by the police for practising *obeah* and placed backwards on a donkey to go to the courthouse. Despite the humiliation of this punishment, the real pain in Dixon's story is that no one had raised a hand in protest. Dixon's story foregrounds the recovery of the past in terms that are far from celebratory, of a people separated — rather than unified — through traditional practices (1996: 23). In contemporary Trinidad, musical practitioners understand the variations in the reception of Orisha. The calypsonian Ella Andall says:

> Watch nah, Orisha songs is the base of ... is calypso, calypsonians who said about me that I am not a calypsonian, no problem, they could say whatever they want to say, but I am coming from inside of the belly of calypso, so I am that, but they don't call me that, a calypsonian will never tell you that, they will tell you that I sing African songs, because Africa is hard for people to identify with, to a great degree in Trinidad still you would not say Africa you prefer to say black, because Africa represent I believe pain to some people, when the whole term with the black and the ugly and the drum not good and everything that was black was not good, so then why do you want to identify with this Africanness that I am bring in their face, but the children love it ... (Andall, cited in Henry 2003: 174)

A shift from a colonial to postcolonial society is marked through the generations. So it is the son of May and Dixon, Alford George, who is able to survey island history in listening to both the manifestos of party politics (evoking Aristotle and Freedom, Plato and Greek city states, Wilberforce and emancipation, indentureship) and steelbands on the streets playing calypso. In this moment, visions of the past promoted through party politics that refer to European histories collide with those practised in performances that look to different kinds of pasts located in Africa (the revival of Orisha performance) rather than in Europe.

Though Alford George talks about 'beauty and promise', he feels loss unlike Bango or Sonan: 'the loss of not having had that loss to lose' (1996: 256). He struggles with the dilemmas of freedom and confinement, unsure whether to see the world in the island or in some more distant location, elsewhere, demonstrating a precarious sense of belonging to the island. Ultimately, he feels trapped by the island, outraged by the power that has twisted what it is to be human and which had retreated into those very categories that had been used to define humanness by invoking the logic of 'racial division' (1996: 259). In contrast, Bango and Sonan are consistently secure in their sense of personal histories and in their visions of unity for the island. Bango hears freedom in the landscape itself, while human sonic production in Cunaripo makes it a 'real town', illuminating a new society in the making. If this chapter suggests an ethnographic reading of *Salt*, based on my ethnographic interpretation of the capacities of regional sounds to emphasise human connections in the reconceptualisation of island society (Ramnarine 2004), it is this soundworld that is captured in Lovelace's sonic narratives. As the soundworld of everyday life, and hence of an everyday politics, it gives rise to optimism about the future of the postcolonial state.

Notes

[1] An ethnographic example lies in the objections of the Maha Sabha to initiatives proposing to introduce the steelpan into schools as part of the national school curriculum during the mid-1990s. In the pages of the local press, S. Maraj argued that if pan were to be represented at this level in the national curriculum, then Ministry of Culture support should similarly extend to the harmonium, an instrument important in 'Indian' musical practice. These arguments did not take into account the involvement of Indian musicians with the steelpan (such as the well known pan arranger for the steelband *Renegades*, Jit Samaroo, and Mungal Patasar's combinations of sitar and pan timbres with his group, *Pantar*). But the pan and harmonium controversy was resolved by 1995, by state agreement to purchase harmoniums for schools too. The important point is that these controversies had been targeted at national policy-making processes, but they rested on assumptions about the island's discrete cultures.

[2] In 2001, Carnival coincided with the Hindu (Saivist) festival of Shivratri and the Islamic period of Hajj. These occasions, Persad writes, 'are strong reminders that we are an ancient people, that we have brought customs and traditions from the "old world", which survive in Trinidad and are in effect Trinidadian' (Persad 2001: 16). This claim leads to an exposition on the origins of Shivratri in Hindu India and the spread of Saivism in the ancient world, including through ancient Egyptian festivals and Islamic Hajj. Persad concludes that the Saivist origins of Carnival and Hajj have been forgotten but that Hindus should remember this history.

[3] Musicians have challenged the separations of such a politics. When Denyse Plummer won the Calypso Monarch competition, for example, she sang 'I ain't no Syrian, Indian, African, White or Chinee, I'm just simply a Trini you see' (*Whole Trinidadian* 2001).

References

Dabydeen, David and Samaroo, Brinsley (1987) *India in the Caribbean* (London: Hansib).

Du Bois, W.E.B. (1999 [1903]) *The Souls of Black Folk*, eds Henry Louis Gates Jr. and Terri Hume Oliver (New York: W.W. Norton).

Henry, Frances (2003) *Reclaiming African Religions in Trinidad: The Socio-political Legitimation of the Orisha and Spiritual Baptist Faiths* (Barbados, Jamaica, Trinidad and Tobago: University of West Indies Press).

Lovelace, Earl (1996) *Salt* (London: Faber and Faber).
Mangru, Basdeo (1987) *Benevolent Neutrality: Indian Government Policy and Labour Migration to British Guiana, 1854–1884* (London: Hansib).
McDaniel, Lorna (1998) *The Big Drum Ritual of Carriacou: Praisesongs in Rememory of Flight* (Gainesville: University of Florida Press).
Nehusi, Kimani (2000) 'The Origins of Carnival: Notes from a Preliminary Investigation', in Ian Smart, Ian Isidore and Kimani Nehusi (eds), *Ah Come Back Home: Perspectives on the Trinidad and Tobago Carnival* (Washington, DC and Port of Spain: Original World Press).
Persad, Kamal (2001) 'Carnival and Shivratri', *Sunday Express* (Trinidad), 25 February.
Ramnarine, Tina K. (2001) *Creating Their Own Space: The Development of an Indian-Caribbean Musical Tradition* (Barbados, Jamaica, Trinidad and Tobago: University of West Indies Press).
—— (2004) 'Music in the Diasporic Imagination: The Performance of Cultural (Dis)placement in Trinidad', in Kevin Dawe (ed.), *Island Musics* (Oxford: Berg).
—— (Forthcoming) *Beautiful Cosmos: Performance and Belonging in the Caribbean Diaspora* (London: Pluto Press).
Williams, Eric (1964) *History of the People of Trinidad and Tobago* (London: André Deutsch).

12
ON THE ROAD TO KUMACA: A REFLECTION

Lawrence Scott

I have travelled the road to Matura Village repeatedly to see Earl Lovelace. Just past Valencia, along that same road, there is a sign to Kumaca, the setting of his second novel, *The School Master*. One of the first times I met Earl Lovelace was at his home in Matura Village. Of course, I had already met him when I read the opening to his novel, *The School Master*. The year was 1978. By then Earl had written *While Gods are Falling* and this second novel. Three things in particular struck me about that novel: the language, the setting, and then the moral imperative of the author:

> Dry season now. Sunlight blazes the hills, and scattered between the hills' valuable timber trees — the cedar, angelin, laurier-matack, galba and mahoe — the poui is dropping rich yellow flowers like a madman throwing away gold. Down on the flat and in the crotches of the land where two rivers stagger through the blue stone so plentiful in Kumaca, the water is clear, and in places, ice cold. The soil is rich, deep and black. The immortelle holds its scarlet blossoms still, and on the stems of cocoa, which it shades, pods have turned yellow or red and are waiting. It is time. The cocoa is ready for harvesting.

We have our own pastorals. What do they say? But this was no mere pastoral here.

I had recently returned to live and work in Trinidad, so I was ready to respond to this evocation of the landscape through its naming, in my rediscovery of the place. The opening to this prose work and the voice which was telling me the names of trees and places was a voice which began: 'Dry season now.' The unmistakeable syntactical lilt of the dialect voice, its elliptical structure — I suppose you could have had 'Is dry season now' — commanded greater attention with which to view what was being described. It directed the ear with its music of the place in that list of names which takes you on to the name of the village where the drama is set: Kumaca, where 'The soil is rich, deep and black'. We are then soothed by the 'immortelle' and shaded as the 'cocoa' is by those tall trees, to be then arrested by the short sentence: 'It is time.' Yes, time for the story to begin. Time for this place to unfold with its 'dry season' when 'the cocoa is ready for harvesting'. Later, as the novel unfolds its tragic tale, we are to learn that 'time' is the historical time of Independence which brings the schoolmaster, who brings formal education, to Kumaca. And we finally learn that this experiment is a 'time' of 'harvesting', a cruel and tragic 'harvesting' which cuts down the young Christiana in her first flowering. In that will lie the lesson of this fable, this moral tale.

We feel all of that in the very opening of the novel through a voice which is beginning to do something with a language made of the landscape, the very place with its own names and music — the parang, if you like, of that region, that Venezuelan Spanish music which is the tender side to Trinidad's cut and thrust of picong, mamaguay, and the satire and comedy with which calypso entertains and upbraids us.

What this author is doing is choosing to create a narrative prose, whose voice and intentions are to remain close to his characters and place, raising them up like a mas is raised up high on Carnival day from the effort with which his characters 'scrimp and save and whore and work and tief to drag out of the hard rock stone and dirt to show the world they is people'. That is Lovelace's voice in *The Dragon Can't Dance.*

Of course, this rhythmic syntax in the language is there right from the beginning. It's there in *While Gods are Falling,* where the sentences want to go the full length that they go, say, in the opening of *The Dragon Can't Dance,* but are cut short by what we must now call the caution of the first novel, the beginning of the craft. The full expression comes in *The Dragon Can't Dance* and then given almost epic (we must be careful with that word) proportions in *Salt*. It is the rhythmic syntactical structure which allows his sentences to build themselves with statement, parenthesis, lists, qualifications and digressions to attempt a simultaneity of the moment: the history which has produced it; the place in which it is grounded; the people who live it; the music and rhythms of a whole culture which has had to be wrested from the most appalling suppression in an experiment of trade, which in its cruelty and moral abandonment attempted to make animals and savages of a people, so as to rationalise its own turpitude and philosophical barrenness.

There needed to be an experiment in language to challenge this history of systematic exclusion — hence the breaking down of the separation between narrative and dialogue.

And so it is in *The Wine of Astonishment* that we hear the voices of those who were particularly excluded for their rescuing of a religious tradition which kept them in touch with their ancestral spirits. That rescuing propelled them into their creative assimilation of what they found on the other side of the Middle Passage in the New World, and helped make their very own Orisha worship, one that both echoes and differentiates itself from what they had left behind. It is a woman's voice, Eva's voice, a Spiritual Baptist woman's voice, which tells that story.

Yes, on the shores of Sali Bay when Oshun, when Mother Oshun, is honoured with garlands of flowers, put upon the waves in her honour, we are taken to the feast by Earl.

Only with Earl, as guide, do we find ourselves at these feasts, led through the doorway of the other I have always known as my people. I was tended in my mother's house by black women who left me to sleep. But I heard them go down the back steps, and peeping, I saw their heads tied with white cloth to catch the spirit in the gully from where the singing and the drumming came, in what I later came to know as the *palais* and the *chapelle*.

It was a night we journeyed, four friends, women's heads tied with the traditional cloth, into the hills at Troumacaque above Port of Spain. We were welcomed into the house with the drumming, passed the lighted candles and the water and oil into that hot room, hot with the drumming and then their silencing with the Catholic prayers I knew as a boy: Our Father, Hail Mary, Hail Holy Queen, My Soul does Magnify the Lord. As the drumming began again, we watched the spirit ride their devotees. In wonder and astonishment, we witnessed these things with Earl, included by those who had been excluded, all now brought in from the cold, bringing us in from the cold.

It is this that, when I began to write my own stories and novels, I wanted to try and get to grips with in my own way, from where I was coming from in the same society. This was the dialogue that I began with Lovelace's writing in myself, and at times literally with Earl in the way those talks could begin late evening after a day at the beach by Rivermouth; relaxing in the hammocks back at the house; slowly sipping Jean's sorrel and cashew wines, to feel a bit of the life which produced the work. The experience of that began in me the desire to write a writing which would choose its stories and its language from 'the soil which is rich, deep and black'. In my apprenticeship, I wrote my homage to him in *King Sailor One J'Ouvert Morning*. The opening sentence of *The House of Funerals*, another of my stories, was trying to track down that Lovelace sense of simultaneity. In *Witchbroom*, of course, and even in *Aelred's Sin*, poised to look back from another place, there is still that keeping on, attempting to find — as I put it in a critical paper entitled *Migrating Voices — The Making of a Literary Creole – The Fictional Writing Process: Loss and Recovery of Primal Nurturing Voices in Language, Literature and Landscape* (a long title!) — a language which can tell our stories as we engage the world, another of Earl's philosophical premises.

It is no surprise to me that, quite soon on in my most recent novel, *Night Calypso* — note the title — we should find three pardners, Singh the Indian, Jonah the African, and Doctor Metivier the French Creole, debating their place in the society, while each has the need to tell his story to the other so that they will gain the respect of each other, and together they can act on behalf of the whole people. I remember C.L.R. James saying that one of the important features of *The Dragon Can't Dance*, in fact what made it one of the most important novels that he had read, was the engagement that an African author had made with Indian characters, referring of course to the creation of Pariag and Dolly and their attempt to engage with the African Yard on the Hill.

To return to *The School Master*, I want to dwell in the closing moments of this reflection on the story of Benn and Captain Grant. For it is in this short story (of course fully integral to the novel's shape), which erupts at the centre of the novel, that we get to the core of the moral imperative of this author and this particular work. To cut to the quick of the story, Benn would rather give away the foal that he has bought and reared into a fine horse, than take money from Captain Grant for it. Captain Grant had not thought to sell it in the first place until Benn himself saw the value in the sickly foal. He does not want to sell it back, but if Captain Grant, who has already sold him the horse, now wants it back because Benn has reared it into a fine horse, he will *give* it to the Captain. Captain Grant can't accept that arrangement because it will make him an equal of Benn's. Benn knows that the Captain has no right to force him to give up the horse. He has 50 horses. Benn has one. When he leaves the horse and goes his way without accepting the money, he then hears that Captain Grant shoots the horse with the lame excuse that it has broken its leg. Benn's refusal to sell the horse is about his selfhood — his sense of himself as a man who is equal to Captain Grant. That sense of selfhood is at the heart of the Lovelace philosophy as he explores the lives of people who have been enslaved to a system of work and values which denies them their selfhood.

To return to my starting point about language and setting, we see in this episode how integral both the language and a proper understanding of the setting are to this drama of Benn and Captain Grant, which ironically is told to one of the servants of the colonial system, the Catholic priest, as they journey towards Kumaca.

In 2005, Earl celebrated his seventieth birthday. We travelled to Matura, stopping at the sign to Kumaca. Then we went further along the coastal road to Toco where Earl had been born in 1935. When the celebrating party arrived in Toco to witness Earl's homecoming to the village of his birth, we stood under the village shop to be welcomed by a group of Spiritual Baptist women dressed resplendently in white dresses with their heads tied in white cloth. They stood and sang hymns, rang the bell, and sprinkled water, accompanied by clapping and the rhythmic swaying of prayer. Their leader spoke and prayed and Earl sat and listened, and allowed himself to be taken back into the embrace of his birthplace by women who reminded him of his own mother. Afterwards, he said he thought he had seen his mother there, as we stood and listened to the women singing, *Over Sion there is music in the air* ...

On the way back to Port of Spain after the celebration, I reflected on the fact that I had never been to Kumaca. There is still some distance along that road that I have to travel with Earl in the creation of a literary Creole which both tells our stories and engages the world.

INSTITUTE FOR THE STUDY OF THE
AMERICAS

UNIVERSITY OF LONDON · SCHOOL OF ADVANCED STUDY

The Institute for the Study of the Americas (ISA) promotes, coordinates and provides a focus for research and postgraduate teaching on the Americas – Canada, the USA, Latin America and the Caribbean – in the University of London.

The Institute was officially established in August 2004 as a result of a merger between the Institute of Latin American Studies and the Institute of United States Studies, both of which were formed in 1965.

The Institute publishes in the disciplines of history, politics, economics, sociology, anthropology, geography and environment, development, culture and literature, and on the countries and regions of Latin America, the United States, Canada and the Caribbean.

ISA runs an active programme of events – conferences, seminars, lectures and workshops – in order to facilitate national research on the Americas in the humanities and social sciences. It also offers a range of taught master's and research degrees, allowing wide-ranging multi-disciplinary, multi-country study or a focus on disciplines such as politics or globalisation and development for specific countries or regions.

Full details about the Institute's publications, events, postgraduate courses and other activities are available on the web at *www.americas.sas.ac.uk*.

Institute for the Study of the Americas
School of Advanced Study, University of London
31 Tavistock Square, London WC1H 9HA

Tel 020 7862 8870, Fax 020 7862 8886
Email *americas@sas.ac.uk*
Web *www.americas.sas.ac.uk*

INSTITUTE FOR THE STUDY OF THE AMERICAS
UNIVERSITY OF LONDON · SCHOOL OF ADVANCED STUDY

Recent and forthcoming titles in the ISA series:

Making Institutions Work in Peru: Democracy, Development and Inequality since 1980
edited by John Crabtree

Right On? Political Change and Continuity in George W. Bush's America
edited by Iwan Morgan and Philip Davies

Francisco de Miranda: Exile and Enlightenment
edited by John Maher

Caciquismo in Twentieth-Century Mexico
edited by Alan Knight and Wil Pansters

Democracy after Pinochet: Politics, parties and elections in Chile
by Alan Angell

The Struggle for an Enlightened Republic: Buenos Aires and Rivadavia
by Klaus Gallo

Mexican Soundings: Essays in Honour of David A. Brading
edited by Susan Deans-Smith and Eric Van Young

America's Americans: Population Issues in U.S. Society and Politics
edited by Philip Davies and Iwan Morgan

Football in the Americas: Fútbol, Futebol, Soccer
edited by Rory M. Miller

Bolivia: Revolution and the Power of History in the Present. Essays
by James Dunkerley

American Civilization
by Charles A. Jones

Caribbean Literature After Independence: The Case of Earl Lovelace
edited by Bill Schwarz

Contesting Clio's Craft: New Directions and Debates in Canadian History
edited by Christopher Dummitt and Michael Dawson

Printed in the United Kingdom
by Lightning Source UK Ltd.
127582UK00002BA/4-6/P